Dear Reader:

The book you are about to read is the latest bestseller from the St. Martin's True Crime Library, the imprint the *New York Times* calls "the leader in true crime!" Each month, we offer you a fascinating account of the latest, most sensational crime that has captured the national attention. St. Martin's is the publisher of bestselling true crime author and crime journalist Kieran Crowley, who explores the dark, deadly links between a prominent Manhattan surgeon and the disappearance of his wife fifteen years earlier in THE SURGEON'S WIFE. Suzy Spencer's BREAKING POINT guides readers through the tortuous twists and turns in the case of Andrea Yates, the Houston mother who drowned her five young children in the family's bathtub. In Edgar Award–nominated DARK DREAMS, legendary FBI profiler Roy Hazelwood and bestselling crime author Stephen G. Michaud shine light on the inner workings of America's most violent and depraved murderers. In the book you now hold, COLD-BLOODED, veteran true crime scribe Carlton Smith details the death of a respected attorney—and the secret, sordid life of his wife.

St. Martin's True Crime Library gives you the stories behind the headlines. Our authors take you right to the scene of the crime and into the minds of the most notorious murderers to show you what really makes them tick. St. Martin's True Crime Library paperbacks are better than the most terrifying thriller, because it's all true! The next time you want a crackling good read, make sure it's got the St. Martin's True Crime Library logo on the spine—you'll be up all night!

Charles E. Spicer, Jr.
Executive Editor, St. Martin's True Crime Library

"Hey, what are you doing?" Debbie called out. Elisa and Sarah seemed surprised to see her. Again, Debbie wondered how Larry was supposed to be getting to Florida—here was Elisa driving Larry's truck, so he obviously wasn't driving there.

Elisa put her head out the window. "We're going to the bank," Elisa said. "I want to make sure that Larry hasn't cleaned out our bank account." Debbie nodded. She couldn't see through the tinted windows into the rear of the truck with its fold-down rear bench seat, but in the truck bed Debbie could see a folded wheelchair, a pair of brand-new pointed shovels, some suitcases, Larry's bag of golf clubs, some laundry bags and an ice chest. *A wheelchair?* Debbie thought. *Shovels?*

Elisa and Sarah said goodbye, and drove out of the parking lot.

Debbie went inside the trailer, and noticed that all of Larry's showing clothes had been removed.

Weird, Debby thought. *This is turning out to be a weird day.*

But Debbie had no idea how weird it really was. That would only come out later, much later, when the body of Larry McNabney, formerly of Reno, Nevada, and a one-time star of the Nevada bar, would surface in a vineyard some 350 miles north of where he had last been heard from—skipping dinner while in Room 916 of the Pacific Palms hotel.

Titles by Carlton Smith

Blood Money

Death of a Little Princess

Seeds of Evil

Dying for Daddy

Death in Texas

Murder at Yosemite

Bitter Medicine

Hunting Evil

Shadows of Evil

Death of a Doctor

Blood Will Tell

Love, Daddy

Reckless

Cold-Blooded

From the True Crime Library of St. Martin's Paperbacks

COLD-BLOODED

Carlton Smith

St. Martin's Paperbacks

COLD-BLOODED

Copyright © 2004 by Carlton Smith.

Cover photograph of couple © Cashman Photo Enterprises, Inc. Photograph of house courtesy San Joaquin County Sheriff's Department.

ISBN: 0-312-99406-0
EAN: 80312-99406-8

Printed in the United States of America

St. Martin's Paperbacks edition / December 2004

St. Martin's Paperbacks are published by St. Martin's Press, 175 Fifth Avenue, New York, NY 10010.

10 9 8 7 6 5 4 3 2 1

When a woman of bad character marries she earns the admiration of her set, she has worked the trick and become respectable, but he, the man, only earns its ridicule . . . he is the mug . . . Believe me, to conduct yourself gracefully in such a position you need either great dignity of character or an unparalleled effrontery . . .

W. Somerset Maugham
Ashenden

September 2001

City of Industry, California

The sun was still below the eastern horizon as Gregory Whalen left his hotel room on his way to the barns and the horses. He always fed at 5, and the horses knew it, so they would be waiting for him. The early morning air was cool, but it would soon warm up.

Ahead in the early morning darkness, on a strip of grass walking her dog, Whalen saw his client—one of them, at least. Elisa McNabney was a beautiful woman—tall, dark, slender, with a vivacity that was inescapably seductive, at least to men. Elisa could look at you with her merry dark eyes and pin you with your own thoughts, even if you were, like Whalen, 72 years of age and old enough to know better.

Elisa looked up as Whalen approached.

"You'll never guess what happened," she said.

"What?"

"Larry's gone," Elisa said.

"Gone? Where the hell did he go?"

"He left last night," Elisa said. "We had an argument. He left. He's said he's going back to the cult."

Nonplussed by this disclosure, Whalen said nothing. Elisa's dog, Morgan, a Jack Russell terrier, sniffed at the grass. "So Larry won't be showing anymore?" Whalen finally asked, coming to grips with the practical implications of this surprise. That was Greg: forget the philosophy, focus on the immediate.

"No," Elisa said. "He said he's done with showing."

Whalen nodded. He turned and headed toward the barns, thinking the whole thing was strange, but then, rich people tended to *be* strange—at least, that was Whalen's experience

with them. After all the work that had been done, all the
money that had been spent, to just throw it all away on a
whim—to go join a *cult*? It wasn't like Larry—or was it? As
he entered the hotel elevator, Whalen thought back over the
past few days, and when he replayed them in his mind, he
realized that something had been brewing, all right.

They had arrived at the horse show in the City of Industry,
about forty minutes east of Los Angeles, on the Wednesday
before, September 5. Whalen had brought the horses down
from northern California in his trailer, accompanied by his
daughter, Deborah Kail, like her father, a trainer, as well as
an insurance broker who specialized in casualty coverage on
expensive show horses, like those of the McNabneys'. Larry
and Elisa had followed them down in Larry's shiny new red
Ford pickup truck, the one with the dark-tinted windows and
dual rear wheels—a "dually," it was called—that had cost
Larry close to $50,000 earlier in the summer. They'd all
checked into the Pacific Palms hotel and prepared for the Pacific Quarter Horse Classic, the first of two four-day shows
where trainers and owners of American quarter horses, like
Greg and Debbie, and Larry and Elisa, put their prized animals on display. "Just like a big dog show," as Debbie Kail
described it later, although it had as much in common with
a fashion show as anything else. As the McNabneys' trainers,
it was Whalen and his daughter's job to get the McNabney
horses ready for the exhibitions. That meant exercising them,
washing them, grooming them, all to make them look pretty
as well as muscular. It was a full-time job, at least for Greg
Whalen.

Whatever one said about Larry and Elisa, the McNabney
horses, at least, were champions. One, Justa Lotta Page,
Larry's yearling stallion, was worth at least $30,000 and
maybe, quite soon, even a lot more. Tall, handsome, well-
muscled, the sorrel-colored colt had a promising future in
the American quarter horse sweepstakes. If things went right,

Justa Lotta Page could eventually be sold to a breeder for many times what he had originally cost—just $12,500—when Larry McNabney had bought him as an 8-month-old colt from Whalen at the first of the year.

Quarter horses were Greg Whalen's business—had been for more than forty years, ever since he'd quit riding rodeo bulls in his native Texas, and started making money from horse fanciers instead. It was a long way from the days when Whalen's father had raised broncos for the U.S. Army, back before World War II. From his ranch near Clements, California, north of Stockton, Whalen was something of a cross between a coach, a confessor, a barber and a chauffeur. His stock in trade was his knowledge of the American quarter horse breed. Greg bred the mares, picked the foals, raised them, trained them, then groomed them, mostly while acting as the agent of a steady stream of paying customers who formed the backbone of the horse show circuit—people, for the most part with a superabundance of both time and money, and an animating interest in displaying both. Exhibiting an American quarter horse wasn't for either the faint of heart or the weak of pocket, as more than one trainer like Whalen had pointed out to a would-be client. In a sense, participating in horse shows was a bit like owning a large yacht: if you had to ask how much it cost, you couldn't afford it. A serious exhibitor, like Larry was turning out to be, could easily spend $100,000 in one year on obtaining a horse, training, board and care, veterinary fees, transportation, accommodations and entry fees, and if the horse was a dog—so to speak—the money could never be recouped.

Whalen had known the McNabneys for about three years. Larry, he knew, was a big-time lawyer from Nevada who had made a pile in personal injury lawsuits, mostly in Reno. Elisa, almost twenty years younger than Larry, was his fifth wife. She was the one who handled all the money. As Elisa had explained it to Greg's daughter, Debbie, Larry didn't like to be bothered with financial details, that was *her* job.

Larry's income, when it came, came in great gushing gobs, Elisa had explained; it was the nature of the business of representing clients in personal injury cases—*feast or famine*, as Elisa put it. Money would grow tight for a bit, then *wham!*—in came a huge settlement for some lawsuit, and the coffers would be filled to overflowing again. It all depended how fast Larry could make the insurance companies settle up, and for how much.

Still, it didn't seem to Greg that Larry was practicing much law these days. Ever since Greg had sold Larry Justa Lotta Page, on January 1, 2001, Larry had spent most of his time—and a lot of money—showing the horse. So far, Whalen and the McNabneys had been pretty much all over the West with the prized animal: Scottsdale, Arizona; Las Vegas, Nevada; Central Point, Oregon; Monroe, Washington; Fallon, Nevada; and a number of venues in California where prize horses were similarly exhibited.

Justa Lotta Page hadn't been broken to the saddle yet. Instead, he had been entered in halter competition, common for yearlings. This was where Larry, or Greg himself, simply led the colt into the center of the ring by means of a head halter. Points were awarded by the judge or judges based on the way the horse looked—it's "conformance," that is, its shape and muscle tone, along with its ability to respond to the directions of the human holding the rope. So, too, was the halter handler judged—on his own looks and demeanor as he directed the horse through a series of paces.

So far, Larry and Justa Lotta Page had done very well, although this was at least as much a function of the amount of money one was willing to spend as anything else—the more shows one entered, the more points might be accumulated. As of that morning, in fact, Larry was leading the nation in halter exhibition points; if he kept up his pace, it was possible that he would win the American Quarter Horse Association's Amateur Horseman of the Year Award to go with his AQHA Rookie of the Year Award from two years before.

The rookie award had netted Larry a prized silver belt buckle inscribed with his name.

But it wasn't the prizes or even the fame that interested Larry in quarter horse exhibitions, although everyone who'd ever known him agreed he loved being the center of attention. The way Larry saw things, this was to be a year off for him, away from the law, which, if the truth were to be told, had begun to bore him. It wouldn't be a total write-off: instead, he hoped to lead Justa Lotta Page into the winner's circle at the AQHA's World Championship in Oklahoma City in October. A champion halter horse, a stallion with his best years still ahead of him, Larry knew, could make him rich. Larry saw Justa Lotta Page as Justa Lotta Dough, at least six figures, maybe even seven, once he had the title. Larry hoped to sell the horse for many times what he'd paid for him, thereby defraying all his exhibiting expenses (and Greg Whalen's not inconsiderable boarding costs and training fees), and making him a healthy profit to boot.

But now, if Elisa was telling the truth, Larry for some reason had decided to throw it all away.

As he thought back, Whelan realized that Larry's behavior had been off almost the entire weekend. True, he had been drinking: Larry was an inveterate imbiber of Chardonnay wine—he always seemed to have a glass in his hand. But Whelan knew that wine was only Larry's cover: the reason the glass never seemed to be empty was Larry's penchant for spiking it with vodka, and Larry's capacity for vodka was prodigious. Bob Kail—Greg's son-in-law, Debbie's husband—had played golf once with Larry, and told Greg that by the time they'd reached the eighteenth green, Larry had swigged an entire bottle of vodka between swings.

But Larry's experience as a drinker didn't account for his behavior that weekend. The booze usually made him ebullient, talkative, even boastful. In contrast, Larry that weekend had seemed withdrawn, quiet—almost spaced out, Whalen thought. Where usually Larry enjoyed interacting with people, that weekend he seemed to want to stay to himself. Even more significant, on Sunday Debbie Kail had chided Larry on his personal appearance—where he was usually extremely well-groomed, on that day he seemed a bit slovenly, at least to Debbie. She'd had to tell him to change his jeans, and in the arena during the halter competition Larry had seemed confused—unsure of himself. In an endeavor that prized how one looked and acted as much as anything else, that was an indication that all was not well with Larry. Debbie thought he was unusually depressed.

And then, on Sunday night, there had been the scene at dinner. Everyone had gone to an Italian restaurant—Greg, Debbie, Larry, Elisa, and Elisa's friend or secretary or whatever she was, Sarah Dutra. Larry had been drinking as always and seemed worse than usual, slurring his words and having difficulty in following the conversation. He seemed mad at Sarah, making faces at her and at one point calling her a "bitch." Debbie Kail thought Larry was drunker than she'd ever seen him.

Debbie had already noticed that Elisa seemed to be spending most of her time that weekend with Sarah, and the two of them well away from Larry. At one point, either on Friday or Saturday, Debbie had overheard Elisa telling another friend that they would make sure Larry had enough to drink so he would pass out, so Elisa and Sarah could go out and party without him. Larry didn't like Sarah, Debbie knew; it was almost as if he were jealous of the pretty 21-year-old blond student, who always seemed to be at Elisa's side. At the dinner, the tension between Larry and Sarah had been obvious to everyone.

"Fuck you, Larry," Sarah had whispered, raising her middle finger to her cheek in a more decorous version of the obscene gesture. Larry didn't say anything. Then, a few minutes later, Larry had grabbed Debbie's arm, and told her she was acting like a "bitch" herself, although he didn't appear to be angry at her. He was apparently trying to make a joke. Greg had been offended, Debbie had been hurt, and Elisa had been embarrassed. Sarah had just rolled her eyes. Greg told Larry to knock it off, and Larry had apologized. Later, Greg had to help Larry out of the restaurant, he was so wobbly. In fact, Larry fell down once on the way to his red truck. That night, after the dinner, Sarah had left, intending to drive back to Sacramento, where she had classes in art at Sacramento State University.

The following day, Monday, Larry seemed preoccupied, again withdrawn. Greg and Debbie both wondered whether Larry and Elisa were having serious marital difficulties, and the more Greg thought about it, the more likely that seemed. It wouldn't be the first time in Whalen's experience a younger wife had been seduced by the atmosphere around the horse show—the large, muscular animals, the smells, the rangy hired horse handlers, the traveling circus aspect of the exhibitions—and knocked something off on the side. Maybe Elisa was stepping out on Larry; maybe Larry had found out about it, and had decided to climb even further into the bottle to kill the pain. In fact, Greg wondered whether Elisa had something going with *Sarah*—Larry had already told him, months earlier, that he wanted his wife to fire Sarah, that they were "too close." What did that mean?

Still, Greg thought, over the weekend Larry had seemed enthusiastic about the immediate future: based on the performance over the weekend, Larry and Justa Lotta Page had passed his main competition for Horseman of the Year. He and Greg talked about taking Justa Lotta Page East, even to Florida, where there were many more horse shows, and the opportunity to win still more points, which would give Larry and his horse a shot at a national championship.

Others also saw Larry the same day, hanging around the barn near the arena, the ever-present glass of Chardonnay in his hand. To some, Larry seemed mellow, feeling no pain. If he was upset about something, he was hiding it well.

Nevertheless, by that Monday night, Larry had taken to his bed in the hotel. Greg called to invite him to dinner with him and Debbie, but Larry said he just wanted to rest, maybe watch a movie on television. Around 6:30 that night Elisa had come down from the McNabney room, just across the hall from the room shared by Greg and his daughter. At the table in the hotel restaurant, Elisa made a call on her cell phone to Larry, trying again to get him to join them, but Larry didn't want to come down. Elisa sat with Greg and Debbie for maybe twenty minutes, then picked up a bowl of soup, a salad and two glasses of Chardonnay, and took them upstairs to her husband. Later, Greg and Debbie went out to check the horses once more before retiring for the night.

Then, in the morning, Tuesday, September 11, Larry was gone, according to Elisa—off to join some sort of cult. To Whalen, it seemed flakey. He hoped Larry knew what he was doing.

About quarter to 7 that Tuesday morning, after his brief conversation with Elisa McNabney on the grass strip in front of the Pacific Palms hotel, and after he'd fed the horses, Greg Whalen returned to the hotel room he was sharing with his daughter, Debbie Kail.

As he came through the door, Debbie's eyes were glued to the television screen.

"You won't believe what just happened," Debbie told her father.

"*You* won't believe what just happened," Greg retorted. "Larry's left. He ran away to join a cult."

Then Greg noticed what Debbie had been talking about—there on the screen was a picture of the south tower of the World Trade Center in New York, smoke pouring from a gaping hole about two-thirds of the way up. And as they stared at the screen, the whole building went down in a tremendous cloud of fire and smoke.

Later, the terror attacks on the World Trade Center were to provide a sort of dividing line for everyone involved in the Larry McNabney mystery—while most everyone in America could recall where they were when the attacks took place, for those involved in the McNabney case, the attacks became a sort of reference point for recalling who did and said what in the hours immediately afterward. And like most such intensive recollections, recounted many times to many people, some portions became hardened in memory, whether real or imagined, and others evaporated. It was only by piecing together the various recollections of a number of individuals that a coherent scheme of the events became discernible, and it necessarily was a tale not unlike *Rashomon,* with different perceptions of truth depending on one's perspective.

Greg, for one, recalled that no sooner had he watched the first tower fall than both Elisa and Sarah Dutra entered the room. He recalled overhearing some vague conversation between Debbie and Elisa about Larry leaving the hotel to join a cult, but it didn't seem particularly important at the time, not with the disaster that had just taken place. Even as they stared at the screen, the second tower collapsed.

Debbie, for her part, recalled things a bit differently. She remembered that when her father came into the hotel room, Elisa and Sarah were already with him. That was when Greg told her that Larry had left during the night. "I said, 'You are not going to believe what just happened on TV,'" Debbie recalled. "He said, 'You are not going to believe what just happened *here.*' I said, 'What do you mean?' He said, 'Larry's gone.'"

Debbie said she asked where Larry had gone, and Elisa told her that he had gone to Florida to join a cult. "What are *you* doing here?" Debbie asked Sarah. Sarah said she'd flown in late the night before from Sacramento, because Elisa had asked her to come back.

"How is Larry going to get to Florida?" Debbie asked. "All the planes have been grounded."

Elisa looked confused. Debbie told her that all flights had been grounded since 6 in the morning. She knew because her own flight to Phoenix, Arizona, had just been cancelled. Elisa said she guessed that Larry had taken a flight that left before the grounding had taken effect.

Debbie didn't say anything, but thought Elisa was lying to her, for some reason. How would Larry have been able to get a plane in the middle of the night?

Sarah didn't say anything.

Greg went into the bathroom to shave.

• • •

A bit later that morning, Greg, Debbie, Elisa and Sarah went out to the barns, where Greg had parked his long white horse trailer. The trailer not only served as a conveyance for the horses, it also had a separate compartment where exhibitors could change their clothes between showings. Debbie wanted to get her show clothes out of the trailer to put them in her room, since her flight had been cancelled, and she was stranded in southern California. Around 10 that morning, she parked her father's white pickup truck near the trailer and began transferring the clothes. As she parked, she saw Larry's red truck pull up nearby. Elisa was driving.

"Hey, what are you doing?" Debbie called out. Elisa and Sarah seemed surprised to see her. Again, Debbie wondered how Larry was supposed to be getting to Florida—here was Elisa driving Larry's truck, so he obviously wasn't driving there.

Elisa put her head out the window. "We're going to the bank," Elisa said. "I want to make sure that Larry hasn't cleaned out our bank account." Debbie nodded. She couldn't see through the tinted windows into the rear of the truck with its fold-down rear bench seat, but in the truck bed Debbie could see a folded wheelchair, a pair of brand-new pointed shovels, some suitcases, Larry's bag of golf clubs, some laundry bags and an ice chest. *A wheelchair?* Debbie thought. *Shovels?*

Elisa and Sarah said goodbye, and drove out of the parking lot.

Debbie went inside the trailer, and noticed that all of Larry's showing clothes had been removed.

Weird, Debbie thought. *This is turning out to be a weird day.*

But Debbie had no idea how weird it really was. That would only come out later, much later, when the body of

Larry McNabney, formerly of Reno, Nevada, and a one-time
star of the Nevada bar, who some considered the F. Lee Bai-
ley if not the Clarence Darrow of Nevada, would surface in
a vineyard some 350 miles north of where he had last been
heard from—skipping dinner while in Room 916 of the
Pacific Palms hotel.

Larry

Reno—"The Biggest Little City in the World," as it calls itself—is a universe away from its southern Nevada counterpart, the glittery Las Vegas. The birthplace of the state's casino industry, it has a history—and an establishment—that long predates its splashier sister to the south.

In its original incarnation, Reno was a railroad town—the offspring of those wild days when the Central Pacific was built just after the end of the Civil War. In 1867, the western part of the transcontinental tracks had just emerged from a four-year struggle to get through the Sierra Nevada mountains, hell-bent for Utah and a future shotgun wedding with the Union Pacific track, when representatives of the Big Four—Crocker, Huntington, Hopkins and Stanford—encountered a man named Myron Lake, who owned a toll bridge in the grasslands of Truckee Meadows, just below the eastern wall of the Sierras. After the long, winding, arduous and expensive effort to punch the railroad through the mountains, the relatively flat lands of northern Nevada beckoned, and the opportunity to lay miles of track fast in the race against the eastern competition loomed profitably. The railroad people decided that this was just the spot for a new station, and Myron Lake eagerly agreed.

Lake had come to the meadows in the early 1860s, just as the mines near Virginia City to the south were hitting their early stride. A man named Fuller had erected a rickety bridge across the fast-flowing waters of the Truckee River, only to see it wiped out by floods on several occasions. Lake bought the bridge, or what was left of it, for a small amount of money, and built a new structure to take its place. Then he sat back to collect—a dollar for every steer, fifty cents for each horse, and a dollar for every wheeled vehicle on their way to the ravening demands of the mines. Soon Lake put up a hotel and a restaurant, then a grist mill. When the railroad people came to Lake's Crossing, as the little enterprise was called, Lake saw the future: and it was the closest thing to a sure bet that anyone would ever make in the city that was to be called Reno.

Lake quickly gave the railroad people title to eighty acres on the north bank of the Truckee for a townsite—provided that he got half the lots. The railroaders agreed, and on May 9, 1868, nearly 1,500 would-be investors swarmed into Lake's Crossing to bid on the lots, and a city came to life literally overnight. The first lot sold for $550, a fortune in those days, and some sales later in the day even exceeded a thousand.

Originally the town was to have been named Argenta, but the name didn't stick. A few weeks after the town sprang into existence in the shape of green lumber and tents, it was renamed for Jesse Lee Reno, a Union Army general killed in the battle of South Mountain, Maryland, in 1862; in those days, the Civil War was still fresh in everyone's mind, and so Reno was honored as a martyr to the Union cause.

By fall of the following year, 1868, the new town of Reno had 240 buildings, a remarkable growth rate. The Central Pacific tracks were well on their way to Utah, but the town prospered on the tons of silver that were then being extracted from the famous Comstock Lode. Lake continued to operate his toll bridge, raking in the money as wagons and miners and cattle went to and from the railroad and the mines. By 1870, the town had grown so rowdy that Lake realized a jail was needed; the county authorities, in Washoe City to the south, refused to pay for it. In response, Lake and others organized an election, and moved the county seat to Reno—and then took the county courthouse with them, brick by brick.

That same year saw the first murder in Reno, when a man named Henry Roth, drinking at the Reno Billiard Saloon, shot bootmaker J. H. Miller "by intent and Henry Clay Phibbs by accident," according to Phyllis and Lou Zauner, authors of *Reno-Sparks, Nevada: The Way It Was Then, the Way It Is Now,* a history of the area published by Zanel Publications in 1978. The unfortunate Phibbs was the keeper of the saloon, shot by mistake when he tried to prevent Roth from killing Miller with Miller's own gun.

Through the next half-century, the fortunes of Reno waxed and waned, dependent first on the largesse from the Comstock, later by the grace (or lack of it) of the railroad. The main thoroughfare, Virginia Street, ran north and south across the river, at first using Lake's toll bridge—until the county authorities revoked Lake's franchise and took over the bridge in the name of the public. North of the river, the town spread out in orderly streets—numbered lanes going east and west, named streets going north and south. Because there wasn't a tree within miles of the place, all the shade had to be imported. By the present day, however, the city is quite leafy.

As the Comstock played out of ore, the town became ever more dependent on the railroad for its prosperity. At one point, taking advantage of its monopoly, the railroad began assessing "backhaul" fees for freight: a surcharge levied against all goods delivered to Reno equal to the amount the railroad would have charged if the goods had been sent from San Francisco, even if the wares had come directly from the East and had stopped 220 miles short of the Bay terminus. Naturally, the townspeople resented this; they especially resented the fact that the railroad refused to pay any taxes. At one point the Washoe County sheriff chained the railroad's locomotives to the tracks to force them to pay up. That did the trick—the money was wired to the county's bank the same day.

By 1886, the state established the University of Nevada

on a low hill to the north, and the town began to expand to south of the river and to the east; by the 1890s, Reno had become the state's largest city. But its fame was still in the future, and it would turn on the twin cards of marriage and money—or more precisely, the ending of marriages and the wagering of money.

Although the original Nevada Legislature had passed a law in 1861 outlawing gambling, and did so once more in 1865, the laws were never enforced. By 1879, the legislature decided to join 'em if they couldn't lick 'em. A law was passed to license gambling establishments, in effect legalizing them. By the turn of the century, Nevada was the only state in the country with legalized gambling—a circumstance that made its taxes among the lowest in the nation. In 1910, Reno was the scene of one of the most famous prize fights in history, at a time when boxing was often outlawed, when Jim Jeffries fought Jack Johnson in a specially built, 22,000-seat wooden arena. To get the arena built on time, the promoters paid the carpenters' overtime in whiskey. Jeffries left town with $127,000 and a stack of unpaid bills, while Johnson—although the decisive winner of the fight—got $110,000. The city, of course, made out like a two-armed bandit, reaping $277,000 from the contest, according to the Zauners' history.

By the same year, the gaming industry in Reno was firmly under the control of gangsters, namely "Big Bill" Graham and Jimmy "the Cinch" McKay. Progressive elements in the state capital at Carson City succeeded in having gambling outlawed once again. This time, the games went underground, and were quickly joined by booze, since Prohibition was soon enacted. Crime began to proliferate, and Reno began to be seen as a congenial spot for outlaws—in the late twenties Baby Face Nelson came to town, along with other desperadoes. The *Los Angeles Times* primly referred to Reno as a "vicious Babylon."

It took until the mid-1930s to get rid of the gangsters; by

that time, the state had re-legalized wagering. After the bad guys went off to the penitentiary, legitimate business people such as Raymond Smith and Bill Harrah took over the gambling enterprises, and moved them back to the main street and made them respectable. Both Smith and Harrah saw gaming as a legitimate tourist attraction, and it turned out they were right.

Just about the same time ordinary people began to come to Nevada to gamble legally, someone noticed that Nevada's mining camp past had engendered a quirk in the law: because so few miners stayed in one place very long, the law only required six months' residence for a divorce. A Reno lawyer began advertising this curious provision in the East as early as 1906. That was when a famous, beautiful, East Coast showgirl named Laura Corey arrived, replete with minks and diamonds, stayed in town for the required six months, and then asked a local judge to grant her a divorce from her husband—the president of U.S. Steel.

Ms. Corey's exploit in the courts of Nevada generated a lot of publicity; by the end of World War I, Reno had become the place to go to get unhitched. By the 1920s, in fact, a regular industry had grown up in Reno, catering to the needs of would-be divorcees. When the society columns of most newspapers in the country reported that so-and-so was in Reno, the readers knew almost without thinking that that meant so-and-so was getting a divorce. Agreeably, the legislature amended the residency requirement to a mere six weeks. Two Reno judges, Thomas Moran and George Bartles, became nationally known as the "Reno divorce judges," granting thousands of decrees while the divorce industry was in its heyday. Among those who got divorced while taking the waters in Reno were Mary Pickford; Liz Whitney, wife of New York scion John Hay Whitney; Orson Welles; the third wife of Cornelius Vanderbilt; an Indian maharaja; and at least one Astor and one Du Pont.

Along with the divorce mill came another new fad: dude

ranches. These were places that offered the six-week "residents" a congenial atmosphere while they waited for the calendar to turn, and were later to become famous in the newspapers and eventually movies of the day: the "Tumbling DW," with its swimming pool (then a rarity); or "The Willows," a place near the mouth of the Truckee River Canyon that offered top-flight cuisine and a chance to while away the days pulling the arms of mechanical slot machines. Also famous were various Reno clubs that catered to the short-term residents, among them the "Ship and Bottle," and the "Cowshed," which had tanks filled with silver trout. Someone suggested the proprietor put some goldfish in with the trout, reasoning that the gold and silver would match the state's mining motif, but the silver ate the gold.

Then there was the tradition of the wedding ring: after getting the short-awaited divorce decree, the newly unwed ex-wife would walk to the Virginia Street bridge over the Truckee, strip the no-longer-valid wedding ring from her finger, and toss it into the river, a scene faithfully reenacted as late as the 1960s by Marilyn Monroe in the movie *The Misfits*.

But if this was the popular perception of Reno, it was belied by what lay beneath the surface. For despite its reputation as a playground for the rich and dissolute, by the middle of the last century, Reno had grown a rather staid foundation—an underpinning of conservative respectability, an establishment who really ran things—"old Reno," some called it; a class of hidden social and economic power who were perfectly content to see people come in from out of state and spend their money. But none of the newcomers, most of them transients, after all, should expect to be accepted as one of the town's elite: there were some things that even money could not buy. Old Reno ran things, and it liked it that way.

And it was among that class of Renoans that Laurence

Williams McNabney was born on December 19, 1948, the second son of James McNabney and Marie Williams McNabney, both of long-time Nevada families with deep roots in the hidden bedrock of the community.

James McNabney—"Mac" to his friends and acquaintances—was himself born in Nevada in 1919, one of two sons of Guy and Alexina McNabney. Guy McNabney had been born in Indiana late in the 19th Century, and by the 1920s, he was living and working in Lovelock, a small town on the rail line about 100 miles northeast of Reno. Lovelock was farming and ranching country, and it appears that Guy McNabney was engaged in one of those occupations; the only public mention of Guy came in the *Nevada Appeal* newspaper in 1922, when the railroad proposed to end its stops at Lovelock, which prompted Guy to protest—losing the rail stop would have been death to any agricultural enterprise.

Guy's son James—"Mac"—was a handsome young man, considered very bright by all his schoolmates, and also a gifted athlete, running the sprints and hurdles. By 1943 he was in military service, as were most able-bodied young men in the first years of World War II. On May 10 of that year he married Marie Williams in San Francisco; Marie was the daughter of the superintendent of a gold mine in Tonopah, Nevada, Laurence Williams, and his wife Frances. Eventually Frances Williams—who would be known to Larry and his older brother Jimmy as "Gamm," or "Gammy"—would as a widow marry a man named Laughenour; by the time "Gammy" died in 1980, she would leave an estate worth about a half a million dollars.

"Mac" McNabney returned from the war to Reno, and began to raise a family. Larry's brother James, Jr.— "Jimmy"—was born in 1947, and Laurence Williams McNabney—"Larry"—came at the end of the following year. Then, while both boys were still toddlers, Mac was recalled to the service for the Korean War.

The details of this call-up and its effects on the McNab-ney family are sketchy, but it appears that the conflict in Korea had a profound effect on Mac. Some people in Reno were later to say, in fact, that on his return to Reno after the Korean War, Mac was never the same person that he had been before being recalled to service. Clearly, Mac had a number of problems, not the least of which was his drink-ing. In short, Mac was an alcoholic.

Alcoholism is an insidious disease, not least because it creeps up so unobtrusively on its victim. This is because the tolerance for the drug grows with habitual usage. Where a young soldier like Mac might be able to polish off a six-pack of beers without much effect, a middle-aged Mac would find himself drinking more and more alcohol, and having a far harder time stopping—in short, it took more booze for Mac to feel its influence.

The alcoholic has two burdens that the non-alcoholic doesn't have: first, a probable genetic condition which causes alcohol to affect the body and brain chemistry more power-fully than it does the non-alcoholic's; and second, a social/ psychological condition which helps create a craving for the drug as an inseparable part of the personality of the afflicted person. A person with the genetic condition who does not have the psycho/social condition is not likely to become an alcoholic; nor is a person with the psycho/social condition who does not also have the genetic condition. The combina-tion of the two conditions in an individual creates a powerful, often overwhelming dynamic. As a general rule, the only way the dynamic can be shattered is to disrupt the psycho/social condition that leads to the consumption of alcohol and re-place it with something else, which is how such programs as Alcoholics Anonymous and similar "rehab" programs es-sentially function. Once the psycho/social condition is al-tered, it may be possible for an alcoholic to realize that they

have the underlying genetic condition as well, but until the
psycho/social condition is addressed, this is information
that isn't particularly useful to the sufferer of alcoholism.

Because of its progressive nature—that is, it increases in
severity over a period of years—it is often difficult for a
person who is an alcoholic to even realize his condition. In
effect, there is a gradual erosion of personality, often so
subtle that it passes unnoticed, even by people who are closest to the afflicted person. This seems to have been the case
with Mac. People who knew him later observed that he was
great fun, the life of the party—particularly among all the
rest of the drinkers. But at home he was a terror—stern, demanding, unforgiving of his wife and two sons.

Outwardly—that is to say, materially—the McNabney
family seemed comfortable. Mac had a job managing the
University of Nevada bookstore, and the family lived in a
very nice house on Brown Street in southwest Reno. The
family had two cars, an investment portfolio, a membership
in a country club. On the surface, then, things seemed fine.
But underneath there were severe troubles. This environment
was to have profound, perhaps fatal consequences later for
both Larry and his brother Jimmy. Larry, for one, was to have
a life-long difficulty with intimacy—he would be married
five times—and he would never be able to define himself
in terms other than what he had—material things—or what
he did: his image to others. These are both conditions that
stemmed from the troubled, distant relationship with his
father.

Both Jimmy and Larry attended Reno public schools, at
Mt. Rose Elementary and later Reno High School. Mac was
a stern taskmaster; those who knew the family recalled that
he demanded both academic and athletic excellence from his
sons. Mac himself had been a prize-winning athlete in high
school, and Jimmy and Larry felt driven to measure up to
Mac's expectations.

In Larry's senior year he met another senior from a cross-town high school, Donna Pagini; unlike Larry, Donna was from a large, boisterous, loving family. Larry and Donna began dating, and by the time they graduated in 1966, were engaged to be married. This, it seems, was evidence of a rebellion against Mac. Neither family approved of the other, and certainly not of the proposed marriage. Donna's father thought little of Larry—he seemed pretty stuck-up, at least to the Paginis—stiff, taciturn almost to the point of rudeness. And Mac disliked Donna—she was the cause of Larry's rebellion. To Donna, Mac was simply intimidating. "I was scared to death of him," she said, years later.

After leaving high school, Larry enrolled at the University of Nevada, Reno; Donna recalled that he majored in business. At the end of the first year, Donna and Larry were married. That at least got Larry out from under Mac's often baleful presence. By the year after that, Donna was pregnant; in July of 1968, she Donna gave birth to a daughter, Cristin.

As the 1960s came to a close, Donna realized that she had probably made a mistake in marrying Larry. He seemed very uncomfortable around her family, with its spontaneity and loving laughter. As long as she was in Reno, Donna could fall back on her family when things with Larry got rough. And things *did* get rough from time to time; just like his father, Larry had begun to drink, and when he drank, he could be belligerent and aggressive, and often insulting when not condescending. Donna didn't like it.

After graduating from UNR in 1970, Larry was accepted as a student at McGeorge School of Law in Sacramento, California, affiliated with the University of the Pacific. In August of that year, Larry and Donna moved to Sacramento so Larry could get ready to attend classes. Donna hated it.

"By that time I knew it wasn't going to work," she said later. "And I missed my family." After several weeks,

Donna moved back to Reno, taking Cristin with her. She filed for divorce from Larry that month, and six weeks later, on September 22, the divorce was granted.

At this point there appears to be some imprecision in Larry's activities, one that is not clarified by the available records. Donna recalled later that as a member of the UNR Reserve Officers Training Command [the ROTC], Larry had an obligation to fulfill in terms of military service. This was during the war in Viet Nam, of course, and exemptions from such service were growing increasingly rare. Donna today recalls that after she and Larry divorced, he went into the Army, traveling to Fort Benning in Georgia; and indeed, several of Larry's friends recall much the same. It appears, therefore, that despite his acceptance in law school, Larry did not actually enroll; or if he did, he dropped out after the divorce and decided to fulfill his military obligation.

But events were soon to overtake Larry, and horrific events they were to be.

By the fall of 1970, with two sons grown—Jimmy had been in the Navy for two years, and had married, Larry was either in law school or the Army at Fort Benning—Marie Williams McNabney decided that she'd had enough of Mac, her husband of twenty-seven years. Mac's drinking had, if anything, gotten much worse over the previous decade. And Mac, when he drank, was abusive. On November 17, 1970, Marie filed for divorce.

"The Plaintiff [Marie] is substantially dependent on Defendant [Mac] for her livelihood," the divorce complaint read. "She has very little means of support other than the amounts that may be provided for her by Defendant . . . the Defendant has earning power of approximately one thousand dollars per month [in those days, a fairly sizeable income, approximately equivalent to perhaps eight or nine thousand a month today] and should be required to pay the Plaintiff during the pendency of this suit and permanently a reasonable sum . . ."

The divorce filing went on to list the McNabneys' community property: the house on Brown Street, two nearly new cars, membership in the country club, eighty-two shares of AT&T stock, thirty-one shares of Pacific Telephone and Telegraph stock, two hundred thirty-five shares of Sierra Pacific stock, and five shares of Northwest Bell stock. Altogether, this represented a substantial portfolio of investments, at least for the times.

Marie asked that she be given the house on Brown Street, along with the alimony; the stocks, she said, should be divided evenly.

Mac made no response to the divorce suit, at least on paper. Instead, he shot himself to death one week later.

Three weeks after that, Larry's brother Jimmy was also dead, the victim of a what appeared to be an intentional drug overdose.

Looking back, it's almost impossible to calculate the effect of these suicides on Larry. Certainly they were powerful influences on his psyche, twin demons that never really left him, and which drove him, on more than one occasion, to contemplate suicide himself. At the very least, Larry felt abandoned by his father and his brother, and whatever limited intimacy he had with two-thirds of his birth family was abruptly ended, under the most unpleasant of circumstances. In the deepest recesses of his mind, Larry was unspeakably lonely, unbearably sad, and this condition drove him repeatedly to the most self-destructive acts as his own life unfolded.

Donna remembered attending the funerals of both Larry's father and his brother, even though she and Larry were now divorced. At Jimmy's funeral, Donna recalled, the boys' grandmother Frances—"Gammy"—cried out in pain and puzzlement: "Why, Jimmy, why? Why did you do it?" But there was no answer, because, as people were to say over and over again, for the rest of Larry's life there was simply no way to know what was really in someone's mind.

"You think you know someone," one of Larry's oldest friends later observed, "but you don't, really. You only think you do. One day you wake up and you look at your wife . . . you've been married thirty years and you suddenly realize that you don't really know this person *at all*, that you only think you do, and that's when you realize that you've only been kidding yourself, that is, when you think that anyone can ever really know another person."

Well, this is all at once profound and depressing, and maybe even true; it *is* true that we are all born as individuals and that we die as individuals, so that we can never know absolutely what is in another person's mind. But it is in the nature of being human that we try, and it is, in the end, the essence of love that we accept one another as we are, even if we don't always understand. That, after all, is the real meaning of intimacy, and it was something that Larry, for all his flair and brilliance, found it difficult to embrace, until, perhaps, the last years of his life.

And then, in a most peculiar way, it may have killed him.

On October 6, 1973, in Virginia City's Silver Queen restaurant, Larry married JoDee Cotton, a young divorcee with a 5-year-old daughter. Cristin, also 5, remembered attending the ceremony with Tavia, who was soon to be her sister, when Larry adopted her. Larry was in the final year of law school at McGeorge, and was being supported by his mother and "Gammy." In June of 1974, Larry graduated near the top of the law school class at McGeorge, and began to prepare for bar examinations in both Nevada and California. In the next year, he was appointed to a clerkship in the Reno District Court, and after passing the bar, joined the Washoe County Public Defender's Office as a juvenile deputy.

In 1977, Larry left the public defender's office to join another Reno lawyer, Ron J. Bath, in a partnership. Bath was also a former public defender, as well as a graduate of McGeorge. A former Air Force fighter pilot, Bath was, in many ways, Larry's polar opposite. Where Bath was conservative, Larry was liberal; where Bath was disciplined, particularly with money, Larry tended to be profligate.

"He was real flamboyant," Bath was to recall. "He used to say, 'Think ink.' He said it didn't matter what they said about you in the newspaper, as long as they spelled your name right."

Larry was one of the most engaging personalities he'd ever met, Bath said. "You couldn't be around him and not like him. He did everything with incredible intensity . . . in the courtroom he was as fast on his feet as anyone I ever saw. He would have been better in the courtroom drunk than most lawyers ever would have been sober, not that he ever came to court drunk."

But Larry did have a drinking problem. "Larry tormented Larry," was how Bath, now a high Air Force official in Washington, recalled it. There were plenty of times that Bath or the secretary they shared had to cover for Larry because of his excesses. Despite Jimmy's death, "Larry was not afraid to abuse substances," Bath said.

In 1979, Larry and Bath bought a venerable Reno mansion at the intersection of Sierra Street and California Avenue not far from the Washoe County Courthouse. The mansion had belonged to the Levy family, descendants of an early day Comstock dry goods dealer who had made millions in the silver rush. The original Levy had two daughters, one of whom had married and had children, while the other never married, living her entire life in the mansion, from birth to death. When she died of old age, Larry and Bath bought the house from the estate, from the other sister's nephew, who turned out to be San Francisco attorney William Coblentz. Coblentz at that time was chairman of the University of California's Board of Regents. Coblentz not only agreed to sell them the mansion, but also to hold a mortgage on the property.

Larry and Bath then began to renovate the structure to make it suitable for offices. Bath recalled removing fixtures like bathtubs from the house, leaving them on the lawn, to the consternation of the neighbors, while they hammered and sawed and painted and wallpapered, then changing their clothes in a rush so they could get to court, then changing back again while they worked until midnight to convert the old house. While Bath was handy with tools, Larry was artistic, Bath recalled. "One of his skill-sets was picking the wallpaper," Bath said. "Larry was left-brained."

Almost from the beginning, Bath recalled, he and Larry

had more business than they could handle. "In those days the town was ripe for lawyers who wanted to try cases," he said. "Up until then, the district attorney's office was very powerful—they had some guys in there that were very good trial lawyers, and so there was something of a tendency to plea bargain . . . but we were willing to try them." One result is that Larry and Bath rapidly became among the most prominent members of the Reno defense bar.

Larry and Bath handled almost exclusively criminal cases, at least at first. There were some drug cases, Bath recalled, but many of their clients had gaming charges—when a casino accused someone of cheating. On the average, Bath recalled, he and Larry also handled about five or six murders a year, rather a considerable number for any attorney.

Then, in early 1979, Larry became the lead defense attorney in one of Reno's most sensational homicide cases—the murder of the son of one of the town's justices of the peace. It was a case that would generate controversy right up until the very end of Larry's life, as we shall see.

On the night of Wednesday, December 20, 1978, Richard Minor, 26, was stabbed to death in his small apartment in Reno. The attack was frenzied, with many different knife thrusts, and the small living room—really, only a little bigger than a large closet at eight by ten feet—was covered with Minor's blood.

The following day, Minor's father, Reno Justice of the Peace Richard Minor, Sr., came to the apartment to check up on his son, and there discovered him lying on the floor, deceased. It appeared that the younger Minor had been dead from six to ten hours.

Over the next several days, Reno police discovered—if they hadn't already known it—that the junior Minor was a dealer in marijuana and cocaine. The murder was seen as some sort of drug rip-off gone very bad, and investigators began trying to identify Minor's customers. There was one thing odd about the case, however—Minor's girlfriend, a young prostitute named April Barber, who was employed at the notorious Mustang Ranch just outside of town, had been reported missing some days before.

Within a few days, the lead Reno detective, a man whose wholly appropriate name was Nevada Wise, began to focus on one of Minor's regular customers, a hairdresser named John Mazzan. Wise discovered that Mazzan had been having financial difficulties, but that a day or so after Minor's murder, he had paid off his back rent from a large roll of bills. Where was Mazzan? It turned out that he had flown to Las Vegas to see his wife, a dancer, on December 23.

Wise put the Las Vegas police on to Mazzan; the Las Vegas authorities contacted him through his wife and told him that he was a suspect in a Reno murder. Three days later Mazzan returned to Reno, and the next day went down to police headquarters to confer with Wise and his confederates. Twelve hours later, Mazzan was arrested and charged with Minor's murder.

Soon thereafter, Larry was appointed to represent Mazzan. Then, even as Larry was meeting with his burly, somewhat unsavory client, the Reno police were discovering new evidence—a suede coat that belonged to Mazzan, stained with blood that matched Minor's blood type, along with a purse and shredded, bloody clothes that had belonged to April Barber. The problem for the police: all the stuff had been found in a trash can near Mazzan's apartment, but it was a receptacle that had been emptied *after* Mazzan had been arrested. That meant it couldn't have been Mazzan who put the bloody clothes and purse in the trash, which in turn meant someone else had to be involved.

The Mazzan–Minor case rapidly escalated into front-page news in Reno—or, as Larry might have put it, "ink." Mazzan's story was problematical, however. He said that he had visited Minor in his apartment the night of the murder, all right, but that he hadn't done the killing. He said he'd left Minor's apartment to go home, only to find that his car wouldn't start. Minor had agreed to let him spend the night in the tiny apartment, and so Mazzan had flopped down behind the couch to sleep. At some point in the middle of the night, Mazzan awakened to see and hear Minor struggling with a shadowy figure in the adjacent tiny kitchen. By the time he got to his feet, the assailant was running out the door, Mazzan said. He heard two people running away, then a car driving off. Minor had been stabbed fifteen times and soon died. Mazzan then fled without notifying anyone that he had seen Minor murdered. A few days later he flew to Las Vegas to see his wife, where he soon learned that he was the prime suspect.

That, at any rate, was Mazzan's story, and he was sticking to it. Larry thought that he might be able to get an acquittal for Mazzan—the discovery of the bloody clothes in the trash can after Mazzan was arrested certainly showed that someone else had to be involved in the case. Larry noted that Minor had been dealing drugs, that Minor's girlfriend April Barber had disappeared, and that April's bloody clothes had been found in the trash can, along with her purse and Mazzan's coat stained with Minor's blood. It certainly looked like someone was trying to frame Mazzan for one if not two murders, he said. Besides, Larry added, Minor had told his sister shortly before his death that he was in trouble with some drug pushers over a deal that had gone bad.

Hogwash! Or so the police said. Mazzan had repeatedly lied to them during their interview of him, they said, and he'd only come up with his behind-the-couch snoozing story when they'd found traces of Minor's blood in his car—the one that supposedly wouldn't start—as well as on his shoes. Mazzan had been broke, suddenly he was flush with a wad of bills. Mazzan had fled the city within two days of the discovery of the body. And besides this, the room where Minor had been stabbed fifteen times was so small that Mazzan had to have known what was happening when it was happening, not after the fact as he had claimed. The facts shouted out a logical conclusion: that Mazzan had stabbed Minor to death in a robbery.

But Larry vociferously contended that Mazzan was innocent, and the bloody clothes in the trash can proved it. Everything against Mazzan was circumstantial evidence, Larry said, even the blood in Mazzan's car and on his shoes. The fact was, Mazzan had stepped in Minor's blood when he was fleeing the scene, so it would have been unusual if there *wasn't* blood in Mazzan's car or on his shoes. Mazzan had won the big roll of money in a casino just before the death, he contended.

The key to the case, Larry told anyone who would listen, was April Barber. If they could only locate April, a 20-year-old from Florida, the police might be able to unravel the mystery, Larry said. Larry said he guessed that she was dead—killed by the same drug dealers who had killed Minor while his client, Mazzan, had slept behind the couch. After all, both Minor and April had been involved in selling drugs. In fact, Mazzan had met April while dressing her hair at the infamous brothel, and April had sold him cocaine, then introduced him to Minor. Mazzan was only the friend, and occasional customer, of two young people who were involved in the drug racket, Larry contended, who happened to be at the wrong place at the wrong time.

It was a miracle, Larry suggested, that Mazzan himself hadn't been killed in the bloody attack. And if April had also been killed, and her body was found, Larry said, there would be new evidence as to the identity of the two mysterious men in Minor's apartment. To that end, Larry told the newspapers, he had decided to hire a psychic to help locate April Barber.

In early March of 1979, a little over two months after Mazzan's arrest, Larry retained the services of Kay Rhea, a California woman who believed she had abilities as a psychic, and whose claims seemed to be backed up by police agencies in California. He met with Rhea for several days, then announced to the newspapers that she had concluded that 1) April Barber was indeed dead; 2) her body would be found near some sort of monument; 3) it would be unburied; 4) the terrain nearby would be rugged, in the foothills; and 5) the body was outside the Reno city limits.

The day after this pronouncement by Larry, he met with Rhea again; neither would say what was discussed. But Larry seemed confident he was on the right track. "We still have a long way to go in the investigation, but the case is solved in my mind," he told the newspapers.

About two weeks later, Larry began a search of a four-hundred-square-yard area in the desert outside of Reno, apparently in search of April Barber's remains; it looked as though Larry was acting on Rhea's information, at least in the view of the newspapers. But Larry found nothing. Late the next month, Mazzan gave an interview to the newspaper, while Larry sat by his side in the jail. Mazzan told his story again, proclaiming his innocence. Larry cut off questions that were too probing, however, and soon Washoe County District Attorney Mills Lane—who would go on to become a nationally known television "judge"—erupted at Larry, saying that he was appalled at Larry's conduct in permitting the interview.

"I think it's improper as the devil to go up there and coach your client," Lane said. "I think he's engaging in trying it in the paper."

Larry shot back: "I don't think the district attorney should be so concerned that Jack [Mazzan] got to tell his story. You don't hear the DA complaining when a story *unfavorable* to a defendant comes out. He'd like to have just the unfavorable comments published."

This was ink, all right.

By September of 1979, Mills had left as district attorney, and a new D.A., Cal Dunlap, was in his place. Dunlap decided to convene a grand jury to investigate April Barber's

disappearance. Larry complained that the district attorney
was attempting to discover attorney–client information he
had learned from Mazzan through the guise of a grand jury
investigation into another matter. Dunlap said Larry was
blowing more smoke.

In October, Mazzan was brought to trial for the murder
of Richard Minor, and after almost three weeks' testimony,
was found guilty. Larry seemed furious. In summing up his
argument to the same jury at the penalty phase, he excori-
ated the jury members for their decision, which he called
"the greatest act of irresponsibility that I have ever seen . . .
if the jurors are the conscience of the community, then I am
ashamed to be a member of it." Naturally, the jury was offended by Larry's tirade. A week later they gave Mazzan
the death penalty.

Three weeks after that, a pair of passing motorists found
the remains of April Barber in a shallow grave just off the
interstate highway east of town.

After April's remains had been identified, one of the reporters for the *Nevada State Journal* who had covered the Mazzan case chided psychic Kay Rhea for her lack of accuracy in predicting the location of the 20-year-old girl's body. **Psychic bats zero in search,** the paper headlined. Reporter John Zappe said Rhea was wrong all the way around in her predictions about April Barber's body. The body wasn't unburied, and it wasn't near a monument—not unless one considered a highway sign a monument. And the body wasn't in the foothills, it was in a gully just off the highway. District Attorney Cal Dunlap couldn't resist a poke of his own, even though only two weeks earlier he had suggested that April wasn't dead at all, that she in fact had been Mazzan's accomplice and was therefore hiding out until the heat died down.

"Technically," said Dunlap, "it was not in the foothills. A gully next to a highway is not in the foothills. In the foothills you would expect to be in the hills, rather than along a highway."

Stung, Rhea struck back, and as she did so, the onus settled squarely on Larry.

She had been right all along, Rhea said—it was just that what Larry had told the papers wasn't at all what she had told Larry, back during his "search" for the body in the spring. Reporters in San Francisco, who had picked up Zappe's chiding story of Rhea, then called the psychic herself for her response, now contacted Larry, and he admitted that Rhea had been accurate in forecasting the location of the body. But once she had told him, Larry said, he couldn't very well announce the information to the world for fear that someone would actually find the body. That was why he had led the papers on a merry chase, far away from the supposed location.

Larry said Rhea had provided a generalized description of the location. "I didn't get into any specifics," he added. "If everybody was misled, then . . . that's unfortunate. What I did, I did for a very good reason. I don't think you [the press] understood that I have a client to represent and I didn't think it would necessarily do him any good to have that body found."

Larry said he couldn't simply have stopped talking about the psychic and the body without people concluding that Mazzan was guilty. That was why he'd led everyone astray.

But there was even more to the story, Rhea said.

"I told Mr. McNabney, 'I will come, I have no idea what I will find. I don't know if I will find your man innocent.' Then, in the very first five minutes, I said, 'Your man is guilty. Your man is very guilty. He's a complete schizophrenic.' " Mazzan had also killed April Barber, Rhea said she'd told Larry.

The day after Larry had put out the information about the body being near a "monument" in March, Rhea added, she'd called Larry to ask him about the remark he had attributed to her. "I said, 'Hey, what's this "monument" business?' He laughed and said, 'Well, I don't want them out there looking for the body, given your description, because right now it's not going to help my client to have them find the body.' And I said, 'Well, I understand that, Larry, but you know and I know I never said that.' "

Well, what could anyone do with this? It seemed pretty clear from the context of all of these remarks that Larry had gone into the Mazzan case believing that his client was actually innocent, and that April Barber was indeed the key to the case, only to discover that Mazzan in fact had done the deed, and that he'd also likely killed April Barber. Why else would he have tried to prevent people from finding poor April's remains if he really believed that Mazzan wasn't guilty? But Larry was true to the defense lawyers' code: he told reporters he still believed in Mazzan's innocence.

This wouldn't be the last anyone heard of Jack Mazzan, Richard Minor and April Barber, as things would turn out.

By 1979, Larry and JoDee were living in Larry's boyhood home on Brown Street in southwest Reno. Tavia had been joined by a little brother, Joey, in May of 1976. Marie had moved into a condominium in south Reno, and had deeded half the equity in the Brown Street house to Larry and JoDee, with JoDee receiving 15 percent as her separate share, and Larry getting the remaining 35 percent. By any standard, this was a curious arrangement, but as Larry admitted later, it was his mother's way of trying to induce Larry and JoDee to have a stable, permanent relationship—the scars from Mac's suicide still cut deep, years later.

After all the "ink" from the Mazzan trial, Larry was one of the most prominent lawyers in Reno. He and Ron Bath continued to do well. By this time they had expanded their practice to include two new partners, among them Fred Atcheson, one of Reno's brightest lawyers, who, for some reason, came to be nicknamed "Frodo," for the Tolkien character. The old mansion also became the home of a second partnership, this one among lawyers Tom Brennan and Peter Durney.

In those days, according to Bath and others, the circle of trial lawyers in Reno was fairly small, no matter what side one was on. Prosecutors and defenders knew one another, and often had a social life together outside the courthouse. "There was a sort of pack," Bath recalled. "We all ate together and pretty much knew each other." Like cops and newspapermen, the trial lawyers also drank with each other. This was another example of the Reno establishment—the lawyers might fight like cats and dogs in court, but outside the marble corridors they tended to stick up for each other against outsiders.

Larry's own predilection for alcohol and drugs continued, and the other lawyers tended to cover for him if things got crazy. By the early 1980s, even Larry realized that his drinking was getting out of hand. At one point he checked himself into a rehabilitation clinic to dry out. While there, he began jogging, then running. When he got out several weeks later, Larry told Bath that he intended to be a world champion marathoner. That was Larry: it wasn't enough to run a marathon, he had to be the champion. Nevertheless, Bath was still shocked several weeks later to realize that Larry meant it: he'd flown to Massachusetts to run in the Boston Marathon, and while he didn't win, he did finish the race. When Larry made up his mind to do something, Bath said, he did it with everything he had.

In some ways, Bath represented Larry's better half. For one thing, Bath ran the business side of the partnership. "If Larry made a buck, he'd spend a dollar-thirty," Bath said. "If he made a hundred dollars, he'd spend a hundred and thirty. If he made a million, he'd spend one point three million." It was just Larry's nature to be expansive, even a show-off, when it came to money. So Bath kept the books and signed the checks, and Larry seemed okay with this. When Bath told him they weren't going to "take any great big [salary] draws," Larry accepted it.

On September 7, 1980, Larry's beloved grandmother, "Gammy," Marie's mother, died in Reno. She was 90 years old, and had amassed a fortune of about $450,000, all in a trust for Marie's benefit. The will outlining the trust arrangement began to make its way through probate, but on March 4 of the following year, Marie disclaimed all interest in the estate. This may have been for tax reasons, however. At the end of April in the following year, 1982, Larry petitioned the court to substitute him for Marie as the will's beneficiary, noting that Marie had disclaimed any interest in her mother's wealth. But this, too, may have been for tax reasons, because it seemed apparent from later litigation that Marie kept control of the money.

Then, in 1982, Larry got involved in another high-profile criminal case—this one stemming from the spectacular extortion bombing that had ripped the venerable Harveys hotel and casino to bits at Lake Tahoe on August 27, 1980.

The "bomb plot," as it came to be known, was one of the most colorful criminal episodes in Nevada history. It all began in the early morning hours of August 26, 1980, when two men wheeled a heavy piece of "office machinery" labeled "IBM" into the old casino, located right on the border between Nevada and California in Lake Tahoe.

Harveys was the pride and joy of Harvey Gross, a onetime butcher who owned a shop that had been bisected by the state line back in the early days of Lake Tahoe. The shop, like most butcher shops, had its floors covered with sawdust, and down the middle of the sawdusted floor was a painted line. On the California side of the line, Harvey sold meat. On the Nevada side of the line, he installed four slot machines. It wasn't too long before Harvey realized that the slot machines were much more profitable than the steaks, and what was even better, they never spoiled.

Over the years, Harvey built his establishment up, mostly by serving great food and hospitality in his "Wagon Wheel Room," with its French onion soup a particular specialty. Over the years the butcher shop had grown into a high-rise hotel, just across the state line, and across the street from his competitor, Harrah's.

But by the late 1970s, both Harvey and his hotel were aging. He wanted to remodel his facility to add more rooms, and the Lake Tahoe planning people were giving him grief. Still, Harvey thought he had a good plan, and was confident that eventually the hotel's remodel would go forward.

That was the situation on Tuesday night, August 26, when the two men wheeled the heavy, draped "machine" into the casino's offices and left it there.

It soon became apparent that the equipment was not equipment, or even made by IBM. It was in fact a sophisticated bomb, and it had been rigged to blow up if anyone tried to disarm it, or even move it. A note left with the equipment said Harvey would have to pay $3,000,000 in cash for the secret of disarming the bomb. Failure to comply, the note said, would cause the bomb to go off, and if it did go off, it was likely to level the entire casino.

Harvey decided not to pay the ransom, but to act as though he would. The money was supposed to be flown by helicopter out of Lake Tahoe, west along U.S. 50, the main highway into the resort area. When a strobe light flashed below, the helicopter was supposed to land and deliver the money. The authorities' idea, however, was that cops on the ground would track the money to the extortionist, arrest him, and then squeeze the secret of the bomb out of him.

But things went wrong almost from the start, when the chopper pilot failed to spot the strobe. Eventually he gave up and returned to Lake Tahoe. Experts from around the country flew in to figure out how to disable the bomb, but were stumped. After more than a day passed, the experts decided to try to use a small charge to blow the triggering mechanism off the diabolic contraption. Instead, the whole thing went off and blasted a huge hole in the side of the hotel, causing an estimated $11,000,000 in damage. As a result, the old Harveys was leveled, and a new hotel was built in its place at a cost of around $20,000,000.

About a year after the bombing, on August 15, 1981, a 60-year-old Clovis, California, man, a former Hungarian freedom fighter and one-time fighter pilot, John Birges, was arrested and charged with the extortion attempt and bombing. So were Birges' two sons, and several other people. Because of massive publicity in the Reno area, the trial was moved to federal court in Las Vegas. Around the first of the year, Larry joined with Fred Atcheson to defend one of the two men accused of actually delivering the bomb to the casino, Terry Lee Hall. Hall was the son-in-law of one of Birges' employees in a Fresno, California–area landscaping business.

As the trial unfolded in 1982 Larry's relationship with JoDee began to go sour. By June of that year, he was in court in Reno seeking to have her and the children evicted from the Brown Street house. Larry asked the court to give JoDee three days to get everything she owned out of the place.

JoDee quickly countersued, seeking an equitable division of the community property. The dispute turned bitter as the summer turned into fall. Larry commuted between Reno and Las Vegas, trying to defend Hall at the same time he was trying to defend himself in the property portion of the divorce action. Larry's drinking increased substantially.

Eventually Hall was convicted of some of the charges in the bomb plot, and given a sentence of 7 years in federal prison. Larry and Atcheson were satisfied. Under the circumstances, Hall could have gotten as much as 20 years, like Birges.

By the winter of 1983, even as he was still squabbling with JoDee over their property settlement, Larry had fallen in love again. On March 1, he married Gail June Fredericks, who was employed as a Social Security administrator in the Reno area. It appears from the record that Gail moved into the house on Brown Street.

Then, a month later, a man named Boatright was arrested and charged with molesting up to fifty small children at the nursery school his mother operated in Reno, an establishment doing business as "Papoose Palace." Larry and his friend Tom Brennan agreed to represent some of the families in lawsuits against the school, Washoe County, and most important, against the school's insurance carrier.

It was, as one of Larry's lawyer pals later put it, every lawyer's dream case: the insurance company, it turned out, had written an unlimited liability policy for the school. Larry and Brennan stood to get rich.

As it turned out, the Papoose Palace cases spelled the end of Larry's partnership with Ron Bath. Bath had for some time felt himself drifting away from his colorful partner, and apparently Larry had felt the same way.

"I was more conservative than he was," Bath said. "We just began to see things differently. When the Papoose Palace cases came up, Larry came in and said he felt he wanted to do them by himself. I said that was all right with me. It was just time . . . time to terminate our partnership." Bath and his wife had been close to both Larry and JoDee. The end of Larry's marriage also seemed to be a factor in the partnership ending.

By June of 1983, Larry reached agreement with JoDee over their property division, and it was expensive—for Larry. To settle the case, Larry agreed to pay $50,000 toward the purchase of a house in Reno for JoDee and the kids, and another $25,000 within the next three years, secured by a second trust deed on the Brown Street house. JoDee agreed to give up the 15 percent interest in the house that Marie had once hoped would cement the couple together. In addition, Larry agreed to pay JoDee $550 a month in alimony, and $600 a month in support for the kids. In addition to a full half-interest in the Brown Street house, Larry got to keep his ownership interest in the mansion–office, and a separate interest in a real estate investment partnership called R3JL Properties.

Another year went by, and the nursery school's insurance carrier began to settle up: indeed, it was an almost indefensible case. The son of the school owner admitted to unspeakable acts with over fifty children, agreed to plead guilty, and drew a life sentence in the penitentiary. The civil liability was open-and-shut. By May of 1984, the Papoose

Palace insurer had settled with the families and their lawyers. Larry began drawing a monthly payment, with escalators, that started at $3,700 a month. The money was in the form of an annuity that would run until 2004, increasing in value every month.

Now he was rich as well as smart, and the only thing that stood between Larry and happiness was Larry himself. What he did not know was that his future life and death would be inextricably tied to a young woman named Laren Renee Sims, who was even then dropping out of high school in Florida, more than two thousand miles away.

Laren

The twenty-seventh state to join the union, on March 3, 1845, Florida is a world away from a place like Nevada. Where the Silver State is dry and mountainous, with snow-clad peaks topping out over 13,000 feet, Florida is wet and flat—its highest point is, at 345 feet, more than a hundred feet lower than the lowest point of Nevada. And it is humid, subtropical and tropical in its weather, its forest and its bugs, the sort of place one might instantly identify with Bogart and Bacall, or with Hurt and Turner—where the steam rises and sultry passions lie mostly dormant beneath moss-laden trees and ominous, pregnant weather.

There, nestled amid a series of low limestone hills some forty-five minutes north of the Gulf Coast cities of Tampa–St. Petersburg, lies the bucolic, *To Kill a Mockingbird*–like town of Brooksville, seat of Hernando County. It was just outside Brooksville, surrounded by rain-dampened cedar, pine, oak and pasture, that Laren Renee Sims grew up, one of four children of Jesse and Jackie Sims.

By all accounts, little Laren was a bright, inquisitive, even precocious child. Born in Attleboro, Massachusetts, when her father was attending the Massachusetts Institute of Technology in the 1960s, Laren as a girl was as popular as she was smart. She also had a willful streak that some thought endearing, while others predicted trouble. At one point, it was said that Laren's intelligence quotient was rated at 140, which certainly put her in the top echelon for brains, if true.

In its early days, Brooksville was the retail center of a rural county that employed most people in its limestone quarries, although some worked in the timber industry—for years the area was the main manufactory for the wooden cases for Eberhard Faber pencils. Brooksville had a long history, even though for most of its existence it had fewer than 2,000 souls. Named in honor of Preston Brooks, a South Carolina congressman who gained national notoriety in 1856 when he beat U.S. Senator Charles Sumner senseless with a cane after the latter had expressed his abolitionist sentiments on the Senate floor, the town was founded as homage to Brooks' violent dedication to states' rights, slavery and later, segregation. During the Civil War, the nearby village of Bayport was used by rebel blockade-runners, and in the aftermath of the conflict Brooksville continued to maintain its color-line traditions, the remnants of which can still be seen today, along with the statue of the Confederate soldier on the county courthouse lawn.

The years after World War II, however, began to bring change to Hernando County and Brooksville. First the population doubled, then redoubled, with much of the new development spreading westward across the low hills between Brooksville and the Gulf, particularly around the community of Spring Hill to the west. As recently as 1970, Spring Hill had only three or four hundred residents; by the year 2000, it had nearly 80,000 people who called it home. All that development did more than just bring money to the Brooksville area; it also brought new ideas and new people.

Among those who moved to the area were three brothers, Jesse, David and Charles Sims, and their families. The Sims brothers began a manufacturing business in Brooksville, Sims Machine and Controls. The business soon grew to be one of the town's largest employers, and was very prosperous indeed; as the years passed, the Sims brothers and their families became socially and politically prominent in Hernando County. Jesse Sims and his wife and their children settled into a comfortable upper-middle-class home northeast of Brooksville, amidst the oaks and pastures of the horse country outlying the town, with every reason to be optimistic about the future.

Later, much of the early background of Laren Sims would be uncertain, not least because Jesse and Jackie, her parents, were intent on keeping it that way. Although a lawyer representing the Sims family agreed to communicate a request for an interview to them, they did not respond to the invitation to share their recollections of their daughter. That certainly was their right, and even understandable, in light of the events that had by then unfolded. Both Simses loved their daughter dearly, and the tragedy that was to occur did nothing to lessen that love. Sometimes talking about the pain doesn't really make it go away—sometimes it only makes it hurt more.

In perhaps the only interview by Jesse and Jackie in the aftermath of the events with which this book is concerned, given to Jamie Jones, a reporter for the *St. Petersburg Times*, Jackie Sims noted only that as she grew older, "Laren's life seemed to change, and she began to make some wrong choices."

According to Jones' account, some of those changes had their origins at Hernando High School, when Laren began to hang out with the boys near the Brooksville bowling alley, Louie's, and drink beer under the nearby power lines. She spent weekends with the fast crowd that liked to hang out at Pine Island, a then-isolated spot on the coast. While this was likely a reflection of typical teenage rebelliousness, a closer look at two photographs from Laren's high school annual seems to tell a more profound story. In one photograph, taken her sophomore year of 1981–82, Laren looks like a naive tenth-grade girl, someone whose innocence is all too apparent. The photograph of the following year, 1982–83, is, by contrast a portrait of a confident, knowing woman. It is almost as if they are two different people. It therefore seems possible that whatever happened to make "Laren's life seem to change," it happened between her sophomore and junior years.

By May of 1984, in her last year of high school, Laren dropped out to marry a young man named Virgil Scott Jordan, who was from the northern, panhandle area of the state. Just how and where Laren encountered Scott, as he was called, wasn't all that clear from the records many years later, but according to the Simses' family lawyer, Thomas Hogan of Brooksville, Laren met Scott at a dance somewhere in north Florida in the spring of 1984. Scott, Hogan said, was in military service at the time. According to the *Times'* Jamie Jones, who apparently got the story from Jackie Sims, Laren married Scott at a ceremony at the Simses' house in Brooksville; the state's official records indicate only that a marriage license was taken out on May 12, 1984, in Jackson County, in north Florida near the Florida/Alabama/Georgia border.

The following January, Laren gave birth to a daughter, Haylei. What next transpired was to be shrouded in the mists of uncertainty and reluctance to discuss it, but it appears that shortly after Haylei was born, Laren and Scott split up, and were soon divorced. Laren returned to Hernando County with her infant daughter.

There, Laren began a relationship with a Brooksville man. Soon she was pregnant again. On March 17, 1986, she gave birth to a son. By early the following year, that relationship had gone sour as well, and Laren was in court seeking child support payments from the father of the boy. In an agreement in June of 1988, the father agreed to pay $165 a month in child support, as well as a $750 lump sum for Laren's lawyer's fee.

Somehow during this period of time Laren found the time to finish high school, obtaining a GED, and if the Hernando County records are accurate, it appears that she also attended college—a later court record notes that she had four years of college (more probably just two years, however) and certification as a dental technician.

Still, from 1988 forward, there would be an ever-widening angle away from the straight-and-narrow for Laren. What began as a small deviation from the law, over time and with continued probation violations, grew larger and larger, more and more serious, and eventually, led to fatal results, like a long-term bond accruing compound interest. Some of this early veering away from a life of honesty was due to Laren's headstrong, independent nature. Some was due to Jesse and Jackie's decision to deal with their daughter in terms of "tough love," as Hogan later put it. Much of it—perhaps most of it—was due to Laren's consistently unfortunate choices in domestic partners, and her apparent willingness to be used by them, at least in the beginning. But some of it was clearly the result of some form of mental illness, as the court records would eventually suggest.

For one thing, in reviewing Laren's subsequent criminal history, one can't help but be struck by the pettiness of almost all the charges. At least half of the scrapes that she would get into between 1988 and 1993 involved taking things that had very little actual value, but were in fact connected to, or owned by someone with whom Laren was having a personal dispute, or some sort of emotional relationship. That there was a psychological dimension to Laren's criminality was obvious to almost everyone. It wasn't as if she were inherently an evil person, it was just that she had problems— *issues*, as the word is now used—with authority, with men, with property and security. In one sense, the stealing might be seen as an attempt to get even; at the same time it represented an attempt to get someone to rescue her.

Among Laren's first criminal escapades was the shoplifting of a hair-coloring kit worth less than $5, in St. Petersburg in 1988. For this she received a fine and probation. By the fall, the problems deepened: Laren took ceramic flower arrangements and a telephone from a neighbor with whom she'd been having a dispute, total value $170. A month later, she burgled the house of her boyfriend's ex-wife, taking a telephone answering machine, jewelry, clothes, a musical instrument, and an all-terrain vehicle. According to lawyer Thomas Hogan, Laren did this to please the boyfriend, not because she wanted the stuff. Indeed, the boyfriend may have felt he had some legal claim to the property, including the ATV, but was barred from the premises, and somehow cajoled Laren into getting the goods for him. Laren's willingness to do this, Hogan would suggest, only indicated her naivete at the time.

But nevertheless, here is a clue about Laren's personality: the apparent desire to please an older man. As she was to progress through the remainder of her life, this would be a pattern repeated again and again: getting close to a man who was older, then either breaking the law in some fashion to please him, or alternatively, getting even with him by using him in some scheme. This would be seen in Hernando County; Las Vegas; Reno; Lodi, California; Nashville; Biloxi, Mississippi; and again in Florida at the end of her life, when her last objective would be Hogan himself.

By January 8, 1989, these early malefactions had caught up with Laren. A Hernando County sheriff's deputy, acting on a complaint by the boyfriend's former wife, went to Laren's home to arrest her, but she fled. The deputy was patient. Eventually a friend arrived to pick Laren up, so the deputy collared him instead. The friend told the deputy that Laren had admitted burglarizing the ex-wife's house, saying it was the ex-wife's own fault because she had left her keys in her car in front of the house, "a fact that only the victim knew about and the perpetrator," the detective reported. Eventually Laren was located near Tampa, arrested and taken to jail in Brooksville. She denied committing the burglary, but admitted being in possession of the stolen goods.

Now that they had Laren in custody, the Hernando County

authorities cleared two more petty burglary cases: the ceramic flower pot caper, and a second intrusion into the exwife's house, in which another answering machine was also taken. In addition, the arresting detectives noticed that two other police agencies, in St. Petersburg and Winter Haven, in Polk County, had holds on Laren for cases they were investigating. It appeared to the cops, at least, that Laren was fencing stolen property at various pawn shops in other cities. When she was booked into the jail, Laren called her father, Jesse. Laren was held on $5,500 bail.

By March, apparently reconsidering their initial inclination to let Laren sleep in the bed she had made for herself, the Simses retained Hogan to represent her on two burglaries, a grand theft, a petty theft, and a charge of dealing stolen property. Hogan, who had represented the Sims brothers in their factory business dealings, negotiated a deal with the Florida State Attorney's Office. Laren would agree to plead guilty to the two burglaries, the grand theft and the petty theft, and the dealing in stolen property charge would be dismissed. In return, Laren would avoid any more jail time, agree to pay restitution to the victims in the amount of $1,184, and be on probation for 5 years.

"Also," said Hogan, "the assistant state attorney has requested counseling, and Ms. Jordan has already enrolled in counseling, so that will be easily fulfilled."

The judge asked Laren if she was willing to agree to this deal, and Laren said she was. "How far did you go in school?" he asked.

"I have a GED," Laren said.

The judge agreed to accept the negotiated plea, and sentenced Laren to serve 5 years probation, concurrent with 3 years she was serving on probation for the St. Petersburg hair-coloring caper, and that she pay court costs of $500 in addition to the restitution. The judge also ordered her to undergo a mental health evaluation, but Hogan objected to this.

"I'd like it to be noted," Hogan said, "that Ms. Jordan is already in counseling of her own volition, and she doesn't need to be evaluated. She's already evaluated voluntarily."

"Okay," said the judge, apparently amenable to this. "Ms. Jordan, do you have anything further to say?"

"No, sir," Laren said.

"That's the order of the court," the judge said, "and you're so sentenced." He struck his gavel. "Good luck," he told Laren.

But good luck wasn't on the horizon for Laren. By May she was flat broke, and began writing a series of bad checks—mostly for food and other necessities, occasionally for clothes. Indeed, a pattern began to reveal itself: when Laren grew depressed, she would go shopping for clothes. It was a way to offset all the anxieties and disappointments, buying something new to wear. Eventually this would become very nearly a mania with Laren. It wasn't clear what became of the counseling—whether she had ended it as soon as the gavel hit the bench, since the judge hadn't required an evaluation, or if it just petered out from a lack of interest. Yet there was every indication that Laren's mental problems were growing worse.

Between May and June of 1989, a period of a little more than six weeks, Laren wrote eighteen bogus checks, every one of them a violation of her probation. In the middle of this spate of depression, Laren's landlady kicked her out of the mobile home she was living in; the landlady later claimed that Laren had taken $1,300 in fixtures and furnishings when she left.

Laren found a new place to live, but didn't tell her probation officer; nor did she file any of the required reports, or pay any of the costs of supervision. The police apparently knew where to locate her, however. She was arrested on the bad check charges on August 24, 1989, and booked into jail. The

booking sheet identified her as 23 years old, five-feet-nine
inches, one hundred thirty-two pounds, build "slim," with a
scar on her upper lip, a Baptist, divorced, a dental assistant
who was unemployed. Jackie was listed as her mother, Hogan
as her lawyer, and each of the bad checks as a separate mis-
demeanor count of obtaining property by means of a worthless check, each count carrying a bond-out amount of $150.
The same detective who had arrested her for the earlier burglaries got her for the bad checks.

A month later, Laren's probation officer filed a warrant
for her arrest on additional charges that Laren had violated
the terms of her probation from the burglary cases. This is
how such situations compound themselves into ever more
serious problems.

It appears from the records of the Hernando County
court that, after getting released from jail on the bad check
charges, and before the probation violation warrant could
be filed, Laren decided to get out of town. The probation violation warrant, for example, wasn't served until October
26 of the following year, 1990. Just where Laren was during
this period of time is something of a mystery, at least as far
as the publicly available records are concerned, although the
arrest report indicates that she had been working as a dental
hygienist for a Tampa-area dentist the previous seven months.
Just how she came to be arrested—again by the same detective who had arrested her twice before—was likewise
unclear.

Now facing the check charges and the probation violation, Laren returned to Hernando County Circuit Court on
November 2, 1990. This time she was represented by the
public defender's office; apparently Jesse and Jackie had
decided that tough love was the way to go, after all.

By the time of the hearing, Assistant Public Defender
Alan Fanter had agreed to a deal with the state attorney's
office, one that would dispose of all the charges. The deal

called for Laren to serve 3 years in prison, to be followed by 10 years of probation. Laren would still have to pay the restitution. Fanter offered to have Laren undergo "mental health and/or substance abuse counseling and/or treatment at the request of her probation officer."

Laren objected to the requirement that she undergo substance abuse counseling. "I don't think I need anything like that," she said. When the judge said she had to be evaluated anyway, Laren meekly agreed. With this, Laren was sent to the Florida Department of Corrections to begin her 3-year sentence.

However, less than three months later she was back in court in Hernando County. This time the state attorney was asking the judge to cut Laren's prison sentence short—in fact, to end it altogether.

"Pursuant to information provided to me by law enforcement of other jurisdictions," the state attorney said, "this defendant has provided substantial assistance to such a degree that she should be given a break as far as the DOC time. Subject to her information and assistance, they are requesting that the DOC time be commuted."

In other words, in return for becoming an informant—"substantial assistance"—Laren would be let out of prison. The judge agreed to this proposal, and custody of Laren was transferred from the state penitentiary back to Hernando County.

But not long after she was released, Laren committed a new theft violation, this one involving the fraudulent use of a credit card in Pinellas County to the south; the story that filtered north to Hernando County was that Laren had befriended a Tampa police officer in a bar, had gone home with him, and while he slept, had picked his place clean, taking his credit cards, which she'd then used to rack up substantial charges. Laren was soon back in prison, at the Jefferson Correctional Institution at Monticello, Florida.

By the fall of 1991, Laren was again trying to get out of prison, asking for a speedy trial on an unresolved probation violation case in Hernando County. She wanted to be allowed to go to work release, but the prison officials wouldn't let her out with the probation violation case still hanging over her head. In one sense, this is illustrative of the compounding nature of Laren's criminal record—every new violation brought additional charges from violating the probation from the one before, and soon the multiplied charges began swirling around her head like a flock of self-replicating vultures.

In November of 1991 she wrote to the Hernando County court clerk, asking that the probation case be scheduled for hearing as soon as possible. The clerk wrote back, saying the case would soon come before the judge to be scheduled for hearing. Laren responded with another letter. As before, it was well-composed, her handwriting neat.

"Thank you for your prompt response concerning my motion," she wrote. "I would like the chance to explain to my judge, anyone who goes to prison and does not learn their lesson deserves to go back."

In January, a Hernando County judge tried to sort out all the conflicting probation terms, to at least get the system on the same page as far as what time Laren owed to various jurisdictions; otherwise, she faced the prospect of a revolving door of release, violation of probation and re-arrest that promised to go on for years. By March 11, 1992, Laren had completed enough of her 3-year sentence to be eligible for parole, and she was allowed to go to work release.

For most of the next year, it appears, Laren stayed out of trouble. But by early 1993, she was again in jail, charged once more with violating her probation—primarily the requirement that she make restitution to her victims, but also in staying in touch with her probation supervisor.

For a hearing held on February 3, 1993, Laren was

represented by a Tampa lawyer, John Fitzgibbons. Fitzgibbons asked for leniency for Laren, saying she was ready to admit the violations, but that there was an explanation for her behavior.

"We would like to briefly give the court an explanation," Fitzgibbons said. "Most of these are financial considerations, and my client obviously has some financial problems, and it's been difficult for her to make restitution. One or two of these deal with her conduct while being supervised, and we certainly admit she has not been the best as far as being supervised, but it's nothing major in terms of committing crime—well, major things.

"In summary we've had a psychologist, Dr. Farzanegan, who's present here in court, examine Ms. Sims. We call her Ms. Jordan, also. Dr. Farzanegan, I would proffer to the court, has conducted a psychological evaluation and has concluded that she suffers from a mild illness, but it is treatable. He has a course of treatment and therapy that he'll be recommending to the court."

Rather than sending Laren back to prison, Fitzgibbons said, the court should let her continue on probation, but this time under a "very strict supervision program which would include the ankle bracelets." The probation department had said it could supervise Laren by the use of the ankle bracelets, which would send a radio signal to tell a computer where she was at all times. "If she deviates from her course of conduct or allowed conduct," Fitzgibbons said, "probation will know it.

"In summary, Your Honor, she has a bad history. There's not a history, though, of violence or other things. It's just a series of relatively minor, financial-type crimes that shows a pattern, that concerned me when I came into the case. That's why I asked Dr. Farzanegan to take a look at her. She's a mother of two children. She's pregnant at the present time . . . I think probation is recommending about a year in the county jail ... we would respectfully submit to the court that there's an opportunity here to salvage this person. That's what Dr. Farzanegan is recommending. I don't think sitting in the county jail is going to accomplish much, Your Honor, and I think with the structured program that we're proposing and the professional assistance that Dr. Farzanegan will tell you about, I think his projections for a successful prognosis are very optimistic and very encouraging." Laren had a job and an apartment waiting for her in Tampa, Fitzgibbons added.

The nature of Laren's "illness" and its "pattern" was never specified in court, at least for the record, so one can only speculate as to what Fitzgibbons was talking about. Dr. Farzanegan later said he could barely remember Laren, and in fact insisted that he wasn't even present when Fitzgibbons made his remarks, although the court record shows he was. Still, there seems to be little disagreement that Laren had some sort of psychological problem, and that there was at least some sort of plan to deal with it.

Perhaps cognizant of the Sims family's political and social prominence, the judge decided to accept Laren's lawyer's plea for renewed probation. While he was inclined to accept the probation department's recommendation that Laren go back to jail for a year, said Circuit Court Judge John Springstead, "I'm also trying to balance the need to get this restitution paid to the victims ..." Fitzgibbons' assurance that Laren would have a job counted for a lot, the judge said. "I have fairly considered the representation of counsel with regard to Ms. Jordan's psychological problems, and that also enters into the equation ..."

Springstead ordered that Laren's remaining jail time be suspended, provided that she prove that she was working, that she agree to the electronic ankle monitors, and that she continue her psychological counseling. Laren obtained a job in Tampa.

Three weeks later, Laren agreed to give up legal custody of her son, then almost 7, to his father, who still lived in Brooksville. The document specified that Laren would retain custody of her daughter, Haylei.

Three weeks after that, on March 16, 1993, she used her boss' credit card to take Haylei out to dinner, and to buy some housewares at a local discount store. The total charged was $180 including $2.95 for a child's plate of macaroni. Nine days later Laren was arrested and charged with credit card fraud, another probation violation. Faced with going back to prison, Laren snipped off the ankle bracelet and disappeared, taking her 8-year-old daughter with her.

Afterward, there would be little clarity, at least in the public record, about where Laren and Haylei had gone. There is some evidence that the pair went to South Pasadena, Florida, on the Intracoastal Waterway near St. Petersburg. At least, a later credit check seemed to show that a Laren Sims Jordan, with Laren's Social Security number, was living in that town as of November of 1993. There was also a report that Laren Sims Jordan, again with the same Social Security number, was holding a post office box in Ruskin, Florida, across Tampa Bay and south of Tampa in July 1994.

But by that time, Laren had already arrived in Las Vegas, Nevada, where, on May 5, 1994, using the name Elizabeth Ann Barasch—the true name of someone Laren had once met in jail—she married a Las Vegas businessman named Kenneth L. Redelsperger. Curiously, while using a stolen name to marry the 35-year-old Redelsperger, Laren completed the marriage license application with her parents' true first names, although she amended their surnames to "Barasch." Laren also changed her year of birth to 1967, apparently to match the real Barasch's birthdate. From the time of this marriage forward, though, Laren would be known as Elizabeth, or "Elisa" for short. Eventually, in fact, she would be known as Elisa McNabney, even when the

Federal Bureau of Investigation made her the subject of a nationwide all-points bulletin as the "black widow" who had murdered her third husband, the once-prominent Nevada lawyer, Larry McNabney.

Shantar

By the mid-1980s, even as Laren Sims Jordan was beginning her downward spiral into a career of petty crime more than two thousand miles away, Larry was learning the truth of the old adage that being rich isn't the same thing as being happy.

Later, even Larry's closest friends would marvel at his penchant for doing himself harm with chemical substances. "It was like he thought he was invisible," one of his oldest friends remembered. "That's the way it is with drunks—they think they're invisible, that nobody notices that they've been drinking. They think they're acting perfectly normally, even when they're blotto."

Friends would recall that when people would tell Larry that he was drinking too much, he often acted insulted—as if he were too accomplished, too perfect to have such a flaw. "You couldn't tell him anything when he got like that," a friend remembered. "You'd say, 'Hey, Larry, it's me—remember me? I've known you all your life, you can't fool me.'" But Larry wasn't capable of taking personal advice from people—especially his closest friends. And it wasn't just alcohol—by the 1980s, Larry was regularly using cocaine, and, according to some contemporaries, also heroin.

There seemed to be at least two subtle factors at work here: one was Larry's psychological condition, still fragile years after the suicides of his father and brother. To some, Larry seemed armored, as if he were holding himself prisoner deep inside, avoiding all the pain. The drinking and drugging numbed all this, made it so he didn't have to think about it. Unconsciously, perhaps, the abuse of drugs

and alcohol was a form of suicide, albeit one that was
more socially acceptable than blowing one's brains out
with a gun. Perhaps because of his upbringing, Larry was
at heart an extremely lonely person. The drink and drugs
had the effect of seeming to lift Larry out of this loneli-
ness, to make him the life of the party, or at least help convince him that he was an entertaining, enjoyable person to
be around. The desire to make contact with other people
made drink and drugs ever more necessary to Larry's mental
equilibrium.

The second factor was likely the times and the culture.
Larry had grown up and come of age at a time when drinking and drugging were seen as part of the persona of the
rebel, something that boiled out of the 1960s' cultural revo-
lution extolling drugs, sex and rock-and-roll; doing booze
and drugs to excess was hip, it was cool. As one of Larry's
lawyer contemporaries put it, it wasn't as much of a challenge to cope with life straight, so sometimes a person put
himself out on the edge by getting a bit crazy with drinking
and drugs to make it more interesting. Therefore there seems
to be a streak of Hunter Thompson's caricature of the drug-
crazed Samoan lawyer in *Fear and Loathing in Las Vegas*
suffusing Larry's image in those years; it was part of his
persona, at least as Larry presented himself to others.

And as a criminal defense lawyer, Larry often found
himself hanging out with defendants who were similarly
walking the edge, sometimes in shady bars and honkytonks,
where the temptation to drink too much and lapse into harder
chemicals abounded. There were plenty of times that Larry
drank to excess, then hired someone at the bar to drive him
home—he knew enough about the law to want to avoid being nabbed for driving under the influence.

Getting picked up and thrown into the drunk tank for a
night simply didn't fit with Larry's self-image. He was the
sort of person, in his own mind, who could handle his drink

and drugs, no matter what, even if that wasn't really true. Larry's friends and supporters tried to cover for him as best they could, because they loved Larry. When Larry was sober, he was a delight to be around, even if he himself didn't believe it. But when he got drunk or stoned, he could be a first-class pain.

As the 1980s unfolded, Larry continued to get "ink," as he had put it, even if some of it wasn't the most positive. For one thing, by 1984, Jack Mazzan, the hairdresser convicted of the murder of Judge Minor's son, had appealed his conviction. The Nevada Supreme Court upheld Mazzan's guilt, but said that Larry's excoriation of the jury for their verdict was so prejudicial to Mazzan's rights that he deserved a new sentencing hearing. The Nevada Supreme Court's language made Larry look bad. Larry didn't care all that much, however, and indeed, in light of later events—including what he later claimed he actually knew about the murder of Minor and also of April Barber—it seems possible that there was a method to Larry's madness: that, realizing there was no way to save his client from the death penalty, Larry had actually insulted the jury as part of a subtle plan to give Mazzan a viable appellate issue. If that was the plan, it didn't work, however; after a new hearing, Mazzan was again sentenced to death for Minor's murder. It wouldn't be the last of Mazzan's case, however, as we shall further see.

Nor was Larry yet done with the Harveys bomb plot. Believing that the federal sentences for the bombers were much too light, the Nevada district attorney for Douglas County, which included the Lake Tahoe area, decided to prosecute the same defendants on state charges.

This time, the bomb-maker, John Birges, advanced a rather novel defense. He claimed that Harvey Gross, despairing of ever getting government permission to build his new hotel-casino, had hired Birges to destroy the facility, which carried the added bonus of allowing Harvey to collect the insurance money. Because he owed a loan shark a lot of money, Birges said, he felt compelled to go through with it. [This defense was eventually rejected by the jury when prosecutors pointed out that the government had already approved the casino renovation by the time of the bombing, and that the insurance was far less than what it actually cost to rebuild the facility.] As the new trial neared in 1985, Larry and his fellow lawyer Fred Atcheson struck a bargain with the Douglas County D.A., according to Atcheson: they agreed to turn their entire file on the bomb plot over to the authorities in return for an agreement not to prosecute Terry Lee Hall, their client. The D.A. took the deal and the file, Atcheson said later. That saved Hall a possible new prison term.

Meanwhile, Larry's mother Marie got married again, to a man named John Murphy. It appears that Larry and Murphy were not on the most cordial of terms. Some of Larry's Reno friends recall that he saw his mother's new husband as some sort of "drugstore cowboy," out to clip Marie's substantial wealth. After the marriage, Marie executed a will, Larry would later say, granting Murphy a life interest in the income from Marie's assets, but without access to any of the principal. A few years later, though, Marie told Larry that she wanted her new husband to have access to all the money, saying that she had to do this in order to keep the marriage together, that Murphy had insisted that she allow him access to her funds to prove her love and trust for him. Otherwise, Larry said Marie told him, Murphy would leave her. According to Larry, Murphy assured him that this change was only for convenience, and that he still didn't expect to receive anything other than a life interest in the money if Marie died before he did.

By early 1986, Larry's own marriage, to Gail, was in trouble, even as the last of the Papoose Palace cases—Larry and his associates were suing the county for their failure to properly supervise the day-care center—were on trial. Whether it was the stress of the trial or simply his nature, Larry's drinking was out of hand again. On January 23, 1986, he filed for divorce from his third wife; the next day; Gail filed an application for a temporary restraining order against Larry, contending that he had verbally threatened her both at home and at work, including making "insulting and harassing telephone calls" that had caused her embarrassment. Gail wanted a court order to prevent Larry from making any more such calls.

This was but the opening gauntlet in a divorce case that would eventually go all the way to the Nevada Supreme Court, and result in a new law being passed by the state legislature, the so-called "McNabney Rule."

The major bone of contention in the divorce was Larry's annuity from the Papoose Palace cases. Gail claimed that since the annuity had been purchased from Larry's fee from the settlement of the child molestation cases while she and Larry were married, she was entitled to half the money.

Not so fast, said Larry, through his lawyer, Reno attorney Fred Pinkerton. Since both parties had entered the 1983 marriage from prior marriages, and both had separate property, there had been an understanding that each side would "retain their separate autonomous estates . . . they did not pool or co-mingle their respective earnings." Larry used his money to pay the mortgage, taxes and other common expenses, while Gail paid for the groceries. She had no right to half of the million-dollar annuity, Pinkerton said, any more than Larry had any right to anything that Gail had earned during the marriage.

Following a trial in Washoe County District Court, a judge ruled that Larry was entitled to most of the annuity as his separate property—80 percent of it, in fact. Gail got the other 20 percent. Unhappy with this decision, Gail appealed to the Nevada Supreme Court, contending that the state's divorce law required an equal division of the money. It would be a year before the case got to the high court, and when it ruled, it voted 3–2 to uphold the 80–20 split, with the majority contending that "equitable" didn't necessarily mean "equal." The following year, the legislature passed a law to require the 50–50 split of such marital community assets in all future such cases, a law that became known as "the McNabney Rule" in Nevada.

But by the time that happened, Larry had been married again, for the fourth time, and in fact, was well on his way toward yet another divorce.

This fourth marriage took place on November 27, 1986, in a custom "log cabin" which had cost a fortune to build, that Larry had hired contractors to erect in the hills south of Reno. The bride was another Reno lawyer, Linda Gardner. Larry's oldest friends gathered, as well as his mother, Marie. After the ceremony was concluded, Marie turned to one of Larry's long-time friends, who had known him since Mt. Rose Elementary School.

"We've been through a lot together, haven't we?" Marie asked.

"Yes, we have, Marie," the friend responded, and he knew Marie was thinking of all the other marriages—Donna, JoDee, and Gail—as well as all the emotional tumult each of the sunderings had brought.

"Well, this is the last time," Marie said, and the friend realized that Marie meant it—she would never attend another marriage for her only surviving son.

Within the next year, Marie sold her condominium in Reno and moved with Murphy to Ashland, Oregon, where, as it turned out, he would become involved in raising American quarter horses.

In time, Larry would follow his mother north, at least for a while. But there would be one more trial to come, the biggest one of all, and one that would come close to costing Larry his life.

In November of 1987, at about the same time the annuity issue was reaching the Nevada Supreme Court and Larry was getting married for the fourth time, the U.S. Attorney's Office for the District of Nevada indicted two dozen people on a smorgasbord of charges ranging from murder to conspiracy to distribute methamphetamine as part of a "continuing criminal enterprise," in other words, racketeering. This was the so-called "Company" case, named after the twenty-four initial defendants, who were said to have been joined together in a common criminal purpose they themselves called "The Company."

By the time the whole thing was over, the Company trial would represent the second-longest criminal proceeding in U.S. history, and certainly one of the largest in terms of the number of defendants and their lawyers, including Larry McNabney.

"There's a saying," N. Patrick Flanagan, a Reno lawyer and at the time of the Company trial, the head of the district's federal public defender's office, "that a lawyer only has so many trials in him. That's a finite number, and once you've used them up, you're done. That's what happened with Larry."

In their indictment, the federal prosecutors contended that a man named Richard Rupley headed a drug ring that extended from San Diego to northern California and Nevada, an enterprise that had grossed more than $4,000,000 since it began in the late 1970s. Flanagan, as the federal public defender, had to recruit more than two football teams of lawyers to represent all the defendants. Larry was one of the first lawyers he contacted. Flanagan and Larry defended two brothers who owned a trucking company that had been caught up in the drug distribution scheme.

The trial began in early 1988, but not before the federal courthouse was extensively remodeled—there simply wasn't enough space in the courtroom of U.S. District Court Judge Edward Reed to allow all the accused to sit at the counsel table in front of the bar. Reed ordered a balcony installed in the spectators' section to seat all the defendants, and then had a complicated sound system installed, one that, once individual headsets were plugged in, permitted the lawyers to talk to their clients by private circuits without anyone else overhearing them. When the accused and their lawyers weren't whispering to each other over their private lines, the circuit carried classical music.

By the time the trial began, ten of the defendants had either pled guilty or had had the charges dismissed, leaving fourteen to face a jury. By almost any standard, that was an almost unmanageable number, even with the unprecedented closed-circuit sound system.

Originally the trial of *United States* v. *Rupley* was supposed to last only three months, but the lawyers had been far too optimistic. By the time the whole thing was over, fifteen months later, more than two hundred witnesses had come to the stand to testify, and each of them was subject to cross-examination by the fourteen defense lawyers as well as the prosecutors. The transcript covered nearly 25,000 pages. Within a matter of months, the incessant droning of testimony, coupled with the piped-over classical music, began to drive everyone crazy.

With so many defendants, with such a litany of contradictory facts, with so many interruptions, objections, side-bar conferences and out-of-the-presence-of-the-jury hearings, the trial swiftly bogged down. Years later, one participant recalled the entire ordeal as mind-numbing: the sort of case that would make almost any lawyer drool with boredom as his or her mind went spinning off into oblivion.

At one point, in the summer of 1988—the case had been under way for almost nine months—Judge Reed declared a routine mid-morning recess. As the lawyers exited the courtroom, Flanagan later recalled, Larry made a pronouncement.

"I can't take it anymore," he said.

Everyone chuckled, Flanagan remembered. They had all felt the same way, at one point or another. "We figured Larry was just blowing off steam," he said.

Fifteen or twenty minutes later, when it was time to reconvene, Larry did not reappear. Because a trial can't go on if one of the lawyers is a no-show, the judge asked the clerk to see if Larry couldn't be found at his office. Some people thought he had just become confused, and had thought they had reached the noon recess instead of the mid-morning break.

About that point, however, one of Larry's closest friends received a telephone call from him. He had gone back to his apartment, Larry said, and was sitting at home with a bottle of Scotch whiskey and a gun. He was thinking of killing himself. The friends rushed over to the apartment and talked Larry down.

With the help of his friends that same morning, Larry checked into a substance abuse treatment facility near Reno. Apparently no one had time to tell Judge Reed what had happened. Larry was still at the treatment facility when Flanagan, under Reed's prompting, began calling around in search of Larry. While he didn't know for sure, Flanagan had guessed what happened. When he reached the treatment facility by telephone, the operators of the establishment refused to confirm or deny that Larry had been admitted.

"Fine," Flanagan said, realizing he now knew what he

needed to know. "Thank you very much." He prepared to hang up when in the background, he suddenly heard Larry's voice.

"I won't go back!" Larry was shouting. "He can't make me go back. I won't do it." Larry had reached his legal overload—he had exhausted his capacity for trial. A week later, he was out of the treatment facility and back in the courtroom, but taking little active part in defending his client. Larry's friend Fred Atcheson, just returned from a two-year stint as a lawyer in Micronesia, was hired to pinch-hit for him for the remainder of the interminable proceeding. The trial ground on. Judge Reed never said a word to Larry; he realized that every lawyer had his limits.

Looking at the events in retrospect, it seems likely that one possible reason for Larry's breakdown in the summer of 1988 was the erosion of his fourth marriage, the one with Linda Gardner. Less than a year after they had been married at the bucolic "cabin" in the foothills south of Reno, Larry had filed for divorce. The "cabin" was sold at a substantial loss. Having gotten his fourth divorce and having avoided doing himself in, Flanagan recalled, Larry had a mordant sense of humor about the whole situation.

"I told him, 'Larry, women are going to be the death of you,'" Flanagan recalled. "He laughed and told me that his life's ambition was to get married, build a house, then have his wife divorce him and take everything he owned in the settlement."

This puckish sense of humor was classic Larry, at least when he was sober. The narrow brush with the Scotch and the gun had apparently convinced Larry that he had to do something about his drinking, and quickly; he apparently went on the wagon after the trip to the treatment facility and managed to stay on, at least until the end of the Company trial.

That came on the last day of March of 1989, nearly fifteen months after it had all started. During that time, several lawyers had gotten divorced, then remarried; babies had
been conceived, then born. By the end, there were about a
dozen lawyers who had been through the whole thing from
start to finish, and each of them would later say the grueling
events had taken them to the extreme, much as they had
Larry.

Having finished the Company trial, Larry himself realized that his own supply of courtroom legerdemain had run
out. The tank was empty. In fact, Larry said, he was sick of
the law and just wanted to get away from it, and even from
Reno, with all its associations and bad habits.

In this Larry was assisted by a new love interest, a woman
who was a well-known Reno hairdresser. Herself a divorcee
with three older children, Cheryl (her last name has been
omitted here to protect her privacy) was widely seen by
Larry's friends as just the sort of person for him: calm, understanding and tolerant. With his annuity, Larry realized
he really didn't have to work anymore, provided he was
prudent with his expenditures. And without the law to drive
him crazy, without its stress, without its proximity to criminal defendants in bars and drugs, Larry's compulsions began to abate. Later he would say the years he spent with
Cheryl were the happiest of his life, particularly when he
took up finish carpentry. Somehow, sawing a piece of wood
or driving a nail had a simplicity that calmed him and kept
his demons at bay.

That fall, as Larry was cleaning out his house in southwest Reno, a longtime friend dropped by to see how he was
doing. There in the Dumpster were all the manifestations of
the old Larry: boxes of files, books, court clothes, even a rack
of expensive ties. "That was then," Larry said, meaning that
his old life as a lion of the bar was finished.

Late in 1989, Larry and Cheryl moved away from Reno
to the small town of Yelm, not far from the city of Olympia

in Washington State. It was in Yelm that Larry first became involved in "the cult," as Elisa McNabney was later to describe it.

This was Ramtha's School of Enlightenment, the new-age enterprise of a woman named JZ Knight. Ms. Knight, the subject of some controversy in Washington State and elsewhere, claimed to be the "channel" for a 35,000-year-old "ascended master" named Ramtha.

According to Ramtha's School of Enlightenment's website, JZ Knight (she prefers no punctuation) was born in 1946 in Roswell, New Mexico, as Judy Hampton, the eighth child of impoverished migrant farm workers. After spending some time in Texas, Ms. Knight's mother took her children back to New Mexico, leaving an "abusive and alcoholic" husband behind. Ms. Knight then grew up in Artesia, New Mexico, and by 1965 was married and the mother of two children. Herself divorced by 1969, Ms. Knight returned to Roswell, where she began a career in cable television. She eventually moved to California, and later to the Pacific Northwest, where she took on the nickname " 'Zebra' due to her ability to make black and white decisions." The nickname later became abbreviated to JZ, apparently for "Judy Zebra."

While living in the Tacoma, Washington, area in the late 1970s with a new husband, Jeffrey Knight, Ms. Knight later claimed, she had been visited by "an extraordinary being in her kitchen."

This was "Ramtha," described as a 35,000-year-old warrior from "Lemuria," a place that appears to have been either where the Pacific Ocean is now, or "beyond the North Star," as Ramtha himself has described it through Ms. Knight (and echoing, somewhat, J. M. Barrie's "straight on till morning" in *Peter Pan*). As a young boy, so his story went, Ramtha traveled from Lemuria through what is today Mexico into the "Atlantic basin," which was then called "Atlantis." There the 14-year-old Ramtha organized resistance to "Atlatian" tyranny, and over the next sixty-three years, conquered "two-thirds of the then-known world," in the process becoming the "greatest of all warriors." Eventually, Ramtha and his forces found their way to India, where he was the victim of an assassination attempt. After recovering from his wounds, Ramtha became enlightened, learning the mysteries of "the unknown god," and eventually "ascended," promising to later return.

Almost two years after first appearing to JZ, Ramtha began "channeling" through her; that is to say, he began to impart his wisdom to the rest of the world, using JZ's mouth and vocal cords. According to Ms. Knight's devotees, the "channeling" isn't the same thing as being in a trance or acting as a medium.

"She actually abdicates her body and experiences a rushing down a long tunnel to a brilliant light; not unlike the death experiences that have been reported by people who have been declared clinically and legally dead but have returned to their bodies," the school's website reports. "Ramtha surrounds her body and, through a process of light synthesis, actually operates through the brain stem and lower cerebellum and he can make it move, talk, and interact with the environment . . . Ramtha is facilitating her body and using its brain not unlike a telephone." In a word, JZ Knight is possessed, at least when "channeling" Ramtha.

The wisdom imparted by Ramtha can only be summarized here, in part by reference to what it is not—it doesn't claim to be a religion as much as a philosophy, a system of thinking and feeling that appears to mesh the arcane language of Gnosticism with modern science, fueled by the power of positive thinking, overlaid with a dollop of Edgar Cayce, and with a pinch of, perhaps, Werner Erhard.

"So what are the teachings of the Great Work that you have come to listen to?" Ramtha has asked, through JZ Knight's voicebox. "They are not about the occult work and indeed they are not about New Age. The message I give you is the foundation of the earth, the cosmos. That is not new at all. The message I am telling you is this: that if you be God—and indeed you are, philosophically speaking, that is—that should be an enticement to experience that nearer to that principle." In brief, then, the idea is that humans are divine, they just don't ordinarily know it. Breathing exercises, visualizations, meditations are practiced to acquaint the aspiring god with the potential within—"a synthesis of science and spirituality," according to the school. Pyramids are also big at the School of Enlightenment.

Propelled by Ramtha, JZ Knight soon became a worldwide enterprise—publishing, lectures, newsletters, and eventually a school. Hundreds, then thousands of people came to partake of Ramtha's observations, and fairly soon JZ Knight and her husband were wealthy, having started a series of businesses designed to offer workshops, retreats, lectures, seminars, videotapes, books—in fact, all manner of spreading the word and cashing in on it. By the early 1990s, when Larry McNabney arrived, channeling Ramtha had become big business for JZ Knight and her husband, a factor which only increased the controversy over the years.

Critics have assailed Ms. Knight and her acolytes for their preoccupation with money, suggesting that the whole thing is nothing more than a modern snipe hunt designed to separate the gullible from their cash, dressed up in a little mild privation, like sitting in cold, darkened, maze-like rooms waiting for enlightenment to strike, and enough mystery to satisfy the psychic needs of the credulous. "Her story is appealing to those who are not comfortable in today's world," sneers one critic, Robert Todd Carroll in *The Skeptic's Dictionary*, a debunker's bible published in 2003 by John Wiley & Sons. "The past *must* have been better. It must have been *safer* then, and people must have been *nobler*. This message is especially appealing to people who feel like misfits."

According to the school's records, Larry participated in ten different School of Enlightenment events during the years 1990 to 1992. Curiously, this was about the same time that JZ Knight's husband, Jeffrey, decided to divorce her; presumably he had become dissatisfied with sharing her body with the god-like Ramtha. In a case that attracted considerable media attention, the two Knights jousted for the Ramtha moneypot; in the end, JZ emerged triumphant, because it was she who held the copyright to Ramtha's pronouncements. There doesn't seem to be any indication that Larry provided any legal or practical advice to JZ Knight during this episode, despite his legal background and personal experience with divorce.

After arriving at Yelm, Larry began to work as a finish carpenter for a contractor who was building houses in the area. This, he later told friends, was probably the happiest he had ever been in his life. There was no stress, simply the enjoyment of a job well done. It seems that Bath's assessment of his former partner as "left-brained" had some validity; Larry's interest in the decorative arts of woodworking doubtless satisfied his own deeper predilection, even if he tended to see it more as a hobby than a vocation. He adopted the name "Shantar" to indicate his break with the old Larry of drugs and drinking.

After attending a number of seminars, retreats and classes at the Ramtha School between 1990 and 1992, sandwiched around his carpentry work, Larry began to weary of the "cult," according to a number of his Reno friends. "At first it was JZ Knight, cocaine; cocaine, JZ Knight," recalled one friend, holding his two hands apart in the classic weighing gesture, suggesting that at first JZ Knight had been the more attractive to Larry. "Then a few years later it was cocaine, JZ Knight; JZ Knight, cocaine," indicating that the drug came out on top the second time around.

But the truth was, Larry was easily bored, especially when he wasn't drinking. Having heard the Ramtha rap, indeed having learned it well enough to spiel it, Larry then lost interest in it. And, too, there were some who thought that Larry felt the school was becoming just a bit too authoritarian for his taste, "a little too controlling," as one of Larry's Reno friends put it. And there were two other things going on as well.

Larry's mother Marie, died. This happened October 19, 1991, at the home she shared with John Murphy, in Ashland, Oregon. Larry was still living in Yelm at the time, looking for enlightenment at the Ramtha-possessed feet of JZ Knight. Marie was 71 years old when she died. Her body was cremated shortly after the death certificate was signed by a local physician, Dr. John Olson. Apparently Larry didn't know about this when it took place; he told friends that the cremation had come so quickly it was impossible to have any other expert verify the cause of his mother's death. Larry told people he was suspicious that Marie might have been murdered.

The records of Jackson County, Oregon, where the death occurred, in fact indicate that no investigation into Marie's passing was made, and that no one from the state medical examiner's office even went to the scene to determine what had taken place. However, this wasn't unusual in a case where the dead person was under the care of a physician, as seemed to be the case with Marie. What is curious, however, is that Larry didn't seem to know much, if anything, about the details of his mother's final illness—why else would he have suspected foul play?

In any event, by the fall of 1992, a year later, Larry had initiated legal action to get control of Marie's estate, which he guessed had to be somewhere in the neighborhood of half a million dollars or more, including the money inherited from "Gammy" years earlier. Larry retained Larry Digesti, another Reno lawyer and an old friend, to represent him in a petition in the Washoe County courts, asking that Larry be appointed special administrator for his mother's estate. Filed on October 13, 1992, nearly a year after Marie's death, the petition outlined the circumstances of Marie's inheritance from her own mother, and noted that, although the original will from Marie was "lost," and John Murphy had in the past agreed to forgo any interest in the principal of the estate, he now seemed to be reneging. Larry said Murphy was contending that the will never existed, and that he "has threatened to dispose of the assets or otherwise conceal the same." After having converted all of Marie's assets to joint ownership before her death, said Larry, Murphy had never bothered to file a probate case in Oregon. That was why he wanted to be appointed special administrator of his mother's estate, Larry said—to see where the money had gone.

Two days later, Mills Lane—Larry's one-time opponent in the Jack Mazzan murder case, and by now, a Washoe County District Court judge—agreed to appoint Larry special administrator, which gave Larry the statutory power to investigate the disposition of Marie's assets.

There the matter rested for almost eighteen months, until May 19, 1994, when Lane issued an order to Larry, requiring him to make a report to the court on his progress in determining and properly disposing of Marie's assets. A week or two later, Larry filed a paper indicating that the dispute with Murphy had been settled.

By that time, Larry had left JZ Knight and Ramtha for good; he had, almost a year earlier, decided to come home to Reno. He had also decided to go back into the legal arena—this time, not as a criminal lawyer, but as Nevada's King of Torts, that is, personal injuries. But then again, that was the quintessential Larry—it wasn't enough to become a run-of-the-mill personal injury lawyer, chasing ambulances and slip-and-fall clients. He had to be the biggest and the best. Before too much time would pass, Larry McNabney's name would be on every television screen in Nevada as the person to see if you wanted to sue someone. He would make his name a household word from one end of Nevada to the other, Larry vowed. He would do it if it took every cent he had.

Which it would.

Larry's decision to re-enter the legal arena in a new incarnation as a personal injury lawyer didn't really surprise his friends in Reno. Unlike some who felt called to the criminal defense bar, it was less the constitutional issues that motivated Larry as much as it was the fame. To many of his closest acquaintances, Larry was a born performer. "He had to have the spotlight on him," one recalled. "He was at his happiest when people were watching him."

To some of his friends, it was also as if Larry missed "the action"—that is, the cut and thrust of litigation, the clash of egos that frame every legal contest. Still others thought that Larry had simply become bored with his life as Shantar the carpenter. His attention span was notoriously short, they said, pointing to his serial marriages, or his flirtation with Ramtha. Larry was extremely smart, a quick study; but once he'd taken the measure of something, he often lost interest in it.

Now, by the winter of 1992–1993, Larry had hit upon a new interest: he wanted to make money at the same time he made himself famous. His idea was to turn Larry McNabney into a franchise of sorts. This idea occurred to him while he and several of his lawyer pals were attending a convention of criminal defense lawyers in Las Vegas in either late 1992 or early 1993; and as they sat in a hotel bar watching the stream of briefcase-toting lawyers come and go, Larry saw money. Before long, he had conceived of an ambitious plan. He would set himself up, first in Reno, then later in other parts of the state, and, by dint of heavy advertising, induce personal injury claimants to hire him to do battle with the insurance companies. Rather than try the cases himself, Larry envisioned, he would farm out the lawsuits to other lawyers—at least those cases that didn't settle almost immediately. In the meantime, he'd get criminal lawyers—like those attending the convention—to ship him their personal injury cases in return for a piece of the action. Those that couldn't be settled right off the bat would be referred to the heavy hitters among civil litigators, like Durney and Brennan, who would in effect pay Larry a hefty fee for screening the cases. In effect, what Larry was proposing was to become something of a lawsuit broker, a sort of pass-through system in which Larry McNabney and Associates—whoever they were—would get what amounted to a commission for putting the injured together with those who could take the biggest and quickest bite out of the insurance people. After all, it had worked before, hadn't it, with the Papoose Palace cases?

What Larry envisioned was a volume business—one that brought in injured parties far and wide, by casting as large a net as possible. That meant advertising, which also meant that Larry would have to spend a lot of money to make his name as well known as any other consumer product or service. But that was okay—money Larry had. He had the annuity, and he had some portion of the inheritance from his mother and grandmother. In late 1992 or early 1993, it appears, Larry had sold the annuity by discounting it for cash. Added to the funds that he likely received from his mother's estate, that meant that Larry had just less than a million dollars to begin his campaign to make Larry McNabney and Associates, Attorneys at Law, a household name in Nevada.

Domestically, things seemed to be going well, too. He and Cheryl and her two daughters found a house in Reno, and it looked like Larry was finally beginning to settle down.

• • •

Early in March of 1993, Larry was introduced to Nancy Eklof, an expatriate southern Californian who was an expert in television advertising. Together Eklof and Larry worked out a series of television commercials for his new enterprise, and by that spring, the spots were running frequently on Reno-area stations. In the course of working with Larry, Nancy got to know him rather well, and in fact, he enjoyed entertaining her with some wild stories about his old days as a criminal lawyer.

One story, in fact, involved Larry's old client, Jack Mazzan.

By the spring of 1993, Mazzan's case was still bouncing around the Nevada courts, as different lawyers came and went, trying to get the death penalty Mazzan had twice drawn thrown out, or even better, to get an entirely new trial. Mazzan continued to claim innocence. To all intents and purposes, Larry was out of the case entirely by 1993; indeed, the newspaper coverage of the case's twists and turns rarely mentioned Larry, if at all.

But one day—perhaps Larry had begun drinking again, Nancy later wasn't too sure—Larry freely admitted to Nancy that Mazzan was guilty of Minor's murder, as he had also been responsible for the murder of April Barber.

Nancy recalled, "Larry said that Jack Mazzan admitted to him that he had killed Minor and that he'd also killed April Barber. He told Larry that he was driving down the road with April Barber sitting next to him in the truck, just stabbing, stabbing her—" and here Nancy illustrated Larry's gesture by punching her right hand, backhandedly, as if it were a knife, into the body of someone sitting next to a driver. Larry told her, Nancy said, that Mazzan had told him that he'd taken April Barber's body outside of town and had disposed of it in the shallow grave where it had been discovered in the fall of 1979.

This was certainly a curious disclosure by Larry back in 1993. For one thing, Mazzan was still appealing his conviction and his sentence, and was still claiming that he had been framed. If Larry was telling the truth, here was Mazzan's own lawyer telling a comparative stranger—certainly someone who wasn't bound by any attorney–client privilege—that Mazzan was guilty as sin. That of course is the sort of thing a responsible lawyer should never do.

Was this evidence of some sort of residual guilt on Larry's part—for his role in trying to defend Mazzan? Nancy, for one, didn't think so: instead, she thought it was just Larry's penchant for calling attention to himself by telling an entertaining or riveting story. Maybe Larry thought it wouldn't make any difference if he told someone that Mazzan had confessed to him—that there wasn't any way Mazzan would ever get a new trial. But if this was what he thought, Larry would turn out to be very wrong.

Rather surprisingly, for its first year, Larry McNabney and Associates did extremely well. The business, in fact, boomed. If anything, Larry had more clients than he could possibly service. Thinking perhaps that he'd stumbled onto the secret of getting rich without having to do much work, Larry paid $575,000 for a top-of-the-line house on Buckaroo Court in west Reno's toney Caughlin Ranch area. He and Cheryl and her children moved in that fall. As far as Larry could see, Larry McNabney and Associates couldn't lose. He began to play a lot of golf, and developed the habit of dropping in at the office from time to time, rather than giving it his close supervision.

The real trick was finding qualified people to process the cases—paralegals and hungry young lawyers, mostly—and to process the cases quickly enough to make them economical. That meant minimizing the expenses and trying to force the insurance companies to settle up. The whole enterprise was time-sensitive—spend too much time on a case and it didn't pencil out, that is, the profit was too low to make it worthwhile, counting all the overhead: the offices, the help, the advertising. Larry McNabney and Associates' cut would vary between 25 and 40 percent of the gross of every settlement; the art lay in guessing how much the insurance people would be willing to pay out, how much the pain and suffering was worth. The firm developed a "pain and suffering formula" to speed up the payoffs: eight times the amount of the medical bills of the injured person. Hospitals and casinos were prime targets, along with automobile insurance companies; so were mining companies. And while a substantial amount of revenue came in the first year, Larry knew that if he wanted to keep getting, he had to keep spending, mostly on television advertising. The downside—if there was one—was keeping the help in line. There was an always-present possibility that the hungry young lawyer would walk out, taking clients with him, even though it had been Larry who'd spent all the money to get them in the door in the first place. As a result, the atmosphere in the office was sometimes strained; Larry could be nasty and belligerent if he felt someone was trying to put one over on him.

Nancy Eklof's commercials were well done: brief and to the point, they featured a casually attired Larry in an outdoor setting. He was handsome, well-dressed; he looked eminently reliable, and his voice—"I'm Larry McNabney. Call me"—was a trustworthy mixture of calmness and confidence.

By the spring of 1994, Larry McNabney and Associates was spending about $50,000 a month on television advertising, according to Nancy Eklof. The idea was, the more the firm spent, the more cases would come in, and the more settlements could be reached. The business had reached a sort of equilibrium, however—meaning that the income was just about equal to the costs. At that point, Larry made a fateful decision—to get more cases, he would begin to advertise in

Elko, in eastern Nevada, and eventually in Las Vegas, where, in the early summer of 1995, he would meet a beautiful woman named Elizabeth Redelsperger, and fall head over heels in love with her.

Who can say what attracts one person to another? When someone tries to put such a thing into words, even when they are talking about themselves, the words swiftly lose any real meaning and become just that—words, poor, pitiful symbols for a range of thoughts and feelings, reactions, some of the most powerful of them barely sensed. One can look at a person and fall in love with them, or at least, fall in love with the way they appear to be, while remaining conscious that what one is falling in love with is only the way one *imagines* the other person is . . . The way they look, the way they talk, the things they laugh about or cry over—each of these is but a part of the whole, and the whole itself may never be completely discernible. That is what Larry's lifelong friend meant when he observed that no one really, truly knows another person, even after years of the closest of contact.

And yet it sometimes happens that a person will meet another human being who has something so rare, so personal, so evocative of something longed for, that one quickly forgets that there is far more to the person than one may be conscious of, a side or sides completely obscured in the excitement of the connection itself. So intense is the experience that all the rest of life seems animated by the connection, and when it is withdrawn, it is as if one has suddenly gone from color to black-and-white; and one may be capable of doing anything to get it back.

This, it appears, is what happened to Laurence Williams McNabney sometime around June of 1995. And, it must be said, it is likely that something very much similar happened to Laren Sims Jordan, who was by then 29 years old, on the run from the law in Florida, and using the stolen name of Elizabeth Ann Barasch Redelsperger, or Elisa for short.

Six months after Larry and Elisa met, after Elisa had taken him to the financial cleaners the *first* time, some of Larry's Reno friends asked him why he persisted in a relationship with someone who was so obviously crooked. After all, it wasn't as if he hadn't had any experience with breaking up before.

"Because I love her," Larry said, and in light of everything that would happen over the five tumultuous years of the marriage between Larry and Elisa McNabney, that would seem to be as good an explanation as anyone would ever come up with. But this was an unusual, perhaps even perverse kind of love: a love that depended to a significant degree on an intimacy that was grounded in the darkness of each partner's deepest secrets. In short, Larry and Elisa loved each other as intensely as they feared each other, and as desperately as each blackmailed the other, until death did they part.

By the spring of 1995, when Larry McNabney and Associates had decided to invade the Las Vegas market for new clients, Larry thought he had the world on a string. He began to drink and drug again; some of his old pals in Reno were sure that if he hadn't tried to do business in the town of the high rollers, Larry never would have fallen off the wagon as hard as he did. Larry rented a swanky pad in Las Vegas, and spending his own money as well as that which came in from the settlements, he eventually leased a jet aircraft to make the frequent hop between the two cities, giving all the appearances of a high roller himself.

The new McNabney office, near Sahara and Rainbow Boulevards in Las Vegas, was almost decadently luxurious, paneled and deeply carpeted. At one point, Larry had a giant aquarium installed as a divider between the entrance foyer and the staff's cubicles; the idea was to present the image of a fabulously successful law firm in order to convince clients to sign up. Larry ordered a state-of-the-art networked computer system installed, leased a lot of brand-new office furniture, and set about recruiting office staff by means of help-wanted advertisements in the Las Vegas newspapers.

One of the Las Vegas jobs that had to be filled was that of office manager. Among those who applied was Elizabeth Redelsperger.

This was about nine months after Elisa had divorced Kenneth Redelsperger, whom she had married in May of 1994. Exactly what Elisa was up to during the intervening months wasn't entirely clear, although it seems possible that she spent some of that time back in Florida, using her true name of Laren Jordan. There are no records to show where Elisa/Laren's daughter Haylei was at this time; as the years were to unfold, Haylei would spend a lot of time in various places around the country, with friends, in boarding schools, and only occasionally with her mother. Whether Haylei, who would then have been just over 10 years old, was with Elisa/Laren when she first met Larry isn't clear, although there is some anecdotal evidence that she was staying with Ken Redelsperger.

In any event, Larry was immediately taken with Elisa. He hired her to manage the Las Vegas office, marveling over how smart she was, how energetic, how quickly she grasped the bottom-line economics of the personal injury business. Elisa had an instinct for the jugular: she seemed to know unerringly how much a case would be worth, how much she could squeeze from the insurance company, and how soon.

And there was something else: Elisa was a risk-taker, just like Larry. There was something about walking on the wild side that made her attractive, Larry realized. In Elisa, Larry thought, he had finally met someone who was very much like himself: someone with the same sense of drama, the same sense of ruthlessness and even abandon, as well as—and this was very important—the same sense of dry, mordant, often fatalistic humor. To Larry, it was as if he and Elisa had been made for each other; Elisa excited him and made him alive in a way that he hadn't felt in years. And . . . Larry knew or sensed she was dangerous . . . that it would take all his wits to keep himself whole. This was a large part of Larry's attraction to Elisa.

Within a matter of days, Elisa had moved in with Larry at the condominium he had rented for his stays in Las Vegas. Soon Larry had leased matching 1995 Jaguars for Elisa and himself, one black, the other white. He began escorting her around the town, showing her off to friends and acquaintances, telling anyone who would listen that Elisa was one of the smartest people he had ever met. To those who had known him a long time, Larry seemed utterly besotted. What Cheryl knew or believed about Larry's bi-city two-timing isn't clear, but it's safe to say she could not have been happy about it.

In retrospect, all of this had to be a huge step up in class for Laren Sims Jordan, petty thief of Brooksville, Tampa and St. Petersburg. Only two years earlier she had been on the lam from the authorities, snipping off her ankle bracelet and running from the law, a small-time grifter on the make. Now she was living large, and if anything, she had somehow evolved the style to carry it off. Perhaps that had been Laren's problem all along: her cons had always been too petty, at least until she met Larry.

Later, some of Larry's Reno pals would recall meeting Elisa for the first time in Las Vegas. Fred Atcheson, for one, remembered being introduced to Elisa by Larry at one of the city's hotels, while they were ringside at a boxing match involving the championship fighter Oscar de la Hoya. "She was introduced to me as the daughter of a wealthy Cuban businessman," Atcheson recalled. "She looked a bit Hispanic, I guess, and was supposed to be able to speak fluent Spanish." But Atcheson swiftly formed the impression that there was more—or perhaps less—to Elisa than met the eye.

"Usually when you're around people who speak another language, and they're around people who also speak that language, as we were at the de la Hoya fight, they take a great deal of pleasure in speaking that language. But she didn't say much at all in Spanish, only a few phrases." That gave Atcheson the idea that Elisa was only pretending to be a fluent Spanish speaker, and made him wonder whether it was really true that Elisa was the daughter of a wealthy Cuban businessman. So, almost from the beginning, Atcheson, along with some of Larry's other friends, had doubts about her. Moreover, she just seemed cagey, somehow, to Atcheson—too cautious, too controlled, by half. But Larry seemed as smitten by Elisa as he was oblivious to the danger signs, so Atcheson decided to keep his own counsel.

In late July, the bookkeeper in the Las Vegas office quit, and Elisa took over the management of Larry's accounts there, including the responsibility for paying the bills and issuing checks. By mid-August, in fact, Elisa had taken over the money management responsibilities for all three offices; in September, Larry named Elisa "chief operating officer" of Larry McNabney and Associates, with authority over Larry's general office account, his client trust account, and even his personal accounts.

"In this regard," the bar association later found, "all financial statements and account information were set up to run through the Las Vegas office and be directed to Ms. Redelsperger [Elisa]. This included all billings, bank statements, and any other financial documents utilized as part of the operation . . ." This included the rubber stamp of Larry's authorized signature. In other words, wittingly or not, Larry had placed a convicted thief in charge of all of his money, as well as the money of people he was representing.

Elisa quickly began to take charge of the Reno office, just as she had muscled her way in in Las Vegas. One of Larry's Reno employees, Myra Nelson, had worked for McNabney and Associates for two years when Larry brought Elisa to the Reno office to introduce her, telling everyone that from then on, Elisa would be the boss. Myra was not impressed.

"She was skinny," Myra remembered, "totally dressed like Vegas, with a short sundress, cut out on the sides of the waist. I had a feeling that was hard to describe. I felt she was very ruthless and cold. She did not say much the day we all met her, but over the phone and for a few weeks afterward, she was not a kind person." Like Myra, all of Larry's employees in the three offices—the associate attorneys, the paralegals, the secretaries—soon realized that Elisa was the real boss, and that if she took a dislike to them, they would be as good as finished at the firm. So when Elisa began juggling the books—as she did almost immediately—no one said anything, at least at first.

In early August of 1995, Elisa met with a young Las Vegas man named Jeffrey Moore. Moore had recently graduated from Seattle University's law school, and had then relocated, with his wife, to Las Vegas, where his mother lived. Moore's marriage soon came apart, and by the summer of 1995, he was somewhat at loose ends, trying to find a job while waiting to take the Nevada bar examination. As the summer progressed, Moore became more and more discouraged about finding a law job. Then, in early August of 1995, a friend of his mother's, a real estate agent, told him about McNabney and Associates, and Moore called to inquire about the prospect of employment as a law clerk. On August 9, Elisa decided to hire Moore for the Las Vegas office, and send him to the Reno office for a short time for training.

Moore explained that he hadn't passed the bar exam yet, but Elisa didn't care. Under the rules, as long as he was supervised by a licensed lawyer, he could start acting as an attorney.

"It was cookie-cutter law," Moore recalled later. "Mostly sending demand letters." The idea was to get the cases in and turn them over as fast as possible.

"How soon can you get to Reno?" Elisa asked Moore. When Moore said he could leave right away, Elisa bought an airline ticket for him. She also told him that Larry McNabney and Associates would start him at a salary of $40,000 a year, and give him a car.

"I was in heaven," Moore recalled. "Only the day before I had no job and wasn't getting anywhere, and now I was on my way to Reno with a forty-thousand-dollar-a-year job and a car."

When he arrived in Reno, Moore said, McNabney and Associates put him up at the Clarion Hotel. The firm gave him the use of one of Larry's vehicles, a brand new Jeep Cherokee.

Over the next month, Moore was trained by one of the McNabney associates in the arcana of personal injury work. It wasn't difficult, and soon Moore was closing cases—that is, getting the settlements and their associated fees—with ease and rapidity. Elisa told Moore that she and Larry were tremendously impressed with his work, and when the associate who had trained Moore decided to leave the office, Elisa asked Moore if he would consider staying in Reno.

Well, why not? Moore thought. The firm was paying him handsomely, putting him up at a first-class hotel, and letting him drive a brand new Jeep. What more could he ask for? So Moore essentially took over the day-to-day operations of the Reno office of McNabney and Associates.

Larry, meanwhile, continued to jet back and forth between Reno and Las Vegas. At first this was all done on commercial aircraft, Moore recalled, but as the fall unfolded, the firm began hiring a Learjet for the shuttle. Larry even began talking about leasing his own jet.

Larry was a moody sort of person, Moore recalled. Sometimes he could be very friendly, but at others he could be gruff, even intimidating. Elisa took advantage of this, Moore recalled, acting as the go-between who insulated the staff from Larry. People were grateful to Elisa for this, Moore said; it was as if she were offering herself up as the whipping girl for Larry's nastier moods, saving the others from Larry's belligerency.

As the weeks progressed and his contact with Elisa deepened, Moore began to pick up a weird vibe. "She began talking to me about her sex life with Larry," Moore recalled. He wasn't sure what to make of this—at one level he thought she might be coming on to him. But on the other, maybe the seductive demeanor was some sort of test—that, if he picked up on Elisa's signals, Elisa would tell Larry, and the next thing Moore knew, he would be canned. Elisa made him nervous, especially when she was seductive. On one occasion, on a trip to Las Vegas, Elisa and a woman friend had invited him to enjoy a hot tub with them at the condo. Somehow the keys to Elisa's Jag got into the water, and the door-locking electronic mechanism of the keys shorted out. Moore was sure that Larry would find out that he'd been in the hot tub with Elisa, and even though it was entirely innocent, he was afraid Larry would get jealous and fire him. Later, Moore said, Larry did chide him about shorting out the keys, and while it was intended to be humorous, Moore realized that Larry *was* jealous. On that trip, too, Moore recalled Elisa's friend offering him a bundle of brown powder as a pick-me-up; he recognized it as crystal, a form of methamphetamine, and concluded that Elisa and her friend, if not Larry, were all using meth, at least while they were in Las Vegas.

Moore also heard about Elisa's previous marriage to Kenneth, that they were divorced, and that Haylei was still living with Redelsperger. At one point, in fact, Moore actually met him. He had the impression that Elisa had told her ex-husband that her relationship with Larry was strictly business, even though it was obvious to everyone in the office that it was more than that.

• • •

By late summer, with the staff of McNabney and Associates jet-setting between Reno and Las Vegas, with the television ads booming out of the box all over Nevada, with billboards bearing Larry's face going up all over the state, with a burgeoning payroll in three cities, with bills from the Clarion Hotel rolling in like clockwork, with the leased cars and three homes, with all this—the money was gushing out of Larry's accounts.

Larry's three offices alone carried an overhead of "at least" one hundred thousand dollars a month, the Nevada State Bar Association would later find. By September of 1995, in fact, Larry was having trouble paying the advertising costs. The television people contacted Nancy Eklof, who called Larry to remind him that the bills had to be paid. Larry seemed unaware of the situation, Nancy recalled. He assured her he would take care of everything, and soon the unpaid bills were satisfied. But the handwriting was on the wall: Larry McNabney and Associates were spending money far, far faster than it was coming in. But Larry didn't seem to care, or even to be able to stop the spending. In October, he and Elisa went to Puerto Vallarta, at least partly on the basis of a promotion offered to heavy television advertisers like Larry. Then in early November, Larry treated the entire staff to a trip to Acapulco, Mexico, including a stay at a first-class hotel, El Presidente.

But by late November, Larry had realized that the foray into Las Vegas had been an expensive mistake. It cost more to get the cases than the cases were netting, and besides, it was too difficult to supervise the widely separated offices. He decided to start winding down the Las Vegas office and concentrate on Reno and Elko. Sometime in that month he brought Elisa and Haylei north to Reno. That meant kicking Cheryl and her children out of the Buckaroo Court house, and moving Elisa and her daughter in.

"Cheryl was heartbroken," one of the friends she shared with Larry later recalled. But this was prototypical, alcoholic Larry: his needs and wants came first. When Nancy Eklof asked him why he was doing this, Larry told her, "I'm so bored, Nancy." Soon Larry and Elisa were tooling around in their black and white Jags, the talk of the town.

Sometime in mid-December of 1995, the staff of the Reno office of Larry McNabney and Associates had a Christmas party. At one point during the party, the office accountant approached Jeffrey Moore. Moore later recalled that the accountant, Barbara Westerlund, was nervous and upset. She asked Moore how serious a legal problem it might be if checks written on the firm's client trust account were bouncing.

Moore hadn't yet passed the bar, but he knew it was indeed a serious problem: the trust account was Other People's Money—that is, the clients'—and wasn't supposed to be used for anything other than paying them their settlements, or reimbursing the firm for authorized expenses on the clients' behalf. The fact that checks on the trust account were bouncing indicated that something was drastically wrong. Under certain circumstances, people could go to jail.

When Moore checked into this further, he realized that Elisa had been writing checks for unauthorized purchases on the trust account—including one check for an American quarter horse, one of the checks that had bounced. Moore knew that Elisa and Haylei both loved horses, so it wasn't hard to conclude that Elisa had raided the trust account, using the rubber stamp of Larry's signature that Elisa by that time was carrying in her purse. Moore didn't know whether Larry knew about Elisa's misuse of the account. He wasn't sure what to do—should he tell Larry? Maybe Larry would tell him to mind his own business, that he didn't understand what was going on, and that he had overreached himself. Maybe, in fact, Larry would fire him. Larry could be intimidating, at least to Moore.

"I was very stressed about it," Moore said.

After mulling this over for two days, on Sunday, December 17, Moore called Pete Durney to tell him what he had learned. He picked Durney because he knew that Durney and Brennan were among Larry's closest friends; besides, since they handled many of the McNabney firm's litigation referrals, especially on big mining accident cases, Moore figured they had a stake in what was going on. Durney asked him to come over in person and explain, so Moore did.

"I was crying," Moore said. He wasn't sure whether he had just killed his chances of ever working as a lawyer in Reno—that he wouldn't get a reputation as a rat. But Durney assured him that he had done the right thing, Moore recalled.

Pete Durney and Tom Brennan were among Larry's oldest friends in Reno. They had shared space in the old converted Levy mansion in downtown Reno back in the days when Larry was just starting out with Bath; later, Brennan had worked with Larry in the Papoose Palace cases. They discussed the situation, and later that same Sunday, they went to the Buckaroo Court house to tell Larry what Moore had said. Durney and Brennan later said that Larry was "shocked" to hear that Elisa had been misappropriating from the law firm's sacrosanct trust account.

Larry confronted Elisa in their presence, Brennan and Durney recalled, asking her about the allegations. At first, Elisa denied doing anything wrong or illegal. She became angry at Larry. But under the insistence of all three men, she eventually broke down and admitted juggling the books, diverting some significant amount of money—she wasn't sure exactly how much—from the privileged accounts into cash.

"This resulted in the physical departure of Ms. Redelsperger from the residence," the Nevada Bar reported later. In other words, Elisa took off in a huff, apparently terminating her relationship with Larry. It appears that Elisa went to stay with a hairdresser friend in Reno for several weeks; it was while she was staying with this friend that Elisa was later alleged to have said that she knew just how to control Larry, and that she would soon proceed to do so.

Later that day, Larry called Moore and asked him to come over to see him. Larry told Moore that he was grateful to him for having exposed Elisa's wrongdoing.

"You're my man," Larry told Moore. Noticing that Moore didn't have a warm coat for the bitter winter weather in Reno, Larry raided his own closet and gave him an expensive suede jacket with wool lining. "He said I'd done the right thing," Moore remembered.

And still later that night, Elisa called Moore at home.

"Thanks a lot," she said, with evident venom.

In retrospect, it seems likely that Larry had some inkling of what Elisa had been up to—in fact, he may even have suggested it. While it wasn't ethical, sometimes lawyers did use their client trust account as a sort of temporary bank— a bridge loan for temporary cash shortages—and what the client didn't know didn't hurt anyone. But this couldn't go on for any length of time, probably not more than a month or so, without being discovered. Now Westerlund and Moore had discovered it; what was worse was that the discovery had occurred when a check—for a show horse, no less—had bounced.

Larry now took immediate steps to deal with the trust account problem. The next day he obtained a $234,000 loan from Reno-area developer Mark Combs, a long-time friend going back to their days together at Reno High School. The day after that, Larry borrowed $50,000 more from Brennan and Durney, and another $9,000 from Fred Atcheson. Larry closed his two existing business checking accounts, including the client trust account, and opened two new accounts, with himself the only authorized signatory. He also hired a professional auditor to go over the books going back to the opening of the Las Vegas office in July.

Larry also went to see Fred Pinkerton, a Reno lawyer who had represented him in the divorce with Gail.

"Jesus Christ, Larry," Pinkerton said, when Larry told him about Elisa and the trust account. "You can't do that."

"I know, I know," Larry said, depressed.

"She can't work in your office anymore, you know that. You're going to have to get rid of her," Pinkerton said. Larry said he knew that, too.

What Larry did not do, however—and apparently neither did Pinkerton, or Durney and Brennan, at least immediately—was notify the Nevada State Bar Association of the infraction. There was a bar rule that required them to do so: "A lawyer having knowledge that another lawyer has committed a violation of the rules of professional conduct that raises a substantial question as to that lawyer's honesty, trustworthiness or fitness as a lawyer . . . shall inform the appropriate professional authority."

Moore was later not sure why no one rushed to inform the State Bar of Nevada that December, although he said he was under the impression that Larry had tangled with the bar's disciplinary board on an earlier occasion in connection with drugs and/or alcohol; it may have been that Larry and his friends considered the violation a technical one rather than one of substance, and since the money had been put back within a day or so of the discovery, there was little point in coming forth.

For the next three weeks, Larry endeavored to save Larry McNabney and Associates from the scandal. If the word got out, it would be the same as throwing all the expensive television advertising broadcast over the previous two years right down the toilet. After all, who would hire a crooked lawyer who would steal from his already painfully injured clients? It would indeed be adding insult to injury. If Larry hoped to save his considerable investment, he had to keep the thing quiet, or at least as quiet as possible. If it did get out, Larry would have to blame everything on Elisa: it wouldn't be the first time some law firm employee tapped a firm's till, and while Larry was responsible for supervising his employees, no one could expect him to watch their every move. All Larry had to do was repudiate Elisa, curse her for taking advantage of his trusting nature, and this, at first, he seemed willing to do. But it was better that no one ever find out. For that he needed Moore's cooperation. "For a while, I was the hero," Moore recalled, ruefully. "I was the golden boy."

So some people thought they had seen the last of Elisa Redelsperger—after having reputedly taken Ken Redelsperger for fifty grand the year before, and then Larry McNabney for a substantial if still unknown sum that next year, the betting in Reno among those who knew the score was that the well-traveled grifter, Elisa Redelsperger—whoever she really was—would get out of town in a hurry.

But on January 6, 1996, Larry married her.

Blanche

The stunning marriage of Larry and Elisa, conducted at the Reno Hilton, with Haylei in attendance, is only the curtain raiser on the central mystery of the McNabney tragedy, which is, after all, why? Why in the world would Larry McNabney have married a woman he then *knew* for certain was a thief? Why would he have stayed with her during all the years that followed? Why was he still with her on September 11, 2001, the day he disappeared from a hotel at a quarter horse show east of Los Angeles, never to be seen again, until months later, when he was finally, indisputably dead?

Indeed, asking why even begs the question: why in the world would Larry McNabney ever have hired Elisa Re-delsperger in the first place, way back in June or July of 1995? Why did he put Elisa in virtually complete control of the law firm he had sunk so much money into, and worked so hard to build up? Hadn't he realized that Elisa was not to be trusted, if not already a convicted criminal? Larry was, after all, an experienced criminal lawyer—he'd had plenty of encounters with the criminal element before. He knew the talk, he knew the walk, and he certainly knew how to find out what someone's past was all about. And by the summer of 1995, Larry was aware, at the least, of Elisa's immediate past: her brief marriage to Kenneth Re-delsperger had to have been a warning flag of the reddest hue. Larry would have to have been a fool not to have consulted the Las Vegas businessman about his own unhappy experience with Elisa the year before, and if there was one thing Larry was not, it was a fool. Indeed, it later became apparent to some of Larry's Reno friends that Larry had actually met Redelsperger and had talked with him about Elisa. The story in Reno was all too familiar: that Elisa had met Redelsperger by going to work in his office, had dazzled him, married him, and then run off with a substantial amount of his money, all in just a few months. It is inconceivable that Larry would not have known this history.

So what gives? Why would Larry not only continue his association with Elisa/Laren Sims Jordan/Redelsperger, but actually make her Mrs. McNabney Number Five?

For the likely answer to this, we'll have to make a brief side trip to the movies.

Later Nancy Eklof could recall the scene, the setting: the Rapscallion Seafood House & Bar in Reno. There Nancy, Larry and Elisa often had lunch in the fall of 1995, before the ill wind of Jeffrey Moore had made Elisa suspect. Elisa, Nancy recalled, would enjoy a plate of "Angels on Horseback," scallops wrapped in bacon, while Larry went for the turkey, mashed potatoes and gravy. Nancy loved to recite well-known lines from famous movies, to the amusement of Larry and Elisa. One of her favorites was from the 1962 cult classic, *What Ever Happened to Baby Jane?* There is a scene in the movie where Joan Crawford, playing the role of Blanche, a one-time movie star, an alcoholic now confined to a wheelchair, is tormented by her younger sister, also a former film star, Bette Davis, playing the role of Jane.

"You wouldn't be able to do these awful things to me if I weren't still in this chair," Blanche tells her sister. Jane is quick to respond:

"But cha AAH, Blanche, ya AAH in that chaiaaah!"

As Nancy voiced these lines, including the accent adopted by Bette Davis, Larry and Elisa roared with delight. And from then on, and for years afterward, right up until the fateful day, each persisted in calling the other "Blanche."

Because they both were in that chair, and there wasn't

a thing either one of them could do about it—not without destroying themselves in the bargain.

The outlines of this pact of Mutually Assured Destruction between Larry and Elisa are vague, it is true, but nevertheless discernible in the events that were to mark the course of their six-year relationship.

First, it seems more than possible that when Larry professed "shock" at Elisa's tapping of the client trust account, he was being disingenuous. By early December of 1995, he had already had conversations with Nancy Eklof about the unpaid advertising bills, and had almost immediately had them paid—nearly $100,000. So it seems possible that Larry had instructed Elisa to dip into the trust money to pay off the advertisers in a sort of float game—planning to repay the money to the account when later insurance settlements came in. But then Elisa's use of the account later to buy the horse resulted in the bounced check, alarming Barbara Westerlund, who told Moore, who in turn, agonizing about what this might mean to his career, told Durney and Brennan. Once the cat was out of the bag, Larry had no choice but to put all the blame on Elisa if he wanted to save his law license and even prevent his possible arrest for criminal embezzlement. Of course, Elisa might well have responded that she'd bought the horse only after Larry had told her to pay off the television advertising bill with the client trust money—in other words, Larry was as guilty as she was, and Larry had a lot more to lose than she did. Elisa had learned the extortion game very well while working for Larry, the personal injury lawyer.

So perhaps the best thing for all concerned was to keep the whole thing secret—television ads and horse alike. Which may have been why Moore emerged, for a while at least, as "the golden boy," why Larry treated him so well— at least up until the time of the marriage. Moore even remembered that a week or so after she was banned from the law office, Elisa called him a second time to tell him how grateful she and Larry both were that he had reported the defalcation to Durney and Brennan; left unsaid was the gratitude of Larry and Elisa that Moore hadn't called the bar instead.

Then, when Pinkerton talked to Elisa to get her side of the story, Elisa asked him if the bar and anyone else could force her to testify against Larry if they were married. This happened, Pinkerton was sure, before the marriage actually took place. Elisa's statement seems to indicate that she had possible knowledge of Larry's involvement in the trust account diversion: that indeed, the price of her silence was a marriage license.

The entire situation over the trust account reeked of quid pro quo, of mutual blackmail. And over the ensuing years, there would be still other clues to the nature of this "wheelchair" alliance. Tom Hogan, the Florida lawyer who had represented Laren Sims Jordan and Laren's family near Brooksville, would say that he was surprised to have received a telephone call from his old client, Laren, in the late summer of 1995. By that point, Laren/Elisa had been out of contact with her family for more than two years. Hogan recalled that Elisa asked him what it would take for her to square things with the authorities in Florida so she could return without fear of going back to jail. Laren/Elisa would only tell him that she was in Nevada, but wouldn't give him a telephone number; she would call *him*, she said. Hogan told her he would check around, and did; in a subsequent conversation, he told Laren/Elisa that if she paid the court-ordered restitution to her victims, the chances were very good that she wouldn't have to do any more time. At that point, the amount was certainly less than $5,000. Laren/Elisa told Hogan that she'd get back to him.

Then, some months later, Hogan said, Laren/Elisa called

him back and said that she had married a Nevada lawyer. When Hogan asked her about her plans for the restitution and recovering her freedom in her own name, she told him that she'd talked the whole thing over with her new husband, the lawyer, and he had told her to sever all contact with Hogan, and not to trust him. Still later, after she was finally arrested in connection with Larry's death, Hogan said, Laren/Elisa told him that Larry had insisted that she not turn herself in on the outstanding Florida charges in order to have something with which to control her. Thus, each partner in the marriage would have something to hold over the other: Larry's involvement in the trust account diversion for Elisa, Elisa's criminal record for Larry, even-steven.

There is also the story that Larry himself told his son, Joe, sometime during the summer of 1998. When Joe observed that Larry didn't seem to be happy with Elisa, Larry—a bit drunk, according to Joe—told his son that he couldn't afford to leave Elisa, that she could "ruin" him. To Joe, that sounded like Elisa was blackmailing Larry.

And finally, there is the most interesting clue of all: throughout their relationship, right up until September 11, 2001, Larry and Elisa/Laren called each other by their own pet nickname: "Blanche."

It also seems clear that by December of 1995, Larry's drinking and drugging and spending were out of control—that is, he'd lost all comprehension of how much he'd actually spent, or even where. Larry's acquaintances during this time repeatedly mentioned that Larry was prone to go off on "runners"—binges of drinking and drugging in which he would simply disappear for days at a time, a sort of *Lost Weekend* of the nineties. By early 1996, in fact, Larry had an unpaid American Express bill of about $80,000 which had to be addressed. By borrowing money from Combs,

Brennan and Durney, and Atcheson, Larry was able to re-
plenish the missing trust account money and to get rid of
the burgeoning American Express bill.

Looking back, some of Larry's closest friends decided
that Elisa had played a critical role in Larry's eventual de-
mise. They believed she'd served as Larry's willing enabler
whenever he went off on one of his binges. In contrast to
the first four wives, some thought, Elisa made no effort to
rein in any of Larry's appetites. Some thought, in fact, that
Elisa played a role in actually fueling those appetites, particularly when they had been in Las Vegas together; there
was a vague sense that Elisa had cocaine connections in Las
Vegas that she had helped Larry tap into, although this
might have stemmed merely from the fact that most people
knew that Elisa had grown up in Florida, associated in the
popular mind with cocaine ever since the days of *Miami
Vice*. Certainly Larry hadn't needed anyone's help before in
locating drugs.

After their marriage, some of Larry's friends tried to get
Elisa to work on him to quit drinking and drugging, but she
said she was powerless to make him stop. At one point,
she told them, she'd tried to get Larry to go back to rehab,
but he wouldn't do it. Later, looking back, some of the same
friends decided that indulging Larry's penchant for drugging
and drinking was part of Elisa's plan from the start: "She got
him coked up to control him," said one friend. Or as another
put it, "She allowed him to do whatever he wanted . . . she
told him everything was under control so he didn't have to
worry, she would take care of it for him."

Nancy Eklof was later to vividly recall a trip to Cancún,
Mexico, that Larry and Elisa took that spring with Nancy
and her boyfriend. There was a gigantic hassle, Nancy recalled, about getting a passport for Elisa, who did not have
one, and who probably couldn't get one as a fugitive felon.
Nancy recalled that Larry did something—pulled some
strings somehow—and a passport somehow was produced,

perhaps under the name Redelsperger; Nancy wasn't exactly sure. But the trip came off. Nancy was to remember Larry and Elisa arguing much of the time, and Elisa crying a lot. Nancy also recalled her boyfriend, who was skeptical of Elisa, mentioning that if Elisa wanted to murder Larry, Cancún was a good place to do it. Nancy thought the remark odd at the time.

What may have actually occurred in the trouble over the passport was that Larry finally and for the first time realized the extent of Elisa's criminal history, including the warrant out for her arrest from fleeing probation in Florida; indeed it was shortly after this trip that Elisa had the conversation with Hogan in which she said that her new husband, the lawyer, had advised her not to trust her old lawyer, and to sever all connection with him.

Whatever transpired on this trip, one result seems to have been that Elisa somehow convinced Larry to let her back into the law office. Nancy Eklof recalled that Larry had assured her that Elisa had no access to any of the law firm accounts or even his own personal credit cards, and others in Reno recalled something similar. In fact, Larry used his control over the money as a means to keep Elisa on a leash, some in Reno remembered; it was a bit like being a lion tamer, with the money as the whip, and it appealed to Larry's appetite for living dangerously.

The re-emergence of Elisa in the law office created fear and trepidation among the staff members, too, Moore said. Most knew that once she was back, it wouldn't take Elisa long to get rid of the people she'd seen as disloyal to her, particularly Jeffrey Moore, his legal assistant Johanna, Barbara Westerlund, and several others. On March 8, 1996, Elisa sent around a memo, telling Moore and Johanna that a staff meeting that had been scheduled for the following day had been cancelled. The memo, said Moore, was seen as undisputed proof that Elisa had regained total control. That evening, he and Johanna and others in the firm who feared Elisa's retribution stayed late, copying documents and checks that Elisa had signed as far back as September of 1995. When Elisa's own assistant caught them making the copies, and ordered them out of the office, the anti-Elisa faction knew their days with McNabney and Associates had come to an end. Within a matter of days all had been fired or forced out, including Moore.

Within a week or so of his departure, Moore contacted the State Bar of Nevada and asked an anonymous question: would a non-lawyer law firm employee (he hadn't yet taken the bar examination) have the same obligation to report a lawyer's wrongdoing as a licensed attorney? The answer was yes. Over the next month or so, Moore composed a letter to the state bar, accusing Larry and Elisa of "numerous" ethical and legal violations. From September of 1995 through December, Moore informed the bar, Elisa had used the McNabney client trust account improperly, "for an extravagant lifestyle, which included routine trips in Lear jets, leased Jaguars, purchase of jewelry, a fur, trips abroad and purchase of equine," or, in another word, the horse.

Moore went on to say that he'd reported the situation to "two attorneys in Reno," and that as a result, Larry had tried to repair the problem by borrowing money to repay the client trust fund. "I know that at least three trust fund checks were returned to the bank for insufficient funds," Moore added. In fact, Moore said, he suspected that the bank also tried to cover up the scandal.

Finally, said Moore, "Mr. McNabney literally threatened my hopes of practicing law in the state of Nevada. This has been a souring experience in my endeavor to pursue a legal career." In other words, Larry had in effect blackballed Moore, so that he was unable to find a law job anywhere in Nevada.

At some point after this, the state bar association began

an investigation of Larry McNabney and Associates, and as it turned out, Elisa did have to testify.

This took place in March of the following year, when the bar's disciplinary board held a hearing to decide what to do. Larry's private audit had been completed on the accounts Elisa had been using, and had shown that a total of $74,000 had been improperly taken from the client trust account, transferred into the law firm's general account, and then paid out on "various liabilities of the firm . . . as chief operating officer for respondent's law firm," as the bar later characterized it. "It was Ms. Redelsperger [Elisa] who actively generated the financial transactions necessary to accomplish the above."

The bar's language in describing the events is as cautious as it is curious: it doesn't say that Larry was unaware that Elisa was using the client trust account in this fashion, it only notes that it was Elisa "who actively generated" the transfers to satisfy "various liabilities of the firm . . ."

For her part, Elisa told the bar, she realized that it was wrong to transfer the money from the trust account. To make up for it, she said, she'd transferred at least $60,000 of Larry's own money back into the trust account, using telephone and facsimile transfers from the various accounts. She told the bar investigators that she anticipated that a "big case" would come in, which would make it possible to put all the accounts back in order. Instead, Moore had spilled the beans to Durney and Brennan.

Although Pinkerton had told Larry that Elisa would have to be kept out of the law office, and Larry had agreed, she had crept back in, which was why Moore and his fellow anti-Elisans were thrown out. True, Larry had maintained iron control over the money. But now that the bar association had had its say, Elisa was finally, definitely, legally barred from the office. Larry wasn't happy; he had come to rely on Elisa running things while he was out having fun. But the bar association made it clear that if Larry wanted to keep his license, Elisa would have to go, and for real this time.

In March of 1997, the bar found Larry guilty of two counts of unprofessional conduct, including failing to properly supervise the employees in his law firm, and improperly permitting his client trust account to be misused. For admitting these counts, the bar proposed that Larry be given a "public reprimand" and two "private reprimands."

These reprimands were more than just a slap on the wrist. In a tight-knit town such as Reno, such a public censure was damaging in the extreme—they certainly would have negated all the expensive advertising that Larry had bought over the previous two years.

In a hearing held on March 6, 1997, Larry, Brennan, Durney, the auditor and Elisa all testified before a panel of the bar's disciplinary board. For some reason, one of the panel members wanted all references made to Elisa Redelsperger McNabney contained in the reprimands to be deleted, and the full panel agreed to this. The purpose of this wasn't entirely clear, although it may have been intended to keep Elisa's name out of the news, and thus, may have been a part of some sort of bargain she'd made with Larry and/or the board. In any event, the reprimands, "as modified," were made part of the public record. From that point forward, anyone who wanted to check the McNabney firm's reliability with the bar would have access to this evidence of the firm's checkered history.

After this, things began going downhill for McNabney and Associates. Some thought Larry was embarrassed by the scandal, while others, knowing him better, realized that he was simply tired of answering the question of why he had married Elisa. By May of 1997, he had sold the Buckaroo Court house, taking a $43,000 loss on the property. He and Elisa moved into another house in Caughlin Ranch, a rental, and then still later, an apartment, definitely heading downmarket, some thought. Larry seemed discouraged, people agreed—depressed. He avoided many of his old friends, and went off on periodic benders. He had tried to become the King of Torts of Nevada, and had failed, and failure wasn't something that a McNabney ever did.

Over 1996 and into 1997, Larry and Elisa grew more and more isolated from Larry's life-long friends. True, Larry was embarrassed about the bar association investigation, and even more embarrassed when people asked him why in the world he'd married someone like Elisa, who had stolen from him. He was never able to explain to people, and eventually he simply stopped frequenting places where he could be recognized.

Later, some thought that this was Elisa's method of setting Larry up: keep him away from those who could protect him from himself, as they had always done over the years. Eventually, in fact, Larry and Elisa would leave town for good, the better to keep Larry isolated from those who could save him, some of his friends thought. On the other hand, there were those who thought Larry was just too ashamed to stay in the town he had grown up in.

Elisa also strove to isolate Larry from his own family—or at least, that's what his adopted daughter Tavia, who also lived in Reno, came to believe. "She didn't like me," Tavia said later, referring to Elisa. It was also clear that Tavia didn't think much of Elisa, either; Tavia later decided that Elisa had kept her away from Larry because she was afraid that Tavia would unmask Elisa as a gold-digger. Eventually, in fact, Elisa convinced Larry to write a new will—one that shared all Larry's assets between herself, Haylei, Joe and Cristin, but which cut Tavia out completely. Larry signed. Then Elisa told Joe and Cristin the news: that Tavia had been "cut out."

Late in 1998, Larry and Elisa decided to move to the Sacramento, California, area and start anew. They opened a new law office on Howe Avenue in Sacramento, re-cut some of the old television commercials for airing in California, and tried to drum up some business. For Larry, there was at least one advantage in starting over: while Elisa had been barred from the office in Nevada, that wasn't true in California—indeed, that may have been the real reason why Elisa's name was deleted from the Nevada bar's reprimands of Larry. That way, Elisa could work in Larry's new office.

Looking back, it doesn't seem that Larry's heart was really in the business anymore.

"He'd lost a step," one of his Reno friends observed, "the way a ballplayer loses it. He just wasn't as fast as he used to be, and it was like he'd lost his confidence in himself. The Larry I knew—he was gone." What remained was a man who was past his prime, at least in the law business.

How much any of this had to do with Larry's apparent Faustian, ball-and-chain bargain with Elisa isn't certain. By the time he and Elisa opened the new incarnation of McNabney and Associates in Sacramento, Larry had turned over almost all of the real responsibility for the law practice to Elisa—someone who wasn't licensed to practice law, and who, indeed, was a fugitive felon. But Larry may have simply given up by this point.

He and Elisa began their life in California by renting a house in Fair Oaks, a small town just east of Sacramento. While Elisa drove into Sacramento each day to operate the law business in her husband's name, Larry spent much of his time playing golf and drinking. The idea was that tort claimants would see Larry's advertisements, call the office to hire him to represent them, and that Elisa would then close the deal with the insurance company. All Larry would have to do was sign the complaints and approve the settlements. Elisa would handle all the paperwork, including the banking.

Later, in 1999, Larry and Elisa would move to a town-house in Elk Grove, some miles southeast of Sacramento. By this point, Haylei and Larry weren't getting along any-more; Haylei, then 15, considered Larry an abusive drunk and could barely stand to be around him. Elisa found places for Haylei to stay with friends, and eventually would rent an apartment for her daughter, hiring someone to stay with her. Haylei wasn't happy, but what could she do? She had al-ways been subject to her mother's mercurial whims.

Meanwhile, Larry's son Joe, who had lived with Larry and Elisa for part of the year in Reno after they were first married, was living in Sacramento. Unlike his sister Tavia, Joe got along well with Elisa. One day in the summer of 1998, Elisa invited Joe over for dinner. After the meal, Elisa and Haylei were in another part of the house, while Larry and Joe watched a game on television. Larry had been drink-ing, Joe admitted later. But he could tell that his father was unhappy in his marriage. In fact, Joe said, he had the im-pression that his father was afraid of Elisa.

"Maybe not quite afraid, but something weird was defi-nitely up . . . " He indicated to me, she's a compulsive liar. I think he says, she takes medication for it. And that he never would be able to leave her. He told me that—I didn't know what he meant. I didn't really want to butt my nose into it. It didn't sound good, the way he was expressing it to me, it didn't look good. I just thought, you know, I don't know what he's doing. I don't know what the two of them are do-ing, but I'm not— I'm not going to butt into their business so— But I knew she was faulty."

Joe was pressed for more details, but he said he didn't know any.

"I don't know how it got brought up, [but] it did. But it wasn't crying a sad story or anything. He was just telling me what this woman was all about."

"Did he tell you why he couldn't leave her?" Joe was asked.

"No."

"Did he mention to you that she knew things about him?"

"No. That's what I probably figured or something. That's what was going through my head."

"Did he mention to you that Elisa—if he left her, Elisa could destroy him?"

"No, he didn't— No. Not in those words, no."

"What words did he use when he talked about that subject?"

"Just that he couldn't leave her. Never would be able to leave her and that was that. I didn't ask him why, he didn't tell me why. I just— That was that."

During these years there had been a number of developments in the case of Larry's old murder client, Jack Mazzan. More than twenty years after his conviction, Mazzan was still trying to avoid the death penalty for the killing of Richard Minor. Even before Larry and Elisa left Reno, new lawyers for Mazzan were contending that the Reno police had withheld critical information from Larry at the time of Mazzan's trial—that in fact, the police had information that two drug-dealing acquaintances of Minor's had come to town just before the killing, and that one of them felt that Minor had ripped him off. The police said this wasn't so—they'd given Larry the information, but Larry had decided not to follow it up before Mazzan's original trial. By the late 1990s, the issue was working its way up to the Nevada Supreme Court, with Mazzan's new lawyers complaining that the "secret" police report meant that Mazzan should get a new trial. It appears that no one bothered to consult with Larry about the matter, however, or for that matter, with Nancy Eklof, who later said that Larry had long before told her that Mazzan was actually guilty, not only of Minor's murder but also that of April Barber.

Then, in January of 2000, the Nevada Supreme Court

held that the actual report on the other two suspects had been improperly withheld from Larry, and that they had never been sufficiently investigated by the police. The court ruled that Mazzan was entitled to a new trial. A tentative trial date was set for the fall of 2001. And while Larry couldn't legally be a witness in any new trial, he certainly knew enough to throw the case into a huge uproar if he ever blabbed about what he knew, as he already had, at least once, to Nancy Eklof.

It was while Mazzan's latest appeal was still winding its way through the Nevada courts that, in 1999, Larry and Elisa decided to move to Elk Grove, southeast of Sacramento. In June of that year, the McNabneys met the Whalens, and Larry developed a new interest: showing American quarter horses.

Just how all this came about was a little fuzzy. There were at least two versions of the events. In one, the introductions were made when Elisa, who had always had an interest in horses since her childhood as Laren Sims, met Greg Whalen's daughter Debbie Kail one day in June of 1999 when their horses were stabled next to one another at a horse show in Oregon.

In the other version, told by Greg Whalen himself, Larry and Elisa were introduced to him by another Sacramento-area horse trainer at about the same time. In any event, a few months after the introductions were made, Greg and Debbie Whalen, along with Debbie's husband Bob Kail, agreed to train Elisa's horse—apparently the same animal that she'd purchased with the bad check from the client trust account, the one that had started all the trouble in Nevada. Greg was to recall that in the spring of 1999, Larry and Elisa bought a second quarter horse from a breeder, who had recommended that they take the horse to Whalen for training. At some point after that, Whalen would recall, Elisa's horse was sold, and then the McNabneys added another to take its place. It appears that Elisa had convinced Larry that a good living could be made from the quarter horse industry; she also handled all the financial arrangements, according to Greg. As Greg would later point out, the care, feeding and training of a quarter horse was not cheap: the tab ran about $2,000 a month—per horse.

As Larry and Elisa hung around the Whalen ranch near Lodi more and more, they got to be good friends with the Whalen clan. Whalen would later observe, "we thought a lot of Larry and Elisa, both of them." At one point, in fact, the McNabneys gave Greg Whalen a gold Rolex watch for his birthday.

As this relationship developed, Larry became increasingly interested in the horse show business. But this was typical of Larry: just like criminal law, just like Ramtha, just like torts, Larry's initial enthusiasm propelled him along. Larry soon learned that the big money in quarter horses—at least for the owners, as opposed to the trainers like Whalen—came from the buying, selling and breeding of the animals. The Whalens taught him how to "show" the horses at the ever-occurring horse shows, and how, by winning points and climbing the ratings ladder, the shown horse could be made to increase in value.

For Larry, this was fun—all he had to do was look good. It appealed to his desire to be the star, at the center of attention. It was practically brainless, too, once one learned the ropes.

Thus, throughout the rest of 1999 and 2000, Larry spent his most sober attention on the horse shows, eventually taking up the showing of a gelding as an amateur exhibitor. As 1999 neared its end, Larry led the nation in first-year amateur points; for an award he received a large silver belt buckle with his name on it, along with the title "AQHA Rookie of the Year." Larry was hooked. Throughout much of 1999 and 2000, Larry and Elisa traveled the country extensively, showing horses, often in the company of Greg Whalen.

Then, late in 2000, when he was starting to think about a
new challenge in life as a horse breeder, Larry himself ran
afoul of the law.

Getting caught while driving drunk is an inevitable fate for
any alcoholic who drives. It simply cannot be prevented as
long as the alcoholic continues to drink. For one thing, the
alcoholic has become so used to having the drug in his or her
system, there is no longer any awareness that one is impaired.
Perceptions, reactions, all circuits seem perfectly normal.
What is more, judgment is eroded: *Since I seem perfectly normal, I must be; if I am, there's nothing to prevent me from
getting in my car and driving off.* It was amazing, given all
that he had drunk over the years, and all the drugs he had
taken, that this was, as far as can be determined from the
record, Larry's first and only arrest for driving under the
influence.

Of course, it may well have been that Larry had been
stopped before—but that would have been in Reno, where
he was well-known as a leading member of the bar (as well
as the bars). But in California, to the California Highway
Patrol, he was just another dangerous drunk on the road.
The CHP had no special favors to perform for an unknown
lawyer named Larry McNabney.

On the afternoon of December 5, 2000, Larry finished
another round of golf at a course not far from the Whalen
Ranch. Larry had been drinking—and drinking seriously.
He got in his car, a 1994 blue Mercedes, and began driving
home to Elk Grove. At one point on Highway 99, nearing
Elk Grove, he swerved in front of another car, causing the
driver to veer into the landscaped center median to avoid a
rear-end collision. Larry seemed oblivious to what was behind him and drove off. The other driver was enraged at
Larry's discourtesy. Extricating his car from the divider, he
called the California Highway Patrol on his cellular phone,
and then set off in pursuit of Larry.

About twenty minutes later, Larry pulled up to the rented townhouse in Elk Grove, followed only minutes later by the aggrieved driver, and then the highway patrol. The Highway Patrol officers knocked on the door, demanding to see the driver of the Mercedes. Elisa told Larry that the police were there and wanted to talk to him. Larry ran out the back door of the house and made tracks as fast as he could. The CHP officers chased him and some minutes later brought him down with an open field tackle.

When he was brought into the Sacramento County sheriff's station for processing, Larry first blew a .28 on the blood alcohol test, then a .27. More than three times the state's legal limit, to achieve a .28, one would have to drink fourteen shot glasses of whiskey in an hour. People have been known to die of alcohol poisoning at .34, which is another illustration of how drunk Larry was.

This arrest seems to have depressed Larry more than almost anything else that had happened up until then. According to Elisa, he lost almost all interest in the law business, and began to spend most of his time drinking at home, only rarely coming into the office. And as he drank, he became more abusive, at least verbally, of Elisa. Yet he still seems to have had some good days. He was able to hire a lawyer, Georgeann McKee, a former Sacramento County sheriff's deputy, to represent him on the drunk driving charge, and McKee, while realizing that Larry had a serious alcohol problem, also saw him as polite and contrite over his situation. She began working to try to extricate him from the arrest, while urging that he get some help. Larry made all the right noises about rehab, but didn't seem motivated.

In the meantime, the driver who had been cut off by Larry was talking about suing. Elisa contacted McKee. McKee advised her to do nothing—let Larry's insurance handle whatever the damages were, which appeared to be minimal. But Elisa insisted that they had to pay the other driver off. McKee was astounded one day to learn from Elisa that she'd given a check to the other driver for $25,000 to $35,000 dollars.

"I told her, 'Elisa, you're out of your mind,'" McKee recalled. "But she was insistent, they had to take care of this guy."

This was certainly peculiar, McKee thought. It was only later that she wondered whether part of the problem was that Larry *had* no insurance—that Elisa might never have bothered to pay the premium.

Or maybe there was another angle: because Larry had been keeping Elisa on a tight leash with checks and credit cards since the State Bar of Nevada fiasco, maybe this was some sort of scam of Elisa's—maybe Elisa saw in Larry's misfortune a chance to pry some mad money for herself from the ordinarily controlling Larry. Maybe it was just Elisa's way of scamming her own husband.

If that was the case, it was an omen of things to come.

On January 1, 2001, Larry paid Greg Whalen $12,500 for an 8-month-old sorrel colt with an impressive pedigree. This was Justa Lotta Page, offspring of Page Impressive and Justa Janie. Bred by a California rancher, William McCrain, the colt was acquired first by Whalen and then sold to Larry on New Year's Day as a "halter horse," that is, a quarter horse bred to be shown by leading it around a show ring.

According to some in the American quarter horse industry, a champion "halter horse" stallion is a rare item, and can bring up to seven figures, depending on his "conformance," that is, the size, color, muscle shape and tone. Part of the Whalens' job was to train the horse—in other words, work it out—so that the horse's muscles stood out, much the same as a human body builder's.

"They're buffed up," notes one expert. "You have to breed a lot of halter horses before you get a good one. They're like a work of art." If the horse's offspring are also of championship caliber, such an animal can be worth several tons of money.

The halter competition at horse shows was relatively simple, but required a substantial amount of practice by both the horse and its holder. The exhibitor had to lead the horse into the ring, then bring it to a stop, making sure it took a straight-up stance, without acting nervous or distracted. Then the exhibitor had to lead the horse around a small circuit, demonstrating walking and trotting gaits. At the end, the horse had to stop once again—almost like taking a bow—before exiting the arena. A horse that appeared to be too spirited lost points; so did a horse that didn't seem alert and responsive to the exhibitor's commands.

Beginning in late January, when Justa Lotta Page was just 10 months old, Larry, Elisa and the Whalen clan began traveling to horse shows throughout the West, exhibiting Justa Lotta Page, as well as a gelding horse that Whalen had leased to Elisa. These shows often featured up to a hundred quarter horses, or even more—almost all of them owned by wealthy people who hired people like the Whalens to train their animals. The shows were as much a social event as a competition, in which people gathered for cocktail parties, barbecues and the like, to dress up, be seen, and share gossip. Later, as police investigators dug into the cultural milieu that formed the backdrop of the McNabney mystery, they would be astonished by the amount of posturing—"showing off," as one detective put it—that the exhibitors displayed.

"It was all about money," one detective observed. "You had to have the best clothes, the best truck, the best trailer, the best horse, the best boots, hats . . . and you had to make sure everyone else knew what you paid for them!"

That was probably a harsh assessment, coming as it did from a workaday cop who probably lived, like most people, from paycheck to paycheck. But there was still some truth to the observation, as there was to an analogy offered by one investigator: the horse show business, it was observed, was like a gigantic fish—as the horse-owning leviathan swam on his lordly way through the small pond of fellow horse fanciers, the "pilot fish," people like the Whalens and others in the service industry behind the horses, such as trainers, blacksmiths, vets, insurance brokers, trailer dealers, feed sellers and the like, gathered around to pick off the crumbs of wealth spilling from the mouths of the monsters—fees for training, feeding, boarding, grooming, transporting, insuring, shoeing, doctoring, photographing . . . the list of enterprises capable of cashing in on the horse-owners' largesse was limited only by the imagination. As one trainer put it, owning and exhibiting an American quarter horse was not "for the faint of heart or weak of pocket."

From this perspective, it was in the economic interest of the industry—the professionals who serviced the horse owners, like the Whalens—to have as many shows as possible, and to dress the whole thing up in as much hoopla as could be arranged. It was, after all, a "show" in every sense of the word.

The main event, the one most people pointed for, was the so-called "world show," or AQHA World Championship in Oklahoma City every fall. Several hundred quarter horses would compete in this show, as horse fanciers from all over the country gathered together for the better part of a week, exhibiting their animals by day and partying by night. If an owner's animal won the championship of a particular class, the value of the horse was likely to skyrocket. That, it appears, was what Larry had in mind when he began the last year of his life by buying Justa Lotta Page.

As he acknowledged later, Greg Whalen liked both Larry and Elisa. While it was true that they were his "clients," as he put it, he also felt friendship for them. To Whalen, Larry seemed entirely normal, apart from his habitual drinking, and indeed likeable. For a rich guy, Larry seemed down-to-earth, readily willing to listen to Whalen's expert advice. One reason he suggested that Larry concentrate on the halter events, Whalen said later, was that Larry tended "to be better" in the morning—meaning that in an afternoon event Larry was likely to be somewhat drunk.

By April, Justa Lotta Page was 1 year old, and Larry and the Whalens had shown him in Scottsdale, Arizona; Las Vegas, Nevada; and Central Point, Oregon; as well as Rancho Murietta, Santa Rosa, Santa Barbara, Bakersfield and Elk Grove, all in California.

By this time Larry and Elisa had acquired their own horse trailer, a long red-and-white caravan that contained

luxury living quarters for the people as well as the horses.
Larry and Elisa bought the expensive trailer on credit, using
Joe McNabney's name. Elisa was later to say they had put
the trailer in Larry's son's name to help Joe establish his own
credit history. It seems likely that this financing scheme was
done without Larry's knowledge. Certainly, it came as news
to Joe, months later, to find that he was the one who owed
the balance due of over $60,000. The outside of the trailer
had the printed legend "Larry McNabney and Associates,
Attorneys at Law." Larry also traded in his nearly new black
pickup truck for a red diesel Ford "dually," similar to a
white truck driven by Greg Whalen, which was powerful
enough to pull the trailer. Once he'd bought a collection of
hats, jeans, boots and shirts, Larry was all set, all ready to
join the American Quarter Horse Association parade.

By the same spring, Larry had almost completely stopped
coming into the law office. Elisa was virtually running the
whole show—processing the complaints, making sure they
were typed correctly and filed, that the correct legal notices were served, the doctors contacted for their medical
evaluations of clients' injuries, the settlement conferences
scheduled—in short, doing everything a lawyer had to do to
move a tort case through the pipeline. All Larry had to do
was sign the paperwork. At the end of every workday, Elisa
would bundle up a stack of papers and drive south to Elk
Grove, where Larry would sign them. Elisa had a secretary
to help her with the paperwork, along with her daughter
Haylei, who worked part-time at the law office when she
wasn't in school, and was paid a salary from Larry's office
funds.

Later, when all of Larry's accounts—there were nine of
them—came under scrutiny by forensic accountants, lawyers
were to notice that some very obvious discrepancies began
occurring in February of 2001—that is, discrepancies that
were obvious to the auditors, but not to Larry. For years,

Larry had insisted on reviewing all the checks issued by the firm, and Elisa had complied with this by bringing home the firm's checkbooks, with their carbons, or "foils," for checks issued. But in February of 2001, it appears, Elisa hit on a new scheme: when writing a check, she inserted a piece of stiff paper between the surface of the check and the carbon, so the writing wouldn't go through; later, she used another, thinner piece of paper to fill in a fictitious payee and amount, so that the information on the carbon copy had no relationship to the check that had actually been issued. Thus, while writing a check for, say, $5,000 in cash, the record seen by Larry might say $400 for, say, car insurance. In other words, Elisa began stealing from Larry's accounts again, and concealing the fact from Larry by means of the spurious carbons.

The accountants who later pored over Larry's books also discovered that while Larry might not have been actively engaged in the practice of law, his firm was nevertheless doing a substantial amount of business. Of Larry's nine different bank accounts, three were in Reno, and the remainder in Rancho Cordova, a Sacramento suburb. The Nevada accounts were largely inactive, although Larry had made a total deposit of $275,000 in one of the accounts, a business checking account, in May of 2000, and another $20,000 in a personal checking account in September of that year. But by October of 2000, all of those funds had either been spent or transferred, and the three Nevada accounts were virtually moribund.

The six California accounts included a personal checking account for Larry, a client trust account, and a general business checking account for McNabney and Associates' new law office, all opened on January 19, 1999, just after the move from Reno. Then for some reason, eleven months later, three new accounts were opened at the same bank—a new client trust account, a new general business checking account, and a business account for an Internet brokerage business that Elisa wanted to start, huntseathorses.com. All three of the new accounts were opened on December 18, 2000—the day before Larry's birthday, and about two weeks after Larry had been arrested for drunken driving.

The purpose of these new accounts wasn't clear. The new client trust account was never used. The other two new accounts, however, had substantial activity in 2001, as did two of the earlier accounts, the original California business account and the first client trust account. It therefore seems possible that the parallel accounts were set up to facilitate a check-kiting scheme by someone, in which a bank is eventually stuck with paying off a worthless check. In a way, manipulating parallel accounts is somewhat like the old pea-in-the-shell game, or three-card monte. The general idea is to keep things confused.

The first client trust account, the one opened in January of 1999, had slightly over $1,000,000 deposited from that month until the day Larry disappeared, September 11, 2001. The bank records showed that $987,000 of this was paid back out, and with one notable exception, all but just over $3,000 of it was in checks. The fact that Larry McNabney and Associates had no major California cases during this time makes this something of a puzzle: where did the money come from, and who was it paid to?

One likelihood is that much of the money came into the firm from cases that had been previously filed in Nevada. As some involved in the tort litigation business put it, personal injury cases can have a long incubation. As the cases were settled and the insurance companies paid out, the money would make its way to the McNabney firm, be deposited into the trust account, and then paid out to the claimants—after Larry McNabney and Associates took its 25 to 40 percent cut, of course. That money would go into the general business account, and then out again to pay "the various liabilities of the firm," including the office rent and other costs of doing business, including Larry's draw and everyone's else's salary.

The records of the office's original general business account show that during the same period, from 1999 to Larry's disappearance, $619,000 was deposited, and $604,000 paid out in checks. The most striking feature of the office account is the fact that nearly 90 percent of these transactions took place in the years 1999 and 2000—$556,000 in deposits and $544,000 in checks. Then, in December of 2000, the new accounts were opened, and the year 2001 saw a drastic drop-off in deposits into the first general office account—only $62,000 in deposits against $60,000 in checks. The parallel new general business account, however, had $171,000 in deposits, and $166,000 in checks drawn against it.

What is more, significant deposits virtually stopped in the first general business account after February of 2001. In the months of April, May and June—the same period of time that Elisa was operating her scam with the cardboard and the check register—there were *zero* deposits made to the first general business account. July had one deposit for $80, and August deposits of $7,500. By the time Larry disappeared on September 11, the first general business account was $348 in the red, and the balance in the new, second general business account was itself minus $200.

The meaning of this set of double books isn't clear, although the obvious possibility is that Elisa, as the office manager and head bookkeeper, was trying to bamboozle her husband by pointing to the dwindling income totals of the office account as an explanation for why the McNabneys seemed to be short of money; or alternatively, by switching the books whenever Larry demanded an accounting, Elisa might be able to better conceal where the money was actually going.

Larry's personal checking account may also provide some insight to what was going on. In the first year after the move from Reno, 1999, Larry made deposits of $161,000—a figure that likely represents his own draw against the firm's revenues. Against this Larry wrote $158,000 in checks. The following year, 2000, Larry's personal account deposits were only $41,000, and were outdistanced by the checks written on the account, $43,000. It therefore seems safe to conclude that Larry's personal draw from the law firm, if not his actual income, took a substantial drop—actually a precipitous drop—from 1999 to 2000. The following year, 2001, was even worse: between January and the end of August, just before he disappeared, only $3,300 was deposited in Larry's personal checking account.

Taking the total spent in both business accounts until Larry's disappearance, it appears that the expenses of running Larry McNabney and Associates averaged about $20,000 a month: this would include office rent, telephones, salaries for the employees, taxes, and Larry's own draw, which would have to pay for the McNabneys' rent, their food, Larry's alcohol, schooling for Haylei, and last but hardly least, the upkeep on Justa Lotta Page, who appears to have been purchased with a $12,300 withdrawal from the general office account in December of 2000—a transaction which put the office account temporarily in the red. The care and feeding of the horse at the Whalen Ranch was $2,000 a month, according to Whalen.

Somehow, too, the McNabneys managed to dredge up the money for the aggrieved driver, however much that was; around $50,000 for Larry's new truck; and later, some $15,000 or $20,000 for a four-door BMW for Elisa. One of the more unusual transactions involved a $14,000 transfer from the client trust account during the month of May—the only time there was ever a substantial cash withdrawal from the trust account, at least before September 11. Where this money went isn't clear, at least from the available records; it certainly didn't go into the first general business account, which at that time and the following month had a balance close to zero.

Of the three new accounts, however, the most interesting

one is in the name of Larry McNabney and "huntseathorses.com," Elisa's business venture. Later, the description of just what huntseathorses.com was supposed to do was vague. At one point, Elisa said the business was intended to sell Western wear to horse fanciers; at another she said it was to be an advertising website for those who wanted to buy and sell American quarter horses. One thing is clear, however: the business made very little money, if in fact it made any at all.

Yet, the bank records for huntseathorses.com shows deposits in 2001 of $145,000—fully half of this, or $76,000, in August of 2001, just before Larry went missing. That same month showed a total of $35,000 for checks written, and withdrawals or transfers of another $36,000, bringing the balance in the account back to near zero. In short, it appeared that Elisa had manipulated the various McNabney accounts to deliver around $140,000 into her own hands, fully half of it just before Larry disappeared.

In any event, with all this cash pouring out, it doesn't take a certified public accountant to realize that the McNabneys' expenses substantially exceeded their income during the year 2001. This was probably why Elisa began bouncing checks to the Whalens and to Debbie Kail, why all the McNabneys' existing credit cards were maxed out, why Elisa began, sometime in the summer of 2001, to fraudulently and secretly obtain credit cards in the names of Greg Whalen and at least one other person, and why, in September of 2001, she began to eye the remaining McNabney assets—principally the red truck and Justa Lotta Page, as the means of raising more cash.

Larry may have believed that he had a way of making sure Elisa kept on the straight and true as far as his money was concerned, at least at first, right after the move from Reno to Sacramento. But by the winter of 2000–2001, about the time the new accounts were opened, Larry began showing ever greater signs of drinking and drugging; indeed, some would later suggest that around that time Elisa, in order to keep Larry from tumbling to her book-cooking chicanery, began putting a drug called ketamine into Larry's wine. True, there is also the possibility that Larry himself began deliberately using ketamine, perhaps willingly assisted by Elisa. Certainly Larry's long history of excessive drug abuse made him a prime candidate for branching into ketamine as a new trip of choice. But being under the frequent influence of ketamine may explain why Larry was oblivious to the financial shenanigans under way in his office.

Ketamine—a horse tranquilizer known to drug abusers as "Special K"—is on the federal Drug Enforcement Administration's schedules as a controlled substance. It is a restricted drug that can only be dispensed by a licensed veterinarian. For all that, it is a drug that has seeped into illicit usage with some regularity over the past few decades, usually through thefts and diversions from veterinarians and their suppliers. One of its major conduits is through Mexico.

"Special K"—the street reference to the commercial cereal of the same name is intended to be ironic—is pharmacologically much like phencyclidine, or PCP, according to the DEA. "Like PCP, individuals anesthetized with ketamine feel detached or disconnected from their pain and environment," observed Terrance Woodworth, a deputy DEA director who testified before Congress on the problems posed by ketamine abuse in early 1999. In addition to blocking pain, ketamine has amnesic effects—that is, people who use it sometimes have no memory of the events that took place while they were under its influence. On the street, this blank in awareness is called "the K hole," and lasts anywhere from half an hour to an hour before the drug passes from the system. The drug can be in a powder form, snorted like cocaine, or mixed with alcohol.

Although "Special K" has been abused since the 1960s, it has gained new currency in recent years as a so-called "date rape" drug, similar in effects to GHB. It has gained favor among some in the "club drug" scene, and at so-called "raves."

Later, Greg Whalen would say that, while he knew what ketamine was, and what it was legitimately used for, he had never used it in connection with any of his horses. His veterinarian would also say that he had never prescribed it for any of Whalen's animals. But Whalen did have other horse tranquilizers on hand, including acepromazine—"ace," as it is known, useful for calming fear and aggression in horses and dogs—as well as a particularly potent horse tranquilizer called xylazine. When Whalen transported horses to a show, these substances were kept in a canvas bag in his horse trailer. If, for example, a horse became agitated during the transit, "ace" might be useful to prevent it from injuring itself. Or if there were a traffic accident, xylazine might be useful to put a thrashing horse into near-sleep to prevent further injury. So sedative, tranquilizer-type drugs were fairly prevalent in the horse industry, and rarely well controlled.

With these facts in mind, it is therefore possible that Larry began using ketamine, readily available from many sources in the horse show–supporting substructure of grooms, stable hands and the like, as a kicker to his wine in the spring of 2001; and that Elisa, ever willing to allow Larry to do whatever he wanted to do, as long as he didn't carp too loudly at her own excesses, knew very well what her husband was up to and did nothing to stop him, or perhaps even assisted him.

That Larry had some experience in mixing wine with pharmaceuticals seems clear, as Elisa herself suggested to Debbie Kail that same spring. When Debbie had been involved in a car crash and had been given a prescribed painkiller, Elisa suggested to her that if she really wanted to "get a buzz," she should mix the painkiller with a glass of wine. The combination was extremely potent. She'd done it

once to Larry's wine, Elisa added. And while it would have
dropped most people into a stupor, it had barely registered
with Larry, she said; but then, Larry had far more experience with doping his wine than most people.

In May, Haylei, who had been living with friends of Elisa's
in Oakdale, California, returned to the Elk Grove house. She
could see almost immediately that it wasn't going to work
out. For one thing, Elisa and Larry weren't getting along very
well with each other. "They weren't happy," Haylei said later.

"He was an alcoholic," Haylei observed, with the pitiless
acuity of the young. "He wasn't a good person . . . He and I
didn't get along at all. Ever."

Larry and her mother fought a lot, Haylei observed. She
put the blame on Larry. "Larry was not a mentally stable
man," she said. "He was very indecisive. He had lots of alcohol problems. He had alcohol- and drug-related problems. He
had been to numerous rehabs and left them." At least five
times while she had known him, she said, Larry had disappeared for a time on a bender of some sort.

So after spending two weeks with her mother and Larry
at the Elk Grove house, Haylei moved into a Sacramento
apartment with her boyfriend. Because Haylei was only 16,
Elisa had to fill out the lease application. She filled it out
under the name of Sarah Dutra, a 21-year-old art student,
who would go on to become the key figure in the mystery of
Larry McNabney's murder.

More than a year later, when people were still trying to sort out what had actually happened in the McNabney mystery, Sarah Dutra would emerge as the key witness—in fact, the only living witness, for much of what had taken place. Unfortunately, by that time, Sarah was also a prospective murder defendant, which made it difficult to evaluate the accuracy of her observations, tainted as they might have been with self-interest.

By the time people tried to assess the truthfulness of her recollections, two of the three principal actors—Larry and Elisa—were dead. Sarah herself had very little independent knowledge of the underlying facts. As she told her story at various times over the next year, what would become apparent—even paramount—in her description of what had taken place was the fact that almost everything she knew about Larry and Elisa was told to her by Elisa, and wasn't necessarily the truth.

As one result, it would become difficult, perhaps impossible, to get a true grip on what had really happened, and that in turn would cause a vast schism between the notions of Larry's believers, and those of Elisa.

In Reno, for example, it would be: *Poor Larry, such a brilliant lawyer, it's tragic—that thieving Elisa first took him to the cleaners, then poisoned him, and abused his corpse to boot*; while in Florida, it would instead be: *Poor Laren, it's tragic—that drunken, abusive, wife-beating ambulance-chasing Larry drove her to first murder, then suicide*. These two popular perceptions, separated by two thousand miles, different cultures, and a natural tendency to defend the native son or daughter, were diametrically opposed.

For her part, Sarah, who was with Elisa throughout much of the time before and after Larry's death, had little understanding of the dynamic of the McNabneys' mutually blackmailing relationship, and whatever understanding she did have was primarily arrived at while she was in a fog of marijuana smoke, as she and Elisa puffed away on joint after joint, both before and after the murder. For example: Sarah kept hearing Larry and Elisa call each other "Blanche," and it never did make any sense to her.

Sarah was born August 14, 1980, one of three children, to Mark and Karen Dutra of Vacaville, California. By all accounts, Sarah was one of the brightest, smartest kids around, as well as one of the most beautiful. By her senior year in high school, she had been voted class president. An honor student, a member of the swim and drill teams, Sarah seemed to have an unlimited future, and people in Vacaville were sure she would go far in whatever she decided to do.

But there was a shadow over Sarah's life: in 1995 her father, Mark, had been arrested and charged with converting some $140,000 from the Valley Evangelical Free Church to his own use. The embezzlement resulted in criminal charges against him, though he escaped imprisonment when he agreed to repay the money, and to perform some five hundred hours of community service.

Her father's difficulty seems to have embarrassed Sarah; in retrospect, it also seems to have opened a vein of contempt for men that she would display throughout her association with Elisa McNabney. Indeed, it appears that this contempt was one of the strongest bonds between the two women as the events of 2001 unfolded.

Sarah first came to work for Larry McNabney and Associates in January of 2000. She had answered a newspaper advertisement seeking a law firm receptionist while in her sophomore year as an art student at Sacramento State University. On paper, the job seemed ideal: it was close to the campus, and paid a hefty salary for someone who was fairly inexperienced: first $11 an hour, then $2,000 a month. "I was thrilled by the fact that I got paid a lot of money, that I got to buy nice clothes, because I didn't ever have any money," Sarah said later, referring to her previous life in Vacaville.

While working at the firm for the first year, Sarah had limited contact with Larry, who came into the office only periodically. When he did come in, Sarah would later recall, Larry called Elisa "Blanche" for some reason, and Elisa returned the appellation when addressing Larry. She quickly formed the impression that Elisa and Larry had a "love–hate" relationship; as time went on, the portrait of Larry that Elisa painted depicted him as increasingly degenerate, even a parasitical drag on Elisa's own success.

In the late summer of that same year, Sarah was accepted as an art student at the Academy of Fine Arts in Florence, Italy, one of Europe's oldest art schools. Before she left, Elisa told Sarah that she and Larry were proud of her, and wanted Sarah to help them get an Internet business started. Sarah was supposed to design a website for huntseathorses.com.

Three times over the ensuing school year, McNabney and Associates flew Sarah home from Italy, ostensibly to consult on the website, the last time in February of 2001. But it appears something else was going on, as well—perhaps Elisa had recognized in Sarah a sort of kindred spirit, an earlier, younger version of herself, before all the troubles in Florida. When Sarah left to go back to Italy, Elisa gave her a fur coat, a laptop computer and a digital camera, paid for by McNabney and Associates. Elisa also told her that she and Larry wanted to buy her a car because they were "so proud" of her for her art talent. Elisa said she and Larry would buy the car, a 1995 Saab, for Sarah, and make the payments on it while she was in Italy to help her establish a credit history. Sarah was to take over the payments from the salary paid to her by Larry McNabney and Associates when she returned from Italy for the summer. To get the car deal off the ground, a check for $2,000 was paid to Sarah from the law firm's restricted client trust account on February 18, 2001, and another $3,000 was issued from the law firm's general account directly to the dealer two days later, to make the down payment on the car.

"She would always tell me, 'Your credit is so important, it's so important to have credit,' " Sarah recalled later, "so I just said okay."

This wasn't the first time that Elisa had offered a car to a law firm employee as an inducement to accept a job, or, more likely, as a means of tying an employee closer than merely by paycheck. Another secretary at the Sacramento office, Stephanie Campos, later said that Elisa had offered her a car as well, but it was never forthcoming. Instead, it appears to have gone to Sarah. That wasn't all: based on a reconstruction of the firm's accounts later undertaken by police, it appeared that a number of checks that the firm's check register showed had supposedly been issued to Stephanie had actually been written to Sarah, via the cardboard ruse. And even after Sarah returned to Italy, checks from the law firm continued to make their way into Sarah's Sacramento checking account. In most of those cases, the payee on the check registers didn't match the payee on the actual check. It appears that Larry was oblivious to this cooking of the books, which could only be accomplished if someone other than him was actually signing Larry's name to the checks.

Before she returned to Italy, Sarah heard from Elisa that Larry had become so depressed over his drunken driving arrest that he no longer bothered to leave the bedroom at the Elk Grove townhome. "Larry was confining himself to his room," Sarah said later. "That's why she [Elisa] was upset . . . you know, 'He won't leave his room' and, 'He hasn't taken a shower in weeks, he's just lying in bed watching porno,' that type of thing."

Sarah said Elisa told her that Larry was drinking heavily during this time, periodically telephoning her at the office and yelling at her, "You bitch, bring me more wine, you fucking bitch," and generally cursing and verbally abusing Elisa. Of course, this is Elisa's account to Sarah, and was probably intended to cast Larry in a bad light in order to cement Sarah's loyalty to her, rather than Larry. Certainly one effect of this disparagement of Larry by Elisa was to convince Sarah that her contemptuous attitude toward men was justifiable, Exhibit A being the immoral and dissolute Larry. Elisa told her that Larry was obsessed with having sex with under-aged girls, and that he had even once tried to put the moves on Haylei.

Elisa told Sarah that Larry occasionally went off on "runners," disappearing for weeks at a time while binging on drugs and alcohol, and that she'd once had to hire a private detective to find him. The detective eventually tracked him down at the notorious Mustang Ranch, where Larry had been staying for several weeks. Elisa also told Sarah that Larry had once become so enraged at her while they were still in Reno that he'd smashed a telephone into her face so hard she'd had to have reconstructive surgery. (That was simply not so, according to Jeffrey Moore and others intimately familiar with the Reno days.) So it seems apparent that Elisa wasn't averse to smearing her own husband in Sarah's presence. The inculcation of contempt was later one reason why Sarah made no objection to Elisa's multiple forgeries of Larry's name, and even did it herself before the year was out.

It's still possible, however, that there may have been some factual basis to Elisa's portrayal of Larry as a remorseful recluse at this time, because he failed to attend either of two horse shows held between early February and late March of 2001. Larry was formally booked and fingerprinted for his

DUI on March 27, however, and his lawyer, Georgeann Mc-Kee, didn't notice anything abnormal about his appearance in any of her meetings with him after that date. So the evidence is mixed on whether Larry really was acting like a drunken recluse during those weeks.

By the time Sarah returned from Italy in June, ready to go back to her job, she had come to believe that Elisa was the one who did all the real work at the law firm. As portrayed by Elisa, Larry was nothing more than a washed-up has-been, a lush who lived off his hard-working wife. Sarah was told that Larry hardly ever came into the office.

"But then he actually came in one day," Sarah recalled, "and I just thought, 'Wow, Larry's here.' We had to have the office spotless for when he got there."

Mostly, though, Larry kept in touch with the office by telephone. Sarah was instructed that if Larry called, she was supposed to get Elisa immediately. "Even if she was on the phone with someone else, I'd go, 'Elisa, Larry's on the phone.' She'd go, 'Oh, let me put you on hold,' then pick up the phone [to Larry] and say, 'Hello, Blanchie.'"

Elisa's seduction of Sarah may not have been sexual—both she and Sarah later denied this, as did others who knew both women—but it was nevertheless a thoroughgoing conversion into attitudes that closely mirrored those of Elisa. Even Haylei became irritated at her mother's fascination with Sarah, as well as jealous of all the time they spent together. In a sense, it was as if Elisa was grooming Sarah to be a grifter in her own image. Certainly by the summer, Elisa and Sarah were both signing Larry's name to checks, some for cash, which Sarah took to the bank, returning with currency for Elisa. She told Sarah that she had to write checks for cash because she had no identification, that Larry had taken all her ID so she wouldn't be able to leave him. Soon money was being transferred among the various law firm accounts by check and by telephone, and the distinction between client money and Larry's money began evaporating once more. Elisa and Sarah began spending a great deal of time shopping, and going to expensive restaurants.

Before meeting the McNabneys, Sarah had had a boyfriend, Jason Cataldo. Until she began working for Larry and Elisa, Jason said later, their relationship was normal; but once she had been to Italy and then returned to work, things began to change. It seemed to Jason that Sarah couldn't say no to Elisa. Jason in turn began to feel a bit like he was Sarah's servant or something. She was short-tempered, even sneerish toward others, Jason thought, especially people without money or good looks.

Once, later, Jason was asked just what Sarah got out of her relationship with Elisa. "Going shopping every single day," Jason said. "Five hundred bucks here and there and whatever, running around doing whatever you want, all day long." To Jason, it was like Sarah had gone on an all-expenses-paid vacation with Elisa.

Until she'd met the McNabneys, Jason added, Sarah was always very frugal with money—her parents had brought her up that way. But with Elisa throwing money around like it was an inexhaustible resource, Sarah was swept away by the largesse. Hanging out with Elisa and throwing Larry's money around was fun, Sarah told Jason. "You know, I live to shop," she said.

Mark and Karen Dutra didn't like Elisa, Jason recalled. They were suspicious of her, wondering why she preferred hanging around with Sarah, who after all was eleven years younger than she was. They wondered why Elisa didn't have any friends her own age and status, and what she really wanted from Sarah. Whatever the attraction was, Mark and Karen were convinced it meant more trouble for the Dutra family.

Worse, Sarah's contempt for her "middle-class" parents was obvious, even to Jason. On one occasion, he'd accompanied Sarah on a visit with Mark and Karen, and when her mother tried to question her about Elisa, Sarah told them she didn't care to discuss it anymore. When Karen persisted, Sarah became angry and dismissive of her parents as people who weren't capable of understanding what life was really all about. Later Jason told Sarah he was offended at the way Sarah had treated her parents, that she was acting pretty stuck-up, and that he didn't want to see her anymore. That was fine with her, Sarah said; Jason was sort of square himself.

Even before Sarah's return from Italy, Elisa's shenanigans with the law firm's books had begun to have consequences. On several occasions, checks she had written to the Whalens for the quarter horse services had bounced. Debbie Kail's insurance firm began pressing Debbie to make the McNabneys pay up, and certainly her father, Greg, wasn't running a charity. Debbie took the matter up with Elisa. Elisa apologized, and said it sometimes happened that the accounts at the law firm got mixed up. She made the checks good with cash (this may have been a possible destination for the $14,000 withdrawn from the trust account in May), and told Debbie not to discuss the matter with Larry. It would only upset him, she said; he didn't like to be bothered with financial details.

By August of 2001, the McNabneys and Whalens had been to a flock of horse shows, many of them also attended by Sarah. Larry and Justa Lotta Page continued to score points, moving up the national rankings. Larry was enthusiastic about his new pursuit, being owner of a champion American quarter horse.

One situation Larry was not enthusiastic about, however, was Sarah Dutra. Even in his usual state of impairment, he could tell that she didn't think very much of him, and he resented it. "He had to be the star," was the way Sarah put it later. He also was jealous of the increasing amount of time that Elisa was spending with her protégée. At a horse show in early June in Oregon, in fact, he'd told Greg Whalen that he wanted Elisa to fire Sarah. They were "too close," he said. It appears that Larry was claiming that he'd caught Elisa and Sarah in bed together, and was convinced that Elisa was cheating on him with the art student. A little later, Larry told Bob Kail that he thought Elisa was trying to "break" him, and that Sarah was helping her do it.

Then, in late August at a horse show in Santa Rosa, California, Elisa had told Sarah to keep out of Larry's sight. Sarah had hunkered down in a used BMW the McNabney firm had just picked up from an auctioneer in Texas, smoking cigarette after cigarette, while Elisa took breaks from the show to come out to the car to complain about Larry.

Sarah's acquisition of the BMW is one of the more peculiar sidelights of the McNabney mystery. Based on her later description of what happened, it appears that Elisa, prowling the Internet, had noticed a four-door red BMW for sale in Texas. Elisa put in a bid for the car, and learned that she'd bid the most. At that point—perhaps sometime in July—Larry had supposedly gone to Texas to pay for the car and drive it back to California.

What happened next was confusing as well as contradictory. Sarah later said that she wanted a BMW too. She said she searched on the Internet, just like Elisa, and discovered another red BMW in Texas. According to Sarah, Larry went back to Texas and picked up that car as well. Sarah said she had arranged her own financing for it, but there later seemed to be contradictory information about this—especially when the car was repossessed on the same day that Larry disappeared.

In any event, in Santa Rosa, here was Sarah, driving her own BMW, and hiding out from Larry. What did this mean?

One possibility is that Larry may have learned that he was on the hook for Sarah's new car. First the Saab, now the BMW—Larry may have formed the impression that Elisa was helping Sarah take him for a ride. When one accepts the

nature of the mutually extortionate relationship between
Larry and Elisa, one can also consider the idea that once
Larry had a new truck—the $50,000 red "dually"—Elisa
considered herself likewise entitled to a new car, the first red
four-door BMW. And while Larry might have been willing to
pay off Elisa in this fashion, doing the same for Sarah was
going too far. In effect, what Larry may have meant when he
complained about Elisa and Sarah getting "too close" was
that Elisa was letting Sarah in on the blackmail arrangement.
Later, in fact, Sarah would say that both Larry and Elisa began referring to her, too, as "Blanche." And there is one other
possibility: that Sarah, having realized that Elisa was busy
cooking Larry's books, in effect horned in on Elisa's extortion of Larry, and so began extorting *Elisa.*

Whatever the truth about the second BMW, by the end of
August, things were getting set to fly apart for all the
Blanches, however many there were.

For some time, Larry and Elisa had been talking about moving from Elk Grove. Their idea was to move farther south
toward Lodi, in between Sacramento and Stockton. That
way they would be closer to Whalen's ranch in Clements,
some few miles northeast of Lodi, and also the horses. At
some point in August of 2001, even before the Santa Rosa
horse show, Elisa and Sarah had looked at a very nice house
in a gated community near Lodi, a development called Woodbridge. The Woodbridge houses backed up against a private
golf course. The house seen by Elisa and Sarah was owned
by a physician and his wife, and was being offered for lease
at $2,400 a month. Elisa conducted the negotiations with the
owners. She introduced Sarah as the girlfriend of Larry Mc-
Nabney, the famous television-advertising tort lawyer, and
herself as Larry McNabney's principal associate in his Sacramento office. The deal was agreed to, and the McNabneys,
Blanches one through two, anyway, made arrangements to
move in around the first of September.

What Larry did not know, however, was that after Elisa had paid the first installment on the rent, the McNabneys were living almost entirely on credit cards, which were rapidly reaching their maximum. In fact, by September 10, 2001, they were very nearly flat broke—down to their last $141, in fact. The client trust account was down to its last $1,645. All that was left was Justa Lotta Page, and Larry's new red truck.

And the Whalens were again demanding to be paid.

Later people would wonder how Larry, by all accounts a brilliant lawyer and a shrewd money manager, could have been so obtuse as to go broke without ever having realized it. It just didn't make sense, some thought—especially since he had repeatedly told everyone that as long as he was married to Elisa, he was going to control all the money. It seemed incredible that Elisa—with Sarah's help—could have spent so much money without Larry knowing.

To understand what happened, though, two things need to be recalled: first, that Elisa had devised a scheme to misinform Larry as to the amount of cash he had on hand, with the fake check registers; and more important, that during the period most of this was going on—say from April through September—Larry was drinking heavily, and apparently using drugs—probably "Special K," the established amnesic. It may well have been that Larry had no capacity to recall what checks he'd actually signed, or for how much. Still, it may be that by the end of the summer, Larry was beginning to suspect that something was out of whack, financially speaking. Some of Larry's Reno friends later speculated that by the weekend he disappeared, Larry had tumbled onto Elisa's creative accounting, and confronted her over it, threatening to send her to jail, which then precipitated Elisa's decision to make her husband vanish. But given some of Larry's other remarks around the same time, that could only have taken place in the hours immediately before his disappearance; up until that point, he seems to have been oblivious to his true financial condition.

What is clear is that by the time he and Elisa arrived at

the City of Industry with Greg Whalen and Debbie Kail on September 5, Larry and Elisa were snipping at each other.

"Larry and Elisa just seemed a little tense," Debbie Kail said later. "As soon as we left the ranch and started making our way down, driving down, they seemed a little bit agitated at each other."

At one point after they arrived at the show, Debbie said later, she'd asked Elisa what the trouble was. Elisa said Larry's drinking was the problem—that when she'd first met Larry he was "a wonderful, charismatic person." But now, she said, he was just a drunk. "I'm getting tired of taking care of him and picking up after him," Elisa told Debbie.

Debbie had heard this from Elisa before, so it didn't strike her as being particularly ominous at the time.

But over the next few days, Debbie Kail noticed that Larry seemed to be unusually troubled by something. "Larry just seemed like he wasn't himself," she recalled. "Larry was very articulate and really on top of things [usually]." But at the City of Industry, "he just was not himself. He seemed kind of depressed. He didn't seem like he was up for the show like he normally was. At one point I had to ask him to go change [his clothing for the horse show]."

When Sarah arrived in her nearly new BMW two days later, Debbie said, it looked to her as if she and Elisa were spending all their time together, without Larry. Debbie already knew that Larry and Sarah didn't get along very well. Now it appeared that Larry's wife preferred to be with Sarah rather than him.

"It just seemed like when Sarah would come . . . it would go from Larry and Elisa being together to Elisa and Sarah being together," Debbie said. "They would just get into their little mode and Larry would be kind of the odd man out, while Sarah was there."

At one point on Friday or Saturday afternoon, Debbie recalled, she overheard Elisa talking to another woman, making plans to go out dancing that night with Sarah. "We'll make sure Larry has enough to drink tonight that he passes out," Elisa told the woman, "so Sarah and I can go meet up with you and party tonight." That same night there was no vacancy at the hotel, so Sarah slept in Larry and Elisa's hotel room.

The next morning, Elisa got up early to help Greg Whalen feed the horses at the barn, which was located within walking distance of the hotel. Sarah, asleep on a sofa in the hotel room, was suddenly awakened by a tapping on her back. It was Larry, and he kept calling Sarah "Blanche."

"Blanche . . . Blanche . . . Blanche," Larry said.

"What are you doing?" Sarah asked. "Larry, it's me."

Larry looked as if he had no idea of where he was.

"And then he did it again," Sarah said later. "I'm like, 'What are you doing, Larry?' And then he did it *again*— three times. I got up and I'm like, I was out of there."

Later she saw Elisa at the horse show. "What's up with Larry?" Sarah asked. "He's acting weird." Elisa said she didn't know. Others asked Elisa the same thing. Debbie Kail, for one, thought Larry was actually disoriented while showing his horse that day—unclear of what to do or where to go. It wasn't like Larry at all, she thought.

By Sunday evening, the bad vibes between Sarah and Larry were obvious to everyone. That evening, when Greg, Debbie, Elisa, Larry and Sarah went to the Olive Garden restaurant for dinner, Larry seemed seriously smashed.

"Larry was just sitting there," Sarah recalled. "Drinking a lot. Everyone was having a little bit to drink, but Larry was drinking a lot more." Sarah remembered that Larry had his usual several glasses of Chardonnay, and was obviously inebriated. Debbie thought he'd had as much as two bottles of wine all by himself.

"He just looks like he has water on the brain," Sarah recalled later, and she made her face go slack to illustrate

Larry's alcoholic vacuity. "Real zoned out, just drunk. He would kind of always slowly get sloppy drunk."

Everyone else around the table was wondering what was going on with Larry to make him drink as heavily as he was that night.

Debbie Kail asked Sarah if it was true that she was going to drive back to Sacramento that night, at least a six-hour trip by freeway, and Sarah said she was, that she had to go back to class and open the law office in the morning. The firm had hired a new secretary, Ginger Miller, and Sarah had to be there to show her what to do; it was to be Ginger's first day on the job. But Debbie got the impression that Larry had made Elisa send Sarah away, that he was jealous of her. Larry and Elisa weren't arguing with each other, she recalled. "They were just sort of staying away from each other," Debbie said later. Larry was talking to Greg, while Debbie was talking to Elisa and Sarah.

Then, something happened—no one could remember later exactly what it was—and Larry called Sarah a bitch.

"Fuck you, Larry," Sarah said, holding her middle digit up to her face.

Then some minutes later, Larry called Debbie a bitch too. But as Debbie remembered it, it wasn't said with anger, but more with wry humor. "You're being a bitch tonight, too," Larry told Debbie, grabbing at her arm. Elisa told Larry, "I can't believe you said that."

No one said anything for a minute, then Greg told Larry to apologize. He did. Later that evening, as Sarah got into the BMW to drive back to Sacramento, Whalen had to help Larry out to the truck for the drive back to the hotel.

The next day, September 10, 2001, was an off day at the horse show. A second show had been scheduled to begin the following Friday, and rather than return to Lodi for four days, the McNabneys and the Whalen clan decided to simply stay on at the Pacific Palms hotel. Larry spent part of the day drinking at the barn, according to Debbie Kail. She and Greg and Elisa helped bathe the horses and groom them, getting them ready for the next show. At one point that morning, Debbie was talking with Elisa about a horse that was "acting up," as Debbie put it; she said she wished she could give the horse acepromazine—"ace"—to calm it down. But the horse show regulations forbade it. At that point Elisa asked Debbie if acepromazine would kill a person. Debbie said, yes, indeed it would. "Elisa," Debbie said, "if it would tranquilize a fourteen-hundred-pound horse, it would definitely kill a person."

Around two or so in the afternoon, Larry talked with Greg. "We talked some about Larry's situation," Greg recalled, "trying to win the [exhibitor] honor roll. And he had been four points behind when we got there and he had, you know, got—won quite a bit there. He was catching—he had this guy [another exhibitor] caught."

Greg meant that Larry was on the verge of overtaking his nearest competition for the amateur halter horse showing title. Justa Lotta Page, in fact, had just qualified for the World Championship show in Oklahoma, which had been Larry's goal from the start.

Greg and Larry discussed it that afternoon: "He asked me if I might not talk to somebody back East, because once that show and a couple others are over out here, there's probably ten or fifteen, maybe, even twenty shows, back East that they count the points. So it would have to be a trainer back there that could take Larry, and we talked about that," Whalen said.

Whalen said he could introduce Larry to a trainer in Oklahoma, who might be able to take over after the "world show" in Oklahoma City and help Larry win enough points to win the national amateur title. Larry seemed pleased about this, and began to talk about heading East with Justa Lotta Page. He seemed enthusiastic about continuing to exhibit the horse. The significance of this conversation is clear: it seems that Larry had no idea he was absolutely dead broke. Why else would he be talking about expensive trips to the East to accumulate more horse show points when he had only $241 in his bank account?

Around 3 or so, Debbie Kail recalled, Larry opened the ice chest that was in the back of his red truck, and began pouring glasses of Chardonnay. He passed around glasses to Greg, Elisa and Debbie. They talked a bit about getting together to eat that evening. Larry said he would pass on dinner. He said he was tired—he just wanted to go back to the hotel and take a nap, maybe watch a movie on television.

That afternoon, September 10, Greg and Debbie went to the coffee shop in the hotel. Around 6 P.M., Greg and Debbie started their dinner, ordering soup. Greg called Larry from a nearby telephone and asked him again if he wanted to eat with them. The soup was particularly good, Greg told him. Larry said no. Greg thought he "didn't sound too good," that he sounded the way he did when he'd been drinking to excess. Greg asked if Larry wanted some soup sent up to him. Larry said he thought that would be all right. A few minutes later, Elisa came to join them. She ordered a cocktail, and the three talked desultorily. Around 6:30 Elisa called Larry on her cell phone and asked him once more if he didn't want to join them. Greg and Debbie could hear Larry's voice over Elisa's telephone, again declining to come downstairs, but asking Elisa to bring him some wine. Greg thought he sounded drunk. A few minutes later, Elisa left, taking a bowl of the soup and two glasses of Chardonnay with her to the room she was sharing with Larry on the ninth floor of the hotel. That was the last time Greg or Debbie ever heard Larry's voice.

Elisa and Sarah

The following morning was September 11, 2001, and as we have seen, the first Debbie Kail heard of Larry's sudden departure from the hotel came that morning, at almost the same moment that the second airliner was striking the World Trade Center in New York. Greg, of course, had heard about Larry from Elisa about ninety minutes earlier.

That same morning, just after 7 A.M., Debbie also noticed that somehow Sarah Dutra had reappeared at the hotel, after having left to return to Sacramento two nights before.

"What are you doing here?" Debbie asked Sarah, and Sarah explained that Elisa had telephoned her the night before and asked her to rush back. Sarah had caught one of the last flights out of Sacramento. As of that morning, of course, every flight in the country was grounded.

What actually happened at the hotel that night, after Sarah's arrival, would remain a matter of confusion for months afterward.

Later, Sarah would say that Elisa had telephoned her in Sacramento on the night of September 10, pleading with her to return to the horse show, and saying that Larry had gone crazy. Sarah went to the airport, got on the plane, and charged the ticket to a credit card belonging to McNabney and Associates. The plane landed around 10:30 P.M., she said. She used the same credit card to hire a taxi to take her to the hotel. When she arrived, Elisa was waiting for her outside.

"So she's telling me how Larry's acting crazy," Sarah said later, "and I was like, 'Okay, where am I going to sleep tonight?' " If Larry was freaking out, Sarah said, she thought she didn't want to go anywhere near him.

Instead, Sarah said, she and Elisa went to the barn to look at the horses, walking around near the area where Greg Whalen had his horse trailer, and smoking a lot of pot. Eventually, Sarah said, they sat in Larry's truck. There they passed the night, she said later—at least that's what she said initially—listening to the stereo in the dually and smoking pot. In actual fact, however, Sarah at first kept much of the real story to herself. It was only later—much later—that the rest came out. It would eventually turn out that Elisa made several trips back to the room "to check on" Larry, and that Sarah had gone with her.

"Probably like maybe one o'clock . . . she [Elisa] says, 'I want to go check on him,' " Sarah eventually admitted, the fourth time she was asked what had happened. "See if he's still there, or what he's doing. So . . . I walked up with her [to the hotel]. I told her, 'I don't want to go in that room.' He's being crazy and drunk, you know. She had often mentioned to me that when he drinks, sometimes he would get violent. So I said, 'Okay, I'll stand here by the door, and if it gets ugly, I'll go get the police.' And she goes in there, and I start hearing some wrestling around, and she [Elisa] kind of goes, 'Ahh—' and he's like, 'I'll kill you, I'll kill you,' and she's like, 'Larry, stop acting like that.' He said, 'I'll kill you, Blanche'—he calls her Blanche—and I was shocked . . . I was paralyzed."

She didn't know what to do when she heard this threat, Sarah said. She was still standing outside the room, she said, when Elisa came out, saying that Larry had kicked her. "She showed me her back," Sarah said, "right on her tail bone, where I guess he'd kicked her. And you know, from that point on, I was *not* going in that room."

Well, that was almost Sarah's final story, and for the most part, she would stick to it. The next morning, when Elisa started telling everyone that Larry had left to "go back to the cult," Sarah began to lie in support of Elisa. When Sarah started lying, though, she would keep it up for quite a while, to her eventual regret.

In one of Sarah's initial recountings of the events, she said that before stopping by the Whalen room, she and Elisa had returned to Room 916 early that morning, only to find that Larry was no longer there. That's why Elisa had told Debbie and Greg that Larry had "gone back to the cult," Sarah said—they thought he'd left for good. But still later that same morning, Elisa had gone back into the room, and this time Larry was there. Or so Sarah said. That was when Elisa came out and told her that they'd have to do something about Larry.

"She says, 'Sarah, Larry's running around the room like a crazy, and I don't know what to do, he's scaring me . . .' " Sarah said later. "She's telling me, 'We can't stay in this hotel, he's just embarrassing me. He's telling me how he wants to run away, but then he tells me he's not running away . . .' So she told me, she's checking into another hotel, and she wants me to help her help Larry out to the car, to get to this new hotel." Sarah said Elisa wanted her to help rent a wheelchair to move Larry to the new hotel, since he was so impaired he couldn't walk.

About 8:30 that morning, Elisa and Sarah drove Larry's red truck to a medical equipment rental establishment not far from the hotel. They were waiting when the place opened at 9. Elisa told the rental agent, Mary Deal, that they wanted to rent a wheelchair to take her husband to a wedding reception at the hotel. They only needed the chair for one day, Elisa said. The rental fee was $6.25, and also required a $125 deposit. Elisa paid the rental fee in cash, and put the deposit on a McNabney and Associates credit card. Sarah had to show her driver's license, because Elisa didn't have one. Then she and Sarah left, put the wheelchair in the back of the pickup truck, and drove back to the hotel.

By this time, Sarah and Elisa had been smoking marijuana for hours; and while it is true that Sarah's later recollection of the events was tinged with willful forgetfulness, it is also true that the events themselves had begun to take on something of a surreal, psychotropic quality. Sarah had a vague memory of going to a store and Elisa purchasing something, but she would say, at least at first, that she couldn't remember what it was.

The next thing Sarah said she remembered was going back to the hotel. They took the rented wheelchair up to the ninth floor. There Elisa opened the door to Room 916, and somehow convinced Larry to sit down in it. Sarah said she watched. Larry was being docile, she said.

"She [Elisa] was just kind of saying, 'Okay, Larry, come on, now we're going to go to the other hotel.' He was saying, 'Okay, Blanchie, okay.'"

Sarah recalled helping Elisa push the wheelchair down the hotel corridor toward the elevator; Larry seemed conscious but drunk, she said. He was saying something about wanting a drink, Sarah thought. "I helped her push him out to the car [the red truck]." She asked him if he was okay, and Larry said, "I'm fine," Sarah said.

As they were leaving the hotel, they went past the reception desk. "I remember Larry going like, 'Wahhh,' and [waving his arms slowly, as if he were trying to get out of the chair] and [Elisa was] like . . . 'Oh my God, Sarah, help him.'" Sarah said she didn't know what Larry was trying to do, if he was trying to get to his feet, or not.

"What's wrong with him?" Sarah asked.

"He's drunk, Sarah," Elisa told her.

They made it out to the truck, and both of them helped Larry into the back seat of the dually, Sarah said. Larry was mumbling something. Sarah said she thought he was saying that he wanted Sarah out of the truck, because he didn't like her—"'Get her out of here . . . Get her out of here . . .'"

Or was it instead: "Get me out of here . . . Get me out of here . . ."? Later, no one could be exactly sure.

Sarah said Elisa told her to drive toward the barns next to the hotel. Elisa, she said, had told her that she'd drop her off near the horse show, then drive to the new hotel, put Larry into a room, and then return to join her.

But when they reached the barns, Elisa told Sarah to drive up close to Greg Whalen's horse trailer. That was when they saw Debbie Kail, who was in Greg's truck, moving clothes from the trailer back to the hotel, since her plane had been grounded. Debbie was surprised to see them. She rolled down the window of Greg's truck and called out to them.

"What are you doing?" she called out to Sarah and Elisa. She thought they looked startled to see her. Because the truck had dark tinted windows, Debbie could not see into the rear seat area.

"Oh," Elisa said, "we're going to the bank. I want to make sure Larry hasn't cleaned out all our bank accounts. We'll be back in a few minutes." Debbie happened to glance into the bed of the red dually. She saw Larry's golf clubs, his ice chest, several bags of what appeared to be dirty laundry, and a wheelchair, along with two brand new shovels. Before she could say anything, Sarah drove off, leaving a puzzled Debbie behind, wondering what in the world Elisa and Larry wanted with a wheelchair.

Keep driving," Elisa told Sarah.

"What about Larry?" Sarah asked.

"Don't worry about it," Elisa said. "We're going back to Lodi."

When Sarah glanced in the rearview mirror to see what was going on with Larry, she realized that he had flopped over on the seat.

"It's drugs, Sarah," Elisa told her. Sarah thought Larry looked zoned out, all right. But he didn't seem to be passed out—just tripping on whatever drug he had taken. Every so often, in fact, Larry would sit up and stare out the window. It appeared that Elisa had told Larry they were taking him home. He seemed very docile, even trusting.

Elisa had Sarah pull onto the San Bernardino Freeway, Interstate 10, headed east. Some distance from the City of Industry, Elisa instructed Sarah to take the Devore Cutoff toward the desert on Interstate 15. Once through Cajon Pass, the freeway headed down into the flatland of the high desert. Soon an interchange appeared for U.S. 395, another highway that headed almost due north through the desert toward the eastern wall of the Sierra Nevada mountains.

"What's going on?" Sarah asked Elisa.

"For your own good, you should forget you ever saw Larry today," Elisa told her. "He was never in this truck."

Sarah at first said afterward that she didn't know what to make of this remark by Elisa, although she knew it didn't sound good. Sarah said she wasn't sure if Elisa was telling her to keep quiet about Larry using drugs because of possible repercussions from the state bar association, or if she

Larry McNabney in his early years as an up-and-coming Reno attorney and part-time law professor. *Photo courtesy of Cristin Becker Olson*

Laren Sims Jordan as a junior at Hernando High School. *Photo courtesy of Hernando High School*

James "Mac" McNabney, Larry's stern and alcoholic father. Within a week after Larry's mother Marie filed for divorce after 27 years of marriage in 1970, Mac McNabney shot himself to death. A few weeks later, the McNabneys' oldest son, Jimmy, killed himself with a drug overdose. *Photo courtesy of Cristin Becker Olson*

The house on Brown Street in southwest Reno, where Larry grew up, and later lived as an adult during his first three marriages. *©Carlton Smith*

TOP: Larry's Reno office during his early years as an attorney. ©Carlton Smith

LEFT: In 1986, Larry and his fourth wife, Linda, had this rustic cabin built south of Reno. Custom-built, the house had enormous cost overruns. Larry eventually sold it at a steep loss. ©Carlton Smith

The house on Buckaroo Court in Reno's Caughlin Ranch development. When he sold it in 1997 at Elisa's insistence, Larry lost about $50,000 on the transaction. ©Carlton Smith

The Hernando County courthouse in Brooksville, Florida. Laren, who grew up in Brooksville in the 1970s and 1980s, was to spend a considerable amount of time in court in the 1980s, answering a variety of theft charges. ©*Carlton Smith*

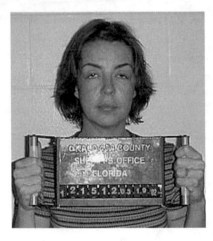

Laren Sims Jordan after one of her Florida arrests. After violating probation once again in early 1993, Laren cut off her court-ordered electronic ankle monitor and fled the state, taking her eight-year-old daughter with her. She eventually turned up in Las Vegas, using the name Elizabeth Barasch.
Hernando County Sheriff photo

By the mid-1990s Larry had decided to become a tort lawyer, specializing in personal injury cases. He advertised throughout the state of Nevada, and his business boomed. *Photo courtesy of Nancy Eklof*

In January of 1996, Laren—now using the name Elisa, short for Elizabeth—married Larry McNabney in Reno. They honeymooned at Caesar's Tahoe. The marriage came three weeks after Larry learned that Elisa had diverted about $140,000 from his personal and law office accounts. *Photo courtesy Cashman Enterprises*

The road to Larry McNabney's next-to-last resting place, a vineyard east of Lodi, California. Laren said she'd buried him in a vineyard "because he liked wine so much." ©*Carlton Smith*

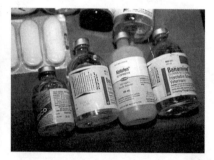

LEFT: Some of the horse tranquilizers found in the McNabneys' horse trainer's vet bag. The bottle on the far left is xylazine, the sedative used to render Larry McNabney comatose on September 11, 2001. *San Joaquin County Sheriff's Department photo*

The Whalen Ranch, where Larry and Elisa kept their horses. *San Joaquin County Sheriff's Department photo*

After giving Larry the horse tranquilizer, Elisa and Sarah drove the comatose Larry back to the rented McNabney house near Lodi. The next morning they decided Larry was dead, and put his body in a refrigerator in the garage and sealed it with duct tape. There is some evidence that Larry actually suffocated to death in the refrigerator. *San Joaquin County Sheriff's Department photo*

After Larry "disappeared," Elisa and Sarah looted a number of Larry's accounts, and enjoyed themselves at a number of horse shows. Here they are with Greg Whalen in Monroe, Washington State in late October, 2001. *Photo courtesy of Don Trout*

Elisa being interviewed by FBI Agent Victoria Harker in Destin, FL on March 18, 2002. Elisa confessed to having poisoned Larry with a horse tranquilizer, and said that Sarah Dutra helped her do it. *Okaloosa County Sheriff's Department photo.*

Two weeks later, Elisa Laren Sims Jordan McNabney was transferred back to Hernando County, where she had a reunion with the family she had not seen for almost a decade. A week later she hanged herself. ©*Carlton Smith*

meant something else. But much later, Sarah would admit that Elisa had told her hours earlier that she had given Larry what she thought was an overdose of "Special K."

As the morning wore on, the red dually flew north, passing mile upon mile of creosote bushes, tumbleweed, sagebrush and later, Joshua trees, branches uplifted as if in mute supplication to the heavens. Large rock formations rose on either side of the road as they drove on, eventually giving way to blue shadows of distant mountains far off to the northwest and northeast as they came into the Owens Valley. Sarah had the truck's stereo on while Elisa rolled more joints. In the back, Larry continued to doze, although he occasionally became alert enough to sit up and look out the window. Based on his fragmented remarks, Sarah had the impression that Larry was remembering things, experiences from the past, asking Elisa if she remembered, too. What Sarah did not know was that Larry was experiencing waves of extremely vivid hallucinations that came and then receded. From time to time he asked Elisa for something to drink.

"I'm thirsty, Blanchie," he said. Elisa reached down to the floor of the truck, found a water bottle, and passed it back to Larry. Larry drank some, then lay back down, back on his mind-trip.

By late in the afternoon, they had passed the small valley town of Bishop and had begun to climb along the eastern escarpment of the mountains. The road climbed higher and higher as the sun angled down behind the peaks to the west, which topped out at over 13,000 feet. At length they came to Deadman's Pass, just over 8,000 feet above sea level, and began going downhill again toward the small ranching village of Lee Vining. Just before Lee Vining, Elisa told Sarah to turn off the highway to head west into Yosemite National Park on State Highway 120. After crossing Tioga Pass at almost ten thousand feet, they arrived at Tuolumne Meadows on the eastern side of the spectacular park. There they filled the dually with diesel, and got something cool to drink. Larry was conscious and exchanged a few more inconsequential words with them. Elisa gave him more water from her bottle, and Larry went back into his semi-trance.

It was well past dark by the time Sarah drove the dually through the guarded gate into the Woodbridge development and pulled the truck into the driveway of the rented house. "We're home, Larry," Elisa said, and Larry seemed glad to hear it. "Oh good," he said, "we're home." Elisa opened the truck's door and helped Larry get out. "I'm going to put him to bed," she told Sarah. Together she and Larry walked toward the front door, arms around each other, Larry staggering slightly. They went inside the house.

Larry seemed happy that they'd finally made it, Sarah said.

In her initial version of what took place that night, Sarah said that after Elisa and Larry went into the house, she next checked her cell phone for messages. Her boyfriend Jason had called. Sarah called him back. Jason told her that Sarah's mother and father had come over to Sarah's apartment, and had taken her new puppy, Ralph, a Maltese terrier about the size of a shoebox. They'd also taken her recently acquired BMW.

Sarah was furious. She called her parents. Elisa by this point had come out of the house and was listening to Sarah as she made the call. Sarah let Mark and Karen know that she was unhappy, and said she'd be over to pick the dog up as soon as she could get there. She didn't understand why they had taken the dog to begin with, since Jason had agreed to take care of it while Sarah was away. She hung up. Elisa told her to use the truck to drive to Vacaville to pick up Ralph, then to come back to Lodi—about a ninety-minute round trip. Sarah had to come back that night because Elisa needed the truck in the morning—she'd already decided to sell it back in Los Angeles.

Which certainly seemed to indicate that whatever was ailing Larry, it might be permanent.

For Mark and Karen Dutra in Vacaville, the day had begun in terror and ended in recrimination.

Not long after the planes hit the World Trade Center, Karen remembered that her son, a student at Georgetown Law, had a job interview scheduled for that day in New York City. She worried that he might have been in one of the towers, or on one of the planes that had been hijacked. When she couldn't immediately reach him, she called Sarah. She guessed that Sarah would also be worried, since the whole country was seeing the devastation in New York City. A little after 7 in the morning, she called Sarah and left a message at her Sacramento apartment. Sarah retrieved the message and called Karen back while she and Elise were still in the Whalens' hotel room at the City of Industry.

Karen thought Sarah sounded strange, even distant. She'd had no idea she had returned to southern California to be with Elisa. When Karen said she'd been worried about her son, Sarah's older brother, Sarah sounded "robotic," as Karen put it later—very preoccupied. In fact, she didn't sound at all concerned about him. Karen was at first mystified as to why Sarah would be in Los Angeles on a school day, and then a little miffed that Sarah was being so blasé about the disasters. "Pray for your brother," Karen told Sarah.

"I will, Mom," Sarah said.

Sarah ended the call fairly quickly, and Karen got ready to go to her job, part of her thinking that Sarah had been acting strangely distant for weeks—ever since she had returned from Italy, in fact.

That afternoon, after the Dutras had determined that their son was safe, they'd received a call from a Texas car dealer. The dealer told the Dutras that a BMW he'd sold to Sarah had been paid for by a worthless check from Larry McNabney. If the Dutras could get the car back, the dealer said, he wouldn't charge Sarah with auto theft.

Auto theft! After all that had happened to the Dutras with Mark's own trouble over the embezzlement charge, that was the last thing they needed. Around 4 in the afternoon, Mark and Karen drove to Sacramento, having only a vague idea of where Sarah's apartment was. Eventually they found the place, and knocked on the door. Jason answered, and the Dutras told him the story about the Texas car dealer. Jason gave Mark the keys and Karen the dog. Then they drove back to

Vacaville. Mark called the Texas dealer and told him he'd recovered the car, and asked what the dealer wanted him to do
with it. The dealer told him to hang on to it—he'd send a car
carrier to pick it up. Of course, Mark would have to pay $600
to transport the car back to Texas, the dealer said.

So both Dutras were somewhat perturbed when Sarah
called later that night to berate them for taking the dog.

About 10 that night, Sarah drove into the Dutra driveway
in the red dually.

"Where's my dog?" she asked. Both Dutras thought
Sarah was very upset, but weren't sure why—whether it was
because of the BMW, or because they had taken Ralph, the
Maltese terrier. They tried to talk to Sarah about the BMW
and the Texas dealer's allegations, but she wouldn't listen.
She took Ralphie and drove away—all the way back to Lodi,
in fact.

When Sarah got back to the Woodbridge house it was
about 1:30 in the morning. Elisa was by herself, waiting up
for her, Sarah said.

"I said, 'Where's Larry?'" Sarah recounted later. "She
just looks at me . . . and said, 'Don't worry about it—just
don't worry about it.' I was thinking, 'Oh my God, oh my
God . . .'

"And I wish I knew more, but I don't. I really . . . don't,"
Sarah concluded. And with that, she burst into tears.

But Sarah did know more—a lot more.

For those who like to think about such things as truth and karma and coincidence, here's a dilly: even as Larry McNabney was to all intents and purposes falling off the face of the earth on that fateful September 11, 2001, another man, one closely linked in the past to Larry McNabney, was having his own day of reckoning. Jack Mazzan, the accused killer of Richard Minor, out on bail pending a new trial after more than twenty years in prison, had been re-arrested on Monday, September 10, and charged the following day with the murder of: April Barber.

Mazzan, who had been driving a taxi in Reno since his release pending the new trial on the Minor murder, was picked up and jailed on a no-bail warrant charging him with the old, previously unsolved murder of Minor's girlfriend. The key evidence was the blood on Mazzan's tennis shoes. Long thought to have been Minor's blood, new DNA tests unavailable back in 1978 had now determined that it had been April's blood all along. The Washoe County District Attorney's Office intended to try the one-time hairdresser for both murders, twenty-three years after they had taken place.

For all that time, Larry had kept Mazzan's secret (except to some, like Nancy Eklof). And now, just when the terrible truth was finally coming out, who should disappear but Larry McNabney himself? All that was necessary for those old, sensational events of the past to come full circle would be the sudden appearance of the psychic Kay Rhea. Doubtless, had anyone asked, she might have developed some insights into what really happened to Larry McNabney, at exactly the same time Larry's old client was being arrested for a crime that Kay had always insisted that Mazzan had in fact committed.

Certainly neither Elisa nor Sarah intended to tell what had happened to Larry, at least on September 11, 2001. The fact is, it's highly unlikely that either Elisa or Sarah even knew who Mazzan was, and why Larry's disappearance on the same day that his old client was re-arrested was so, well, *synchronous*—to use a 1970s word that would have meant something to someone like Larry McNabney. It was one of the tartest of ironies that a lawyer who had always striven mightily to get "ink" wasn't even mentioned in the news stories about Mazzan's latest arrest, and even more ironic that by the time the news was published—on the morning of September 11—Larry was no longer capable of reading it.

After their all-day drive north behind the Sierras in the dually, spiced with all of Elisa's seemingly cryptic remarks to Sarah about "forgetting" she had seen Larry that day, the next morning, September 12, Elisa drove Sarah over to the Whalen Ranch to pick up the Saab. It had been left there more than a week earlier by the McNabneys before the trip to the City of Industry.

Sarah had some instructions from Elisa—drive the Saab back to Sacramento, open the law office, and search the place for the title to the red truck. The truck couldn't be sold without the title, which Elisa was sure was in the office. According to Sarah, Elisa had first begun talking about selling the truck over the weekend, while Larry was getting drunk.

At the ranch, Elisa told Greg's wife, Mary, that Larry had left her after a fight. She showed Mary Whalen the bruise on her back. Sarah didn't contradict her. Then Sarah drove off in the Saab, and Elise drove off in the truck, on her way back to the horse show, and the prospective purchasers of the dually.

. . .

Debbie Kail later recalled that Elisa returned to the horse
show sometime on the afternoon of Wednesday, September
12. She returned to the barn and began helping Greg and
Debbie with the horses. If Elisa was bothered by Larry's
decision to leave her, neither Greg nor Debbie noticed it.
Both noticed that Elisa was wearing Larry's gold Rolex
watch. Debbie saw that the two shovels and the wheelchair
were still in the back of Larry's truck.

Greg was still puzzled by Larry's abrupt disappearance
from the show. Both Greg and Debbie thought it was very
unlike the sociable Larry to have simply left without saying
goodbye to either one of them. The whole thing seemed
strange, disorganized, even frantic to Greg. After Sarah and
Elisa had left in Larry's red truck the day before, Greg
had noticed one of Larry's cowboy hats, abandoned under
the horse trailer. And at one point—either right after Elisa
left, or after she'd returned—Greg had noticed that his trailer
was stuffed with Larry and Elisa's clothes, along with Larry's
golf clubs. (This was contradicted by Debbie, who said she
thought all the clothes had been removed.) Greg said later
he'd also found two pointed shovels in his trailer, both still
with the store tags on them. He had no idea where the shovels had come from. There were boxes of boots, too. One pair
of boots, in fact, Elisa soon gave to another horse trainer,
Casey Devitt, a friend of Greg's. She gave Larry's golf clubs
to Greg. She seemed bent on giving away as many of Larry's
belongings as she could.

Devitt wasn't sure whether he should accept the boots. "I
don't think I want them," he told Elisa, "because when Larry
gets it together and comes back, what if he wants them
back?"

"You'll never see Larry again showing horses," Elisa
told him, in front of Greg and Debbie. "He's going to quit
playing golf and quit showing horses."

That night, Greg, Debbie and Elisa all went to dinner together. Greg and Debbie were still curious about Larry. Elisa told them they didn't really know Larry—that he was very impulsive, that in the past he'd once run out on a trial to go do drugs, that he'd spent a couple of years in the "cult" working as the happy carpenter "Shantar."

"Elisa said that Larry just needed to clear his head and that he'd be— that we would never probably see him again," Debbie recalled. Larry, Elisa said, was going to start a new life for himself.

Late the following afternoon, Sarah set out from Sacramento, driving the Saab. The plan was for her to bring the title to the red truck to Elisa at the horse show. But somewhere near Fresno, the cruise control went haywire and the car speeded up, even as the traffic ahead was slowing down. Sarah, with Ralph beside her on the front seat, swerved into the grass on the freeway median to avoid a collision and went into a violent spin. By the time the car came to rest it was totaled. Neither Sarah nor Ralph was hurt, but both were very shaken. After the highway patrol came to clear away the wreckage, Sarah called Jason on her cell phone and asked him to come and pick her up. Then she called Elisa and told her that she'd been in a wreck. Elisa was glad to hear that Sarah wasn't hurt. Then she made arrangements for Sarah to fly down from Sacramento the following day. She needed the title to finish off the deal for the truck, which, it appears, had begun to come together even before Larry had left the horse show, and almost certainly without his knowledge.

The week before Larry disappeared, one of Devitt's clients, Alan Van Vliet of Carpenteria, put out the word that he was in the market for a truck, and Devitt told Greg Whalen about it. Greg offered to show Van Vliet his own truck, so he could see what one looked like. Elisa volunteered to take Van Vliet out the parking lot to look at Greg's truck, and ended up striking a tentative bargain with him to sell him Larry's red truck. Elisa asked for $30,000, a steep discount from the fifty-something Larry had paid only a few months earlier. Van Vliet offered $27,500. Elisa took it. It appears all this took place while Larry was stumbling around the arena with Justa Lotta Page on Sunday, September 9.

Now, with Larry gone, Elisa forged Larry's name on the truck's title transfer, and made arrangements to deliver it to the Van Vliets on Sunday morning, September 16. Elisa told Debbie that she needed the money, and was glad she'd been able to sell the truck, even if it was at a big loss.

On Sunday, Elisa drove Sarah to the Los Angeles airport, on the way to Carpinteria, a beach town northwest of Los Angeles. There Sarah rented a new green Mustang on a McNabney and Associates credit card. She then followed Elisa in the red truck to Carpinteria, where the Van Vliets gave her a check for $27,500. Before turning the truck over, Elisa stopped by the side of the road and removed the rented wheelchair from the back. She abandoned it on the sidewalk, telling Sarah they didn't need it anymore.

That same afternoon, Sarah and Elisa drove the green Mustang back toward Interstate 5. Around Newhall on the freeway, they saw Greg Whalen in his truck, pulling his long white trailer. They honked, Greg stopped, and Elisa got out of the Mustang to ride most of the rest of the way home with him.

A few days later, Greg removed Larry's golf clubs from his trailer. As he tipped the bag, a small vial fell out of one of the pockets. Greg wasn't sure what it was, but it looked like dope to him. He took it to one of his workers and asked if he knew what it was.

It's heroin, Greg was told. *It's probably worth a lot of money*. Greg said later he threw it into the trash.

Two days after Elisa and Sarah returned to Sacramento and the law office, an old acquaintance of Larry's motored down from Reno at Elisa's invitation. This was Ed Horn, another Reno lawyer, who had known Larry since the late 1970s. Elisa told him that Larry had left, and that a lawyer's services were urgently needed by McNabney and Associates. Since Horn had previously taken some of Larry's spillover cases while the office was still in Reno, he saw no harm in answering the summons. Elisa told him she needed him to take a deposition from a doctor in a car accident claim, and that she'd pay him a reasonable fee for his time.

On Tuesday, September 18, Horn took the deposition of a doctor in the car wreck case. Horn thought it went well, especially when the insurance carrier offered to settle the whole thing for $150,000. Elisa, who was present at the deposition, told Horn that the clients would accept that amount of money to square their claim—that she had their authorization to settle the case. Hands were shaken all around, and the representative from the insurance company said the checks would be mailed shortly. Horn's fee for a morning's work was to be half of McNabney and Associates' 8½ percent of the take. The rest of the one-third or so legal fee was supposed to go to another Sacramento lawyer who had previously represented the client, a man named Michael Carter. When the insurance company agreed to settle, that meant Horn's fee was $6,200—not bad for a morning's work, except that it would later be said by other legal experts that the case was probably worth as much as half a million dollars. Even

Larry, in an arbitration meeting late in August, had said the case was worth a minimum of $300,000.

After the deposition, Horn went with Elisa and Sarah back to the Woodbridge house. Exactly why he did this wasn't clear later; investigating police believed that Horn had a romantic interest in Elisa. Horn said that nothing intimate transpired, that he was only agreeing to handle several more cases for McNabney and Associates, as he had in the past. Horn said Elisa told him that Larry had gone off to join a cult. Horn didn't question this, apparently—he knew Larry's reputation for impulsive behavior.

After spending the night at the Woodbridge house, Horn returned to Reno the following day, carrying the files on four other McNabney and Associates cases. Then he waited for a check to arrive for his part of the fees.

On September 25, the insurance company in the Carter case issued three separate checks, payable to Carter and McNabney and Associates, for $50,000, $99,000, and $950. The two large checks were deposited into the first client trust account shortly after they were received; the third check seems to have vanished.

By that time, however, Elisa and Sarah had mastered the arcana of moving money between accounts by forging Larry's name, and by telephone transfer. The money went into the whirligig of the various McNabney accounts, and eventually back out again in the form of checks to Elisa, Sarah, Ginger Miller, various credit card companies, rent on the apartment for Haylei, and a couple of car dealers. Two used BMWs were purchased, including one for $18,277, which replaced the one that had been repossessed from Sarah by the Texas dealer. Some of the checks were made out to Larry McNabney and signed by Larry McNabney. The bank turned them into cash, no questions asked.

By the end of October, in fact, all but $593 of the trust account had been spent—none of it going to Michael Carter, who had now been victimized twice, once in a car wreck and then later by his own attorney.

As September turned into October, Elisa and Sarah continued to haunt the horse show circuit, traveling with Greg Whalen to shows near Elk Grove, California; Portland, Oregon; Lancaster, California; and Snohomish, Washington. From the day of Larry's disappearance, Elisa had been eager to sell Justa Lotta Page. Greg continued to lease a gelding to Elisa for her to show. Wherever they went, though, they were followed by whispered gossip—rumors about Larry's sudden disappearance, and also, about Greg and Elisa.

At the Lancaster show, in fact, someone saw Greg and Elisa locked in what appeared to be a passionate embrace in one of the horse stalls. The witness had no idea who they were, but was impressed by the fervor displayed. "Boy," she said, "those people should get a motel room." That was when she was told that the smoochers were Elisa and Greg, and that there was a wild story going around that Larry might have been murdered by his wife.

The origin of these stories among the horse set seems to have stemmed from Elisa's question to Debbie Kail about whether "ace" would kill someone. Overheard by someone on the day the conversation took place, the remarks began to assume potential significance after Larry's sudden disappearance. Elisa and Greg seemed oblivious to any of the rumors, however.

Throughout much of the first few weeks of October, Elisa frequently called the Whalen Ranch. Greg later said these calls were made because Elisa was anxious to sell Justa Lotta Page to raise more cash. "She put quite a bit of pressure on us to sell it in a hurry," Whalen said later. "And so she was calling a lot. . . . She called in the morning, she'd call at night. She'd call my wife. She'd call Debbie. She said with Larry gone, she couldn't afford to have this horse there with us anymore, and she needed to sell it. And it was a stud besides, so it wasn't an easy horse to sell, because you're only going to sell a stud to somebody who needs one."

Eventually, however, a buyer was found: Maynard Alves, like Greg Whalen, another horse rancher. Alves had a stud ranch near Redmond, Oregon.

"I'm a friend of Greg's," Maynard said later. "I've known him since I was a kid. I heard through a friend of a friend about a lady who wanted to sell some horses, because her husband had joined a cult. I went to Clements, looked at the horse, thought he was a good horse, and I bought him."

Alves already had one stud on his Oregon ranch, but guessed another couldn't hurt. He and his wife joined Greg, Mary and Elisa for dinner in Clements. Then Maynard brought out his checkbook. "It's nobody's business," Maynard said, when he was asked how much he paid. "I can tell you this, it wasn't a gift."

Later, though, Greg would say that Justa Lotta Page brought around $15,000 in cash—"plus trade." While Greg didn't clarify what he meant by his amendment, it appears that Elisa and Larry may have owed Greg as much as $40,000 in unpaid horse expenses at the time the stallion was transferred to Alves; later it would be rumored in the horse show circuit that Greg and the Kails had taken a half-ownership position in Justa Lotta Page with Maynard. Although Greg would later say that Justa Lotta Page had been moved from his ranch to Alves' place, in fact the horse was kept at the Whalen Ranch for almost seven months after the transfer. Greg showed the horse until May of 2002, at ten more shows, including the World Championship show in Oklahoma City in November. After that, Alves took physical possession of the horse, and began showing him himself.

While Alves wouldn't say how much he'd paid for Justa Lotta Page, it does appear that he was dealing in distressed property. Elisa needed to sell the horse, and was hardly in a position to hold out for top dollar—not if Greg was going to get his money. If one adds the rumored $40,000 owed by Elisa ("trade") to the $15,000 paid by Alves, the resulting $55,000 sales figure seems closer to the McNabneys' equity in Justa Lotta Page at the time. But as Maynard Alves later pointed out, buying a stallion was a gamble: whether it was a gamble that paid off depended on Justa Lotta Page's own offspring. "If he turns out to be a dud, I may cut his throat," Alves joked.

The day before the horse was transferred to Maynard Alves—Whalen said the title could be assigned by Elisa, as Larry's wife, without the need for his signature—Elisa, Sarah and Haylei drove to a Sacramento Jaguar dealer. Elisa had her heart set on a brand new, carnival red XK8 convertible. The price of the car was $68,148. Salesman Richard Wiedel talked to Elisa, and learned that while she wanted to lease the new car, she didn't want it in her name, but rather in Sarah's.

"Elisa and Sarah and Elisa's daughter arrived," Wiedel recalled, "and the car they eventually leased was sitting on a porch area. After they looked it over, and were excited about it, Elisa made the statement that they wanted to lease the car on a two-year basis, and pre-pay it. So it was— I mean, that's a very straightforward and simple transaction . . . Elisa was definitely the leader and the decision-maker, absolutely."

Elisa told Wiedel that Sarah would guarantee the two years of the lease with a check from Larry McNabney and Associates. The arrangements would be made to wire-transfer the money directly from the law firm's bank account to the dealership, at which point the dealership would give the check back to Sarah. This didn't make any difference to Wiedel—how the customers paid for the wheels was their problem, not his. Sarah went into a back room with the dealership's finance manager, produced a check written on the second business account for $30,000, signed with Larry

McNabney's signature, and began to fill out the paperwork. The dealership called the bank and verified that there was a sufficient amount of money in the account to back up the check. Then Elisa and Haylei drove away in the red Jag, followed a few minutes later by Sarah in her BMW. The next day, the money was wired from the bank to the dealership, and on the same day someone from the law firm returned to the dealership and reclaimed the check.

At Clements that night, having dinner with the Whalens and the Alveses, Elisa told everyone that the shiny new red car was her "divorce settlement from Larry."

After the Lancaster show, the rumors among the horse set that Greg and Elisa were having an affair gained much wider circulation. Greg said he heard the rumors, but "that stuff with Elisa never bothered me and it never bothered my wife. We both knew it wasn't true."

But the rumors would continue, and take on even greater spice and frequency at the AQHA World Championship show at Oklahoma City in November.

The plan had been for Elisa and Sarah to travel with Greg and the Kails to Oklahoma City for the big show, which was scheduled to begin the first week of November, and last about two weeks. But Elisa called the ranch around the end of the month and told them that there had been an accident, that she and Sarah wouldn't be traveling with them after all. Instead, Elisa said, she and Sarah would meet Whalen and the Kails in Oklahoma City.

By this point, Debbie Kail had heard the rumors surrounding Elisa and her father, and her friendship with Elisa was cooling rapidly. She was also increasingly puzzled by Larry's disappearance, particularly because Elisa kept providing so many different explanations for what had happened to him. After the first "cult" story, Debbie had asked if Larry had gone "back to the cult in Washington State"— the one he had previously told Whalen and the Kails about.

Elisa said no, it was a different cult—a cult in Florida. Then Debbie heard that Elisa had told other people among the horse show set that Larry had gone to a cult in Costa Rica . . . that he was in Minneapolis when the World Trade Center was hit . . . that he was in rehab . . . that he was hiding out from drug dealers . . . the story seemed to change depending on who Elisa was talking to.

At one point Debbie decided to try to talk to Larry himself. She called his cellular phone and left a message. No one ever called her back.

By late October, Elisa had told her that Larry was divorcing her—in Florida, of all places. Elisa told Debbie she didn't care—she had a new boyfriend, another trainer, not Greg, as it turned out, but someone from Washington State. It was fairly common knowledge in the horse set that Elisa had given the Washington man a gold Rolex watch.

Overall, Debbie had the impression that Elisa and Sarah were using the horse shows to meet men. Elisa was dressing younger, more provocatively. She had begun to lose weight and lighten her hair color—it was as if she were trying to close the gap in age between her and Sarah.

Then came the World Championship show in Oklahoma City, and by the time that was over, relations between Debbie and Elisa would be thoroughly ruptured.

By the middle of November 2001, nearly half a thousand American quarter horses and their owners and trainers had descended on Oklahoma City for the big event of the year. Greg Whalen arrived, pulling his long white horse trailer behind him, followed by Debbie and Bob Kail, and their son, Ryan. The Whalen trailer held a number of horses, including Justa Lotta Page and the horse Elisa had leased from Greg, a gelding named Team Design, along with some vests Elisa hoped to sell, and a lot of Elisa's show clothing—boots, hatboxes and the like. Elisa didn't have to pay anything for the horse lease, Greg said later, just the horse's upkeep. When Whalen and the Kails arrived, Elisa and Sarah met them. They had driven the new red Jaguar from California to Oklahoma.

Elisa showed Team Design on November 9, and went out to party with Sarah that night. The next day, at the barn where Whalen had stabled the horses, Greg met Elisa and Sarah in the tack room they shared. Greg was not happy with Elisa. He thought she and Sarah had been dressing cheaply and acting vulgarly while partying the night before.

"I think they were doing some drugs," Greg said later. "I smelled some in my tack room." Greg told Elisa to take the marijuana out of there pronto—all the straw around made it dangerous as hell. Elisa told Greg to stop being so un-hip. That ignited Greg and he ordered Elisa to get all her stuff out of the tack room.

"She made a comment that she owned a fourth of that tack room and she didn't like to be moved out of it," Greg said later. "And I told her I'd refund her money, but to get her stuff and get out. And she said, 'Boy, you are not treating us very well. Larry and I gave you that Rolex watch,' and it made me mad. I just took it off and threw it at her." The same day, Greg ended the lease on Elisa's horse.

"I didn't think she would do it [smoke marijuana] in the tack room," Greg said. "Because, you know, there's a lot of other people, about two hundred people in that same barn, and you are twelve feet apart, each stall, and there were a lot of my friends there, and they also smelled it. And it wasn't good for our barn." Greg didn't want the prospective clients at the show to think that the Whalen Ranch was populated by potheads.

Afterward, Elisa had a confrontation with Debbie and Bob Kail in the parking lot. Debbie criticized Elisa for smoking marijuana, dressing cheaply and, it appears, flirting with both Greg and Bob. Elisa apparently told Debbie to mind her own business. But from then on, Debbie was definitely not on Elisa's side.

Despite the watch-throwing, it appears that Elisa and Greg temporarily patched up their problems for the rest of the show. Attendees at the show later told police that Elisa and Sarah seemed to spend much of their time with Greg. Greg later said it wasn't his doing—everywhere he went, they were sure to follow.

Then, one night at the hotel, Greg got into a huge beef with Elisa in the hallway. The circumstances of the fight weren't ever made clear, but it appears that Greg might have had too much to drink. There was some shoving between him and Elisa, with Greg calling her bad names—"a slut" and "a whore" according to a hotel maid who witnessed the confrontation, and "a bitch," according to Greg himself—and a hotel security guard had to come and break it up.

And on this same night, or another night, it wasn't clear, Greg chased Sarah and Elisa out of the arena parking lot. Sarah was driving the red Jag, Greg was in his white truck. The Oklahoma City police came and gave tickets to both of them. Sarah said later she and Elisa had no idea who was chasing them, while Greg's story was that he thought the Jag was being stolen. It seemed, however, to some who later investigated Larry's disappearance that the incident had some of the qualities of a high school lovers' spat.

By the third week in November, the World Championship show was over. Justa Lotta Page turned out to be an also-walked—not finishing in the top ten, according to the American Quarter Horse Association, in Greg's Open class, although he might have done better in Larry's Amateur class had Larry still been around. But by the time the show was wrapping up, the rumors about Greg and Elisa—and Larry—were rampant.

"You know, it [the rumors] got pretty bad in Oklahoma," Greg said, "because my daughter got pretty upset, because every time I'd go sit down in the stands, Sarah and Elisa would come sit down behind me." That only made people believe all the more that he was having a fling with Elisa, Greg indicated—especially his competitors in the horse training industry, who were more than glad to lay manure at his feet.

Late in November, the Whalen contingent, including Elisa and Sarah, returned to Lodi and Sacramento, where, it turned out, the affairs of the firm of Larry McNabney and Associates were turning into a first-class mess.

One problem was with Ed Horn, the Reno lawyer who had helped settle the Carter case. Weeks had gone by and he still hadn't seen his share of the money. He called the McNabney and Associates office on several occasions, only to be told that Elisa wasn't in. Horn began to think he was getting stiffed by Elisa. He knew the story of the Reno defalcation, and knew that Elisa was prone to cut corners with money. Horn finally yelled at Sarah, near the end of November, accusing her and Elisa of being dishonest. Whatever else Horn may have accused them of is unclear, but by the end of the day a messenger had hand-delivered a valid check for $6,200 to Horn's office in Reno.

Horn ran into the same problem that many other people were having with the McNabney law firm—finding anyone who could make a decision and stick to it. Partly this was because of the absence of the firm's principal—i.e., Larry—but there also seems to have been an effort by Sarah and Elisa to keep people in confusion. When someone would call for Elisa, Sarah might pretend to be her; at other times, Elisa might pretend to be Sarah. At other times they would identify themselves as Ginger. Sometimes they even made up names when they took messages for Elisa or Larry or Sarah. Later they would say they never got the message. It was maddening for the callers, who felt like they were being given the royal runaround, which, of course, they were.

Carter and his wife Joyce felt particularly abused. Part of the settlement agreement called for the McNabney firm to pay Carter's outstanding medical bills from the accident, as well as other bills that had accumulated during Carter's recuperation from his injury. By early October, the Carters began receiving dunning notices from various creditors. They called the McNabney office to find out what to do, and Sarah and Elisa came to the Carter house to sort through the bills and devise a plan to pay the creditors off. Several checks were filled out by Elisa and Sarah, with the amounts payable to various of the creditors. They told the Carters that they would make sure the creditors got the checks.

But later the Carters began receiving complaints from the creditors—some of the checks had never been signed, it appeared, and in other cases they'd bounced. In still others, they had never been mailed at all.

At that point, Mrs. Carter realized that there seemed to be a problem at the McNabney firm. She went to see the insurance adjustor, who assured her that the insurance company had indeed mailed checks for $150,000 to the McNabney law firm, for the benefit of Michael Carter, in settlement of his accident claim. From this point forward, Mrs. Carter kept after Elisa, who kept dodging her. She reached Sarah instead. Sarah assured her that the problem would be taken care of. Then Elisa and Sarah went off to Oklahoma. When they returned, Mrs. Carter went personally to the office. At that point Elisa gave her a $5,000 check, and said more would be coming as soon as all the bills were settled. Mrs. Carter immediately took the check to the bank and cashed it. She went back to the office, and Elisa invited her to lunch. At lunch, Elisa told Mrs. Carter that they'd been having problems in the office since Larry had left—to attend a "golf clinic" for ninety days. Then Elisa offered Mrs. Carter a job in the law office; she declined.

Meanwhile, there was also a minor tax matter involving the Carters; Elisa kept telling people, Sarah said later, that they couldn't release most of the money to the Carters because the IRS would get it all. And it appears that Elisa had told Mrs. Carter that Ed Horn, the Reno lawyer, would handle the tax matter for $350, but the bill logged by the McNabney firm was actually for $6,000. Horn, of course, didn't get this money—it was just that Elisa used Horn's name to bamboozle Mrs. Carter on where the money had actually gone.

As November progressed, Mrs. Carter developed an ally inside the McNabney office—Ginger Miller. As Ginger put it later, she began to suspect something was wrong at the McNabney law firm when, some weeks into her employment, she realized that she had never actually seen Larry.

"I thought it was peculiar," Ginger said later. "They talked about him like he was alive every day—'Larry's doing this or Larry's doing that.'"

At one point, on the same day, Sarah and Elisa both gave different excuses as to why Larry wasn't coming in. "Sometimes they had the same story," she said. "But one day Sarah said he was skiing and Elisa said he was golfing . . . They changed so often, they did not make sense."

Ginger thought Elisa was mentally unstable, especially over money matters. "I thought she wasn't right in the head," she said later. "She had temper tantrums often . . . she could be very, deeply angry—a rage, in my terms. She would clench her fists. Her face would turn red. She did not like talking about Larry."

When she did talk about Larry, she alternated between being angry and sad.

As October turned into November, and things became increasingly chaotic at the office, Ginger discovered that the rent hadn't been paid. Clients and creditors alike were continually calling to complain, and Sarah and Elisa kept dodging the calls. One particularly persistent caller kept asking about a wheelchair that Elisa had rented that had never been returned. Meanwhile, Elisa, with Sarah's assistance, kept kiting money from account to account. While both Elisa and Sarah were out shopping, seemingly on a daily basis. At one point, Ginger said, Elisa invented a fictitious employee named Tessa to take the heat for all the apparent foul-ups. "She said if we ever have any mistakes in the office, we can blame it on Tessa," Ginger said. "My job was pretty much talking to irate clients."

Then Ginger's paychecks began bouncing—about the same time that Joyce Carter was calling repeatedly, asking to speak to Elisa. Ginger and Mrs. Carter began to confide in one another, and Ginger soon realized there was some sort of scam unfolding at McNabney and Associates. Ginger took Sarah aside to complain about her bounced paychecks.

"Hungry mouths talk," Ginger told her, apparently a reference to the conversations that she'd had with Mrs. Carter. After this, Sarah wouldn't talk to her anymore, and shortly thereafter, Elisa invited Ginger to attend a party at Greg Whalen's ranch. To Ginger, who had never hobnobbed with

Elisa and Sarah socially, this seemed ominous. Was it really possible that Elisa had made her husband disappear? If she went out to the ranch, was she likely to come back?

Thus, on the last day of November 2001, Ginger Miller called the Sacramento Sheriff's Department. She reported Larry McNabney a missing person, and suggested that Mrs. McNabney and her playmate, Sarah Dutra, were up to no good.

Sometime in late November, just about the time Ginger was developing her qualms, Debbie Kail decided to put her own suspicions about Larry's disappearance into words. In talking to a close friend, Debbie said Larry had dropped out of sight abruptly on the day of the 9-11 attacks, and hadn't been seen since. Debbie told her friend that she suspected Elisa had done something to make Larry disappear permanently—in fact, Debbie wondered if he might actually be dead.

After mulling this over for a bit, on December 14 the friend made an anonymous call to the San Joaquin County Sheriff's Department, not mentioning her informant's name, but suggesting that there was something peculiar about the disappearance of the friend's male friend, who wasn't named. No address was given, either, but the friend asked the detective she spoke with whether anyone had been reported missing from the Woodbridge neighborhood.

Later the question would arise: with two different police agencies receiving two different tip-offs that something might be up with Larry and/or his law firm, why didn't someone move in on Elisa and Sarah immediately, before Elisa could do any more damage to the firm's clients, and before she could take steps to flee?

The answer seems to be, first, that Ginger's report was not initially taken very seriously by the Sacramento County Sheriff's Department, coming as it did from a disgruntled employee, not a close relative; the initial investigation of Ginger's report was handled rather desultorily, and didn't

really begin in earnest until a month later. Second, the anonymous call to San Joaquin County—a different jurisdiction—
was put down as just that: an anonymous call. In the absence
of any useful details, no official report was taken. No one in
either department knew what the other department knew.

As the fall of 2001 neared an end, Larry's son Joe McNabney thought it was peculiar that he hadn't heard anything
from his father. It wasn't as if they were accustomed to having daily or even weekly contact, but still Joe expected to
hear from Larry from time to time. The last time he'd seen
his father was at the Elk Grove house in August, apparently
when Larry was just about to return to Texas to pick up one
of the BMWs. Larry told Joe that he'd like to have a ranch
in Texas. "In Texas," Larry told Joe, "you can drink and
drive and have a gun in your car." Larry was kidding, of
course, but it seemed that the arrest for the DUI still
rankled.

    After the move to the Woodbridge house, the only way
Joe had to contact his father was through the law office. Elisa
gave him the 1-800 number for the firm, and told him to call
that when he wanted to speak to Larry. Joe thought Elisa was
just trying to save him some money, because otherwise,
phoning from Sacramento would have required a toll call.
Over the years, Joe usually left it to Elisa to arrange the
father–son get-togethers, but as October turned into November, Elisa didn't call. Eventually Joe called Elisa. Elisa told
him that Larry had taken off, partying in Las Vegas or Reno,
and no one was sure when he'd be back. Joe accepted this; it
was simply part of his father's flamboyant nature. Then Elisa
told him she'd heard from Larry, and that he was soon coming home.

    "She told me he was going to be checking himself into
rehab," Joe recalled. "She said my dad was out on a binge.
'He's been drinking, he's been doing whatever else, and he

wants to do better.' She kept saying, 'You know your dad, he wants to do better. He is going to do better. He is going to come home and he is going to rehab.' I go, 'Good, if he is out there getting in trouble drinking and doing whatever, that's good, rehab.' So I was happy. I just left it at that—'That's good, a wise decision.'" Elisa began discussing arrangements for Larry's birthday on December 19, and celebrating Christmas a week later, a time when Joe traditionally got together with his father. As far as Joe could tell, things seemed normal—normal for the McNabneys, anyway.

Then in late November or early December—about the same time that Ginger received her invitation to the Whalen Ranch—Sarah called Joe. Sarah said she and Elisa were at the Woodbridge house, and wanted to know if Joe wanted to come out and party with them. Joe was flabbergasted by the invitation—first, because he didn't know Elisa and Sarah well enough to party with them, and second because his father still wasn't around. It seemed weird.

"Where's my dad at?" Joe asked. Sarah told him that Larry was "out of town."

Joe declined the invitation, then called his mother, JoDee, and told her what had happened. "I never got a call like that before," he said later. "It came out of nowhere . . . I wasn't friends with them." He wondered what was going on. He had the impression from Sarah's voice that she and Elisa were high on pot.

At some point just after this, around December 13, Elisa and Sarah took another trip, this one to the National Finals Rodeo show in Las Vegas. Sarah arrived at the Woodbridge house in her BMW, and she and Elisa subsequently drove in the new Jag to Las Vegas, where they met Greg Whalen and his wife and spent the weekend attending the rodeo together. Some later thought that after the fiasco in Oklahoma City, and all the rumors, Mary didn't want Greg going anywhere out of town with Elisa unless she was there to keep an eye on him. Sarah and Elisa first tried to check into the Bellagio hotel. The attendant at the parking garage asked Sarah to pop the trunk open for inspection, a widespread practice since 9-11, and Sarah released the catch, opening the Jag's trunk. But Elisa hopped out of the car and slammed the trunk lid down, telling the attendant that they'd changed their minds, and wouldn't be staying at the massive hotel after all. They found another place to park, and Sarah and Elisa stayed somewhere else. Elisa bought several gifts for Sarah, who spent most of her time in the hotel room. As it turned out, this was to be the next-to-last trip that Sarah would take with Elisa.

After Elisa and Sarah returned from Las Vegas, Joe and Elisa continued to exchange telephone calls. Elisa told Joe different stories as to Larry's whereabouts—sometimes he was on a binge, sometimes he was with the cult, Joe couldn't make much sense of it. Elisa set aside a time for Joe to come to the Woodbridge house for Christmas dinner, and to exchange Christmas gifts and birthday gifts with his father. Then, two days before Christmas, she called and told him that Larry wouldn't be able to make it after all. Joe had the distinct impression that Elisa was lying to him about his father. He didn't know what to make of any of this, and wasn't exactly sure of what to do about it.

One who was likewise convinced that Elisa had been doing some serious lying was Joyce Carter. In early December, Joyce talked again with Elisa. She'd taken another check given to her by the law firm to the bank, and the bank had informed her that another check with the same number had been passed through the bank previously, and for a far smaller amount. When she called Elisa, Elisa gave her some sort of story that Mrs. Carter knew had to be false. She told Elisa that if she didn't fork over the money the firm owed her husband, she'd complain to the State Bar of California, and Larry would lose his license. After that, Elisa refused to talk to her.

Mrs. Carter was by now highly suspicious. In addition to hearing some of her grave doubts about the McNabney law firm confirmed by Ginger Miller, she enlisted a friend who lived across the street from the law office to keep tabs on the comings and goings of all the employees, but most of all Elisa. Every time Elisa would be at the office, the friend would call Mrs. Carter, who would therefore know when Elisa was avoiding her telephone calls by pretending to be out. It did not appear that Larry ever went to work. Then Elisa and the office staff seemed to disappear altogether, and Ginger told Mrs. Carter that Elisa had moved most of the office work to the Woodbridge house, in part to avoid Mrs. Carter and people like her. At length, Mrs. Carter went to the Sacramento County Sheriff's Department to complain about Larry McNabney and Associates, but no one there seemed very interested. It was a civil matter, they told Mrs. Carter. She should take it up with her attorney.

Judging from the account ledgers later dissected by the financial experts, by the middle of December 2001 Elisa was beginning to run short on cash again. On December 14, when Elisa and Sarah were in Las Vegas for the rodeo, the landlord at the law office building sent a demand letter for a total of $7,250. The firm was being evicted for non-payment of four months' past-due rent. Had Elisa been there when it arrived, she probably would have gone into one of her money rages. But the cupboard was almost bare. The account summaries showed that by the end of November, the huntseathorses.com account was in the red, the new business checking account had only $87, Larry's personal account had only $104, and the first business account just $15. The only account with any appreciable money left was the original trust account, and that balance was down to $6,518. To try to keep Joyce Carter pacified, Elisa had taken cash advances on various credit cards, sending dollops of money her way, but still far short of what was owed.

Money was maneuvered between the various accounts, and Sarah—or someone using Sarah's name—cashed checks for around $5,000, including one for $300 dollars from Larry's all-but-dormant personal account, which had been momentarily replenished, apparently just for the purpose. But it was clear that the law firm of Larry McNabney and Associates was on its last lap. Around the middle of the month, Haylei moved out of her apartment and in with Elisa at the Woodbridge house. At the same time, Elisa began making plans to move out of the Woodbridge house to live in the McNabney horse trailer, which of course had human living quarters included in its configuration. Late in December, it appears that Elisa, Sarah and Haylei drove the Jag to Salt Lake City to visit one of Elisa's friends. Elisa and Sara then drove back, while Haylei stayed on until after the first of the year.

When they got back, Elisa told Sarah she intended to close down the law office. It couldn't be run without a lawyer, she said. Horn hadn't worked out—after the argument over the money he was supposed to be paid, Horn had returned the other four cases Elisa had given him and told her to forget it, she'd have to find someone else. Mrs. Carter, meanwhile, had finally hired a lawyer who was doing her some good. This new lawyer let Elisa know in very plain terms that the McNabney firm had better make the Carters whole, or there would be dire consequences—no rubber checks, please.

To raise this cash, Elisa had Sarah arrange a finance company loan for her BMW. The loan proceeds, for $14,000, were disbursed on December 27. On her loan application, Sarah had listed Greg Whalen—by all accounts a millionaire—as her brother. According to the account ledger, Sarah then took this cash, and deposited it into the trust account. The very next day, a check was written on Larry's client trust account in the amount of $14,000, and taken to the bank to purchase a cashier's check for the same amount. Then Ginger Miller delivered the money personally to the Carters' latest lawyer.

By that point, the client trust account was for all practical purposes exhausted, as were all the other accounts. Virtually all the money was gone—just like Larry.

Sometime just after the first of December 2001, Larry's DUI lawyer, Georgeann McKee—a former Sacramento County sheriff's deputy—got a call from one of her former colleagues in the department. Detective Steve Hill, who had been assigned to investigate Ginger's report of Larry's disappearance, had run a computer check on Larry and discovered that there was a warrant out for his arrest. As part of his sentencing on the DUI, Larry was supposed to turn up for community work service—picking up trash by the side of the freeway, that sort of thing. Larry had never bothered, and as a result, a warrant had been outstanding on him ever since the spring. When Hill also discovered that Georgeann was Larry's lawyer, he called her, asking for information on Larry's present whereabouts, given the report of his apparent disappearance.

This disappearance stuff was news to her, Georgeann told Hill. But then, she said, Hill had to know that Larry was an alcoholic with a history of going on benders. "I wouldn't be real concerned," she told Hill. "Apparently he does this all the time." Georgeann suggested that Hill go to Larry's office to see if he was there, or failing that, to the McNabneys' home in Elk Grove.

A day or so later, Hill called her back. He'd called the office, he said, but nobody was answering the telephone. Then he'd actually gone to the office, but no one was there. He'd been to the house in Elk Grove, only to discover that the McNabneys had moved. McKee told Hill he'd gone to the wrong house—Larry had told her in April that they'd planned to move.

Well, said Hill, where did they move *to*? Georgeann said she'd check around and find out. Over the next several days, Georgeann made several calls to Elisa. In Georgeann's mind, Elisa was the stable one in the McNabney marriage. She'd talked to Elisa perhaps fifteen times since Larry had been busted, and on every occasion Elisa seemed friendly, reasonable, and highly articulate. When, in the spring, Georgeann had asked Elisa if she'd ever considered leaving Larry, Elisa shook her head, no.

"I felt really bad for her," Georgeann would later recall. "She would tell me she couldn't leave him, she really loved him . . . that he was a really good person."

Thus, in December, when Elisa didn't return her calls, Georgeann guessed that Elisa was probably just preoccupied with Larry and the holidays. She didn't really think too much about it.

On December 12, Hill called once more, and left a message for Georgeann. "I really need to talk to her," Hill said of Elisa. He said some people in the horse show set were exchanging rumors that Larry was dead.

"I called her again," Georgeann remembered. "I left another message. I said, 'Goddammit, the cops are looking for you, they think Larry's dead—you need to call me right *now*.'" The next morning at 5:45 A.M., Elisa called back and left a message on Georgeann's machine.

"Why would they think that?" Elisa asked. "You know what he's like"—meaning that McKee knew that Larry was prone to periodic benders. According to Georgeann, Elisa began to cry on the recorded message, saying, "I don't know where he is . . . he calls me once a week . . . he joined a commune." Elisa indicated to McKee that everything was in a big mess at the office because Larry had simply abandoned everything, and that she was running short of money. Elisa sounded very unhappy and stressed out, according to McKee.

Georgeann called Elisa back once more and left another message, telling her to tell Larry the next time he called to

call the Sacramento Sheriff's Department to get the matter
straightened out. Then she called Hill to tell him what she'd
told Elisa, and explained once again that Larry was unpre-
dictable. Hill seemed to accept that, and there the matter
rested for several weeks. It does not appear that anyone in
the Sacramento Sheriff's Department ever communicated
Mrs. Carter's complaints about the McNabney firm to Detective Hill—at least in December, when it might have done
some good.

Near New Year's Day, two young women jogging in Sacramento noticed a shiny object on the pavement as they ran
nearby. Stopping, Kimberly Thomas picked up the object
and realized it was a large silver belt buckle engraved with
the name "Larry McNabney," and the words, "Rookie of
the Year 1999." Kimberly and her fellow jogger decided the
buckle was probably valuable, and that it might have at least
sentimental value to whoever it belonged to.

Returning to their office, Kimberly and her friend looked
in the telephone book and found the listing for Larry's son
Joe, the only McNabney they could find. They called and
told him what they'd found. Joe came over to the office
and picked it up. He thought it very odd that his father's
prized silver belt buckle would be lying in the street. He
didn't then realize that the buckle had been found less than
four blocks from Sarah's apartment and quite near the Mc-
Nabney law office.

On January 2, 2002, Elisa informed the landlord at the office
that the McNabney firm would be moving out. The plan,
said Elisa, was to wind up the rest of the cases from the
house in Woodbridge. Soon thereafter, Sarah, Haylei, Elisa
and Ginger began moving boxes of files out. Some were
taken to the Woodbridge house, while others were put into
the McNabney horse trailer, which was undergoing repairs
at a shop near Lockeford. Elisa called in an office supplies

dealer, who bought all the McNabney and Associates fur-
nishings, and gave Elisa a check. Most of Larry's law books
and a number of personal items, including pictures of Larry
and his horses, were left behind.

Around the same time, Sarah and Haylei began dumping
various items of Larry's clothing and personal effects in
Dumpsters or at donated clothing collection bins. That was
probably how the silver belt buckle wound up on the street,
dropped inadvertently. "It was just large amounts," Haylei
said later. Some of the better quality items were taken to
thrift stores and sold for cash. When Haylei asked why they
were doing this, Elisa told her that Larry didn't want them
anymore because the marriage was over. Elisa sold all the
McNabney living room furniture, too, saying she didn't
want it because it reminded her of Larry.

On January 8, Sarah rented a U-Haul truck, and drove it
to the Woodbridge house. There, she and Elisa and Haylei
loaded up clothes and other things from the house, then
took the stuff to the McNabney horse trailer, where they
stashed it. Then they took the truck back to Woodbridge.
Several of Greg Whalen's ranch hands arrived, and more
stuff was loaded into the truck to be taken to the dump.
Elisa gave the ranch hands several items for their own use
back at the Whalen bunkhouse, including an old refrigerator from the garage.

The next day, a woman—probably Elisa, but possibly
Sarah—drove the truck to the nearby dump and began
throwing things out. A crew of trustees from the county jail
watched, agog, as the good-looking woman pitched piles
into the trash, including plaques and trophies from horse
shows. Then the truck drove off, and was returned to the
U-Haul outlet a few hours later. While this was going on,
Ginger Miller called the Sacramento County Sheriff's Department and let them know that Elisa was leaving town.

Late that afternoon, Elisa called a man she'd hired to
haul the horse trailer from Lockeford to Scottsdale to tell

him that she was on her way to Arizona, and asking when
he could get the trailer there—she and Haylei planned to
live in it for a while.

But the trailer would never make it to Arizona. Early the
following morning, January 10, 2002, deputies from the
Sacramento Sheriff's Department descended on the Whalen
Ranch in search of Elisa, as well as the by-now empty house
in Woodbridge. At the ranch they learned that Elisa was on
her way to Scottsdale in the Jag, and that her trailer was due
to follow. Where was the trailer? At the repair place in Lockeford. At that point a squad of deputies rushed to Lockeford to
impound the trailer before it, too, eluded their grasp.

At about 1:30 P.M. on January 10, Elisa called Georgeann McKee, apparently from Scottsdale. Georgeann wasn't in, so Elisa left a message asking her to call back. But when Georgeann tried to return the call, she discovered that Elisa's cellular telephone had been disconnected.

About two hours later, though, it appears that Elisa found a workable telephone. She called the trailer repair place in Lockeford to find out whether the trailer had been picked up by the hired hauler. By that point the Sacramento County Sheriff's Department was all over the trailer, looking for evidence relating to Larry's disappearance, and finding a number of legal files. It appears that the repairman told Elisa that the sheriff's department had impounded the trailer, and that someone had filed a missing persons report on Larry. Elisa was furious. She called Joe and demanded to know whether he was the one who had made the report.

Joe was astounded. This was the first he'd heard of any missing persons report involving his father. He denied having filed it. Elisa berated him some more, and told Joe that Larry had run off to a cult in Costa Rica. Everything was in a huge mess and it was all his father's fault, Elisa told Joe. "That's when I knew for sure she was lying," Joe said later. After finishing with Elisa, Joe called the sheriff's department and made his own missing persons report. Just why the Sacramento Sheriff's Department hadn't yet bothered to talk to Joe McNabney is something of a mystery, however.

After this, things became rather murky. Greg Whalen was later to say that while he'd seen Elisa from a distance at Scottsdale, he had no conversation with her. But others said that Elisa had actually been with Greg and another man when she received a call on her cellular phone. At that point, these witnesses said, Elisa appeared to become nervous about something, and soon excused herself.

That same night, Bob Kail called Greg Whalen in Scottsdale. The Sacramento cops had come to the ranch, looking for Elisa, Bob told his father-in-law. They wanted to know where Elisa's trailer was, and Bob had told them. They intended to impound it, Bob told Greg, as part of their investigation into whatever had happened to Larry McNabney.

Then, when Greg and a friend looked for Elisa, they discovered that she had checked into the motel under a name that neither of them had ever heard of—Elizabeth Barasch. But whoever Elisa was, she had vanished.

Laren Renee Sims Jordan Barasch Redelsperger McNabney was on the run once more—and thinking of coming up with yet another new name.

After police just missed Elisa before she went to Arizona, authorities in Sacramento had a number of suspicious circumstances, but very little else to work from—especially since Elisa and her daughter had simply seemed to disappear from Scottsdale.

There was a missing persons case involving Larry—no one had seen him since the afternoon of September 10, it appeared. They had what appeared to be a series of possibly fraudulent actions at the law firm, if the Carters, their newest lawyer, and Ginger Miller could be believed. They had a fraud suspect, Elisa, who seemed to have no legitimate history prior to meeting Larry in Las Vegas in 1995—no real name, no driver's license, no true Social Security number, no indication of any family, other than Larry, and he, of course, was missing.

In fact, the situation had all the earmarks of some sort of bust-out embezzlement scam, except for the fact that the scammer, Elisa, had been married to the scammee, Larry, for almost six years. That last was unusual, to say the least. For the somewhat disorganized Sacramento Police Department, there were therefore two possible sources of information: Greg Whalen and Sarah Dutra.

Sarah herself called the Sacramento County Sheriff's Department on January 15, saying she'd heard that a missing persons report had been turned in on Larry. Sarah said she wanted to come in and tell detectives what she knew about the disappearances of both Larry and Elisa. Among other things, Sarah said, she was worried about the Jaguar that had been leased in her name. What if Elisa had stolen it, or had gotten into an accident with it? She would be financially responsible, Sarah said. So she wanted to know where Elisa was.

This would represent Sarah's first version of the events surrounding Larry McNabney's death. Eventually there would be five more, and each time Sarah would add new details she hadn't revealed previously. But as a detective observed later, it was like pulling teeth.

Whether because of some mix-up or because the Sacramento Sheriff's Department was badly organized, Sarah was not directed to Detective Hill for this first interview, although it was Hill who could have most profitably questioned her at that point. Judging from Detective Maryl Lee Cranford's interview, no one in her department had briefed her about the McNabneys, or even the fact that the McNabneys' trailer had been impounded five days earlier. In fact, it appears that everything Sarah had to say was news to Cranford.

What this seems to show is that the Sacramento County Sheriff's Department had a significant internal communication problem, because while Hill had been looking for Larry, and the Carters had been complaining about being defrauded by Larry's firm, and deputies had been to the Whalen Ranch, and still other deputies had impounded the trailer, Cranford, in interviewing Sarah, appeared to know nothing about any of these events. Nevertheless, Cranford was an excellent detective, and it didn't take her very long at all to sniff out that something was out of whack with Sarah's story.

Cranford began by asking if Elisa still had the Jaguar, and Sarah said as far as she knew, she did.

"She told me after Larry left her and she and Larry were getting a divorce," Sarah said, "she asked if she could put the car in my name to protect herself from him taking it. And also, she didn't have any ID when we were at the dealer, so she said, 'Can I put it in your name? You can drive it some-times.' And I said, 'Okay.' I was stupid . . .'"

"When did Larry leave her?" Cranford asked.

"You know," said Sarah, "the last time I saw Larry was down at the horse show in Los Angeles."

And with this, Sarah embarked on the first of what would turn out to be a series of lies that would eventually entrap her in a nightmarish web of her own making.

When a person is subjected to questioning by police in con-nection with a crime, especially when it is a crime that he or she knows something about, there are really only two choices available: either clam up and ask for a lawyer, or tell the truth—the whole truth. Lying is simply not a viable option, because the police are certain to find out. There are just too many cops, and they have the time and means to verify or expose every single statement, no matter how small. This is particularly true when it comes to murder cases—exactly the sort of crimes detectives are most determined to solve.

True, Cranford at that point had no evidence that Larry was dead. But the interview was being recorded, and Sarah, with every word, was locking herself deeper into a story that would have to stand up—especially if Larry ever turned up . . . dead, that is. Just why Sarah offered herself up for this interview at all is somewhat curious. It may have been that she'd heard that Ginger Miller had reported Larry missing, and she wanted to convince the police that she was in the same boat as Ginger—innocent workers at an ethically wob-bly law firm. But based on what Sarah really knew at the time, it would have been far better for her to have consulted an attorney before volunteering any information. Later, in fact, the lawyer who eventually would represent Sarah when she was charged with murder, Kevin Clymo, acknowledged that had he been involved in the case from the beginning, there was an excellent chance that a plea for a far lesser

crime than homicide might have been negotiated with the
authorities.

But Sarah didn't have Clymo's experience with the criminal justice system, or even Elisa's for that matter. It appears
that Sarah thought she could answer a few routine questions, and that the police would then direct their attention
elsewhere. After all, what was Sarah?—a 21-year-old art
student, seemingly naive, or at least not very worldly. That
was the impression that she sought to give to Cranford, and
later, to others, including her jury.

Cranford may not have known much of the background
of the case, but she knew enough to want to pin down Sarah's
version of the circumstances of Larry's disappearance.
Sarah meanwhile wanted to give the impression that she
had no real information to offer. She said Elisa had told her,
when she returned to the horse show on the night of September 10, that Larry had left to join a cult. Or maybe, said
Sarah, Larry was hiding from drug dealers. "She had some
suspicions like maybe drugs, people were after him for drug
money," Sarah said. "I mean, she was trying to think of
everything, where could he be?"

"How did she know they were getting divorced," Cranford asked, "if he'd just 'disappeared'?"

Sarah didn't have a useful answer for that one. "Yeah,"
she said. "Yeah."

Cranford asked Sarah if she'd ever seen any divorce
documents.

"No," said Sarah.

Cranford pressed for more details about the supposed
divorce—the property settlement, for example. "She
didn't . . . She didn't tell me," Sarah said.

"But she didn't want to have a car in her name because
she thought he would take that?" Cranford's skepticism was
obvious.

"Yeah."

"Was she the major money-maker in the relationship?"

"Probably," Sarah said. "She did—did a lot of the work, settled all his cases, that kind of thing, dealt with all the adjustors."

"Was she an attorney?"

"No."

Cranford returned to the horse show. "Do you know how Larry and Elisa got down there?"

"I think they drove down."

"Okay, do you know what they drove?"

"Uh, a dually."

"Okay. And how did Elisa get back if Larry left her down there?"

"Uh, Larry didn't take the dually."

"So he left on foot?"

Sarah didn't say anything.

"Somewhere, where he didn't live?" Cranford prompted. Cranford's doubts about this were apparent.

By this point, Sarah was doubtless regretting her decision to call the police at all. Cranford had asked obvious questions that she should be able to answer, but couldn't.

"I don't know," Sarah finally said. "I mean, I didn't really ask her how he left."

"So you haven't seen him since?"

"No," Sarah said. "Huh-uh."

Cranford said that if there really was a divorce, there ought to be a lawyer around who knew where Larry was, or how to get in touch with him. Sarah said she didn't have any information about that. Cranford asked about the dually.

"The dually was sold."

"Okay. Do you know who she sold that to?"

"No. Or Larry might have sold it, I don't know," Sarah said, although she'd been there when the Van Vliets gave Elisa the check for $27,000.

Sarah said that Elisa had paid for two years of the Jaguar lease with a check for $30,000.

"I'm trying to figure out how she thought she could hide

that," Cranford said, "if she writes a check to Jaguar for thirty thousand dollars."

Sarah went into dumb blond mode: "I don't know," she said. "She was just . . . She was trying to say, so he couldn't take it, so he couldn't sell it, 'cause, you know, for the drugs and all that. And, I mean, I really didn't think much at the time, and I was stupid. She told me I'd get to drive a brand new Jaguar sometimes and I said, 'Sure,' you know? I mean . . ." Sarah gestured at Cranford as if to say, Hey, I'm just a kid . . . Wouldn't *You* want to drive a Jaguar from time to time?

"Did you ever get to drive it?" Cranford asked.

"Yeah. I got to drive it on Thanksgiving."

"That was it?"

Cranford wanted to know what else Elisa had obtained in Sarah's name. Sarah wasn't sure how to answer this one. She didn't want to go into the credit card area, for some reason.

"That's the only thing I can think of," Sarah said, meaning the Jag.

"You sure no credit cards?" Cranford asked. Cranford already smelled some sort of fraud in the wind, even without the details.

Sarah backed off almost at once. She said she was waiting to get a credit report "to see how many credit cards I have, in my name."

"Do you have a feeling there are more?"

"I suspect there might be some," Sarah admitted.

"Why do you suspect that?"

"Well, because Greg Whalen . . . he's uh . . . a friend of mine, too, and he said that they found a credit card with his name on it. So that's why I'm starting to think, oh man . . . I'm just keeping my fingers crossed."

"When was the last time you saw Elisa?"

Sarah said she thought she'd last seen Elisa on Tuesday night, January 8. "She was going to Arizona to the horse show," Sarah said. "I was going to fly down to meet her on Friday."

"This past Friday?"

"I was going to fly down there," Sarah repeated, "and she'd told me that my ticket was ready at the airport. And when I got there it was just on reserve [not paid for] and so I tried to reach her on her cell phone, but the number's disconnected."

Sarah didn't tell Cranford that she'd called repeatedly throughout the afternoon until the battery on the cell phone ran out, or that she then and there began to suspect that Elisa had left her to take the blame for everything.

Cranford said it sounded as though Sarah had talked to Whalen about Elisa.

She had, Sarah confirmed.

"He saw her at the horse show. I mean, he saw her there and then I guess . . . I guess she left. I mean, he said that she was talking to someone on the phone and she looked real worried and then she left."

After some additional discussion about people at the horse shows, including the Washington State trainer Elisa was supposed to have had an affair with, Sarah was asked if she thought Elisa was ever coming back.

"I don't know," Sarah said. "I hope she is."

"Are you worried that she's not?"

"Yeah."

"Do you think something happened to her? [Or] do you think she just left?"

"I don't . . . I mean, I have so many things going through my head, like what if she got into an accident or something? . . . I don't know . . . Maybe she went to . . . she was in an accident or is in hiding or . . . I don't know . . . I couldn't even tell you where she would be hiding. I was wracking my brain thinking of places, but . . ."

This is probably an indication of Sarah's own true

objective in calling the sheriff's department, and volunteering for the interview. What she really wanted was to find out whether the sheriff's department had caught Elisa, or if they were even looking for her, and if an arrested Elisa was saying anything about Sarah. Sometimes, waiting for bad news can drive a guilty person crazy and make them take risks, like volunteering for an interview. At the same time, Sarah hoped to convince the detectives that she had no idea where Elisa might be, to turn their attention away from her. But her use of the word "hiding" is significant.

"Why would she be hiding and where?" Cranford asked.

"I . . ." Sarah stopped herself and restarted. Cranford's question seemed to suggest that the sheriff's department had no information that could be damaging—if they hadn't, why would they ask why Elisa would be hiding? But now she had to suggest some plausible and innocent reason for Elisa to be hiding.

"Maybe from Larry," Sarah said. "That's the only person I can think of. You know, maybe Larry's after her, and she's running from him . . ."

"Okay," Cranford said. "Sarah?"

"Uh-huh?"

"Are you leaving some stuff out?"

"No."

"I'm trying to understand," Cranford said, "because it seems like there's some big old missing pieces in here. I don't understand why you're so worried that she left."

Sarah tried to explain why she was worried, but wasn't able to find any words that convinced Cranford that there was any reason to believe that Elisa might be in danger.

"Did she say that he had ever harmed her?"

"Yes," Sarah said. "He's been abusive to her."

"Have you ever seen that?"

"No."

"Have you ever seen any bruises or anything on her?"

"No, I haven't."

Pressed for examples of Larry abusing Elisa, Sarah could only quote Elisa. She said Elisa had told her that Larry'd threatened to kill Haylei, then Elisa.

"So she was . . . you think she was somewhat afraid of him, of what he might do to her?"

"Yeah," said Sarah. "And I think that's why she didn't want to tell me everything, because she didn't want Larry to come after me, you know what I mean?" Like someone who was worried about being buried alive, Sarah saw the daylight and ran for it . . . The reason she didn't know answers that should have been obvious was that Elisa was trying to protect her!

A second detective who had been sitting in on the interview—apparently someone who might have been at least slightly familiar with the Carters' complaint about the law firm—now began to ask some pointed questions about the way the firm was run. But after Sarah admitted that Elisa had obtained a Bank of America credit card in her name—apparently "the company credit card," as Sarah would refer to it later—the rest of the questions and answers were lost to posterity: the department's tape recorder for some reason shut off, and Sarah's first attempt to answer questions about the firm's financial fiddling went unrecorded.

Greg Whalen, meanwhile, was probably just as glad that Elisa had disappeared. A week before he'd seen the last of Elisa and Haylei in Scottsdale, around January 2 or so, Greg had been out in his breeding barn when the telephone rang. It was Mary, Greg's wife.

"You got both your credit cards?" Mary asked.

Greg checked his wallet and found that both were present and accounted for.

Mary told him that she'd just had a call from one of the credit card companies. Elisa had tried to get a $10,000 advance on a third credit card that was in Greg Whalen's name. Not only that, but someone had used it to buy a one-way

airline ticket from Salt Lake City, as well as a $150 pharma-
ceutical prescription—for Viagra of all things. Greg hustled
into the house and called the credit card company back and
got all the charges voided on grounds of fraud.

Over the next two weeks, the Sacramento detectives assembled some more facts about the disappearing McNabneys, their bilious law practice, and their most recent activities. By this point, Joe and Tavia were convinced something was seriously wrong. They had contacted various people in the news media to drum up public attention to Larry's disappearance, and had hired a private detective, a retired FBI agent, to see if he could locate either Larry or Elisa. By the time the story made the news, the Sacramento Sheriff's Department had moved the McNabney mystery to the department's homicide unit for investigation.

In a story published on January 24, 2002, *The Sacramento Bee* reported that the sheriff's department was "looking for a local attorney who was last seen in September and is considered a missing person at risk.

"Friends last saw Laurence William McNabney, 53, at a horse show Sept. 10 in the Los Angeles County City of Industry," the paper reported. "A horse enthusiast, he frequented horse shows and rodeos across the state. Since his disappearance, detectives have tried to contact his wife, Elisa McNabney, with no success . . ."

The following week, Sarah was invited in for a second interview, this one with homicide detective Lori Timberlake and Sergeant Mikhaela Links. Apparently for moral support, Sarah brought her dog, Ralphie, the Maltese terrier. Ralphie would accompany Sarah to several of her subsequent interviews. The dog seemed to have an unusual psychic affinity for Sarah's tension—every time the questioning got too close for comfort, Ralphie would set off a racket or otherwise create a disturbance that had the effect of drawing attention away from Sarah.

For this second interview, Timberlake and Links were mostly interested in establishing as many facts as they could, in a case that seemed to be gaining public attention—and therefore, pressure. They were, at least initially, quite sympathetic to Sarah.

After she described her work at the McNabney law firm, and a bit of her own background, Sarah was asked what happened at the horse show when Larry disappeared. Sarah told of returning to Sacramento on September 9, and said she'd flown back the next night.

"Okay," Timberlake asked. "And did you stay with them [Larry and Elisa] again? In that room?"

"Yes . . . Yes, I did," Sarah said.

"Okay. How long were you there then?"

"I was there for maybe two days and then the September eleventh thing happened, and I was, like, not going to be flying anywhere. So I was like, 'Elisa, you're driving me back,' so she drove me back up."

"Okay. So did she drive you up on September eleventh or the next day?"

"I think it was . . . It might have been September eleventh she drove back, or the day after. I'm not sure."

"So she drove you . . . What car did you take?"

"The dually."

"So she drove you all the way back to Sacramento on either the eleventh or twelfth?"

"Uh-huh."

"And dropped you off? And where did she go from there?"

"She went back down to L.A."

"What did Larry do for a car, since she had the truck while he was down in L.A., and she was up here taking you home?"

"Uh . . ." Sarah said.

"Would he have needed a car?"

"I don't think so," Sarah said. "I don't think so."

"So Larry stayed down at this horse show?"

"Correct," said Sarah.

"Did you talk to Larry any time after that? After she brought you home? When was the next time you saw or talked to Larry?"

Sarah said she hadn't seen or talked to Larry after that.

When she returned on September 14 after wrecking the Saab the day before, Sarah continued, Greg and Elisa picked her up at the airport. Elisa took her to a different hotel.

"And that's when I . . . asked her, I was like, 'Where's Larry?' and she's like, 'Oh, he's off doing his own thing,' you know, because I guess he had, she told me later he would have a lot of prostitutes and stuff."

At this point, on January 31, 2002, the date of this interview, Timberlake and Links had no way of knowing that Sarah was lying to beat the band—that in fact, Larry had been with them in the dually all the way back to Lodi, and that Sarah had seen and talked with Larry that day, and even worse. But with these lies, Sarah was on the record, which later helped demolish her credibility when a jury had to decide her fate.

Sarah went on to say that Elisa told her that Larry had gone off on "a runner."

"Yeah," said Sarah, "a runner." She'd asked Elisa what she meant by a runner, Sarah said, and Elisa told her it meant that Larry was off somewhere on a drug binge. To illustrate Larry's drug propensities, Sarah told the "Blanche . . . Blanche . . . Blanche" story of Larry tapping her on the back as she awoke.

Sarah was asked if she'd observed any problems between Larry and Elisa before Larry disappeared. Sarah said that she'd overheard Larry tell Elisa to get out of their room.

Ralphie chose that moment to puke.

After appropriate comments of sympathy for the dog from the two detectives, Sarah continued that Elisa had claimed that Larry had beaten her before, and brought up the phone-in-the-face story. Ralphie threw up again. Even the detectives noticed that the dog seemed stressed out, apparently catching Sarah's anxiety.

"Uh, I lost my train of thought," Timberlake said. "Okay, so then the last time you're back there, Larry's not there, she tells you he kind of went and did his own thing . . . What happened to the truck, the red truck?"

Sarah said Elisa had sold it. Afterward, she said, she'd followed Greg and Elisa back to Sacramento in the rented green Mustang. Elisa paid for it in cash, Sarah added.

Timberlake said it sounded like Larry and Elisa had been very generous with Sarah.

"It was like . . . kind of like they were almost a second mom and dad to me," Sarah said.

Sarah said Elisa told her that Larry had taken all of her ID.

"She never had an ID?" Timberlake asked.

"Is that her real name?" Sarah asked. "McNabney or Jordan?"

"We're not sure," Timberlake said.

Sarah described some of the events in the office in October and November, and said that Elisa was the one who always got the mail, that it was Elisa who would tell clients that she was Sarah or Tessa.

"Okay," said Timberlake, "was there ever a time when you thought maybe Elisa was not being one hundred percent honest with you?"

"You know what?" Sarah said. "I must be really naive because . . . I believe everyone. I never had a reason not to believe her. I mean, she's always nice to me, her and Larry both were nice to me."

"Okay, did you think it was weird that she sold Larry's truck?"

"I thought it was her truck," Sarah said.

Sarah described the trip to the Jaguar dealer when the XK8 convertible was leased in October. She said Elisa asked if she minded if it was put into Sarah's name. She said Elisa told her that she and Larry were getting divorced.

"Was this the first time she'd ever mentioned divorce?"

"No, she had mentioned divorce . . . down at the horse show in L.A. She said that she was served with divorce papers."

"So she told you—?"

"No, no, no, no," Sarah said. "It was after L.A. that she was served with divorce papers."

Timberlake asked if Sarah had ever asked Elisa if Larry was coming home. Sarah said Elisa had told her that Larry called from time to time to curse at her and hang up.

Then, said Sarah, she formed the impression that Larry had come back to see Elisa.

"What made you think that?"

"Because she told me," Sarah said. "She just said that Larry had come back to the house, and I was like, 'Oh, he's back now?' And she says, 'No, but he left again.'"

"Did you ever see Larry at the house?"

Sarah said she hadn't. "I haven't seen Larry since down in L.A. That was the last time I saw him."

"Okay, when was the last time you talked to Elisa?"

"It was on a Wednesday," Sarah said, referring to January 9, "and she was leaving to Arizona and I was going to fly down the next day. She told me, 'Your ticket's paid for,' and all that. So I went to the airport and they said, 'Your ticket is only on reserve.' And I thought maybe she forgot to pay for it. So I went to call her and . . . it was no longer a number. And I was like, 'God, that's weird . . . Maybe she didn't have money to pay for the phone . . .'"

Sarah said she'd called the office number and then the number to Elisa's cell phone, and both had been disconnected.

A lot of her own clothes had been put into the trailer, Sarah said. She didn't know what to think about the numbers being disconnected. Since the trailer had been seized, Sarah had been unable to get to her clothes for nearly three weeks. She went back to the day at the airport, when Elisa had left her holding the bag.

"I'm sitting there at the airport," Sarah continued. "And I stayed there until noon because I just kept trying the numbers, trying the numbers, trying to tell her my ticket . . . And then I just went home and I got my friend's cell phone and called Greg." When she couldn't reach Greg, Sarah said, she'd called Mary Whalen and asked her where Greg was staying in Scottsdale.

"So then I finally got hold of Greg," Sarah said, "and he said Elisa left. I said, 'What do you mean, Elisa left?' And he said that she was getting some phone calls. And she was, you know, looking worried, or something."

Greg told her, Sarah said, that after the phone calls he and several others went to Elisa's hotel room to pick her up for dinner ". . . I don't know why they went there . . . he said that she was gone. Greg told me that she checked in under a fake name."

"How did he know it was fake?"

"Because he went to pay the hotel bill," Sarah said. "And he was trying to figure out, you know, Elisa McNabney, Elisa Jordan, and they're like, 'We don't have anyone staying here' . . . and he's like, 'Well, they're in this room.' And they're like, 'That room is under this name.' And I don't remember what last name. It was something way off the wall. Something I never would have even guessed."

Sarah said it made her sad to think that Elisa had left her

on the hook for the Jaguar payments, and possibly other bills.

"She has screwed you, basically," Timberlake said. "You're not the only one, if it makes you feel any better. Okay, I think she took advantage of your friendship with her, as she did others.' We are obviously concerned about Larry. His son is very concerned about him."

Even though Elisa was probably on the run after having scammed a lot of people, Timberlake said, "I couldn't care less about that. That's not my job. My concern is to find Larry. And we were hoping that Elisa could help us with that."

"Yeah," Sarah said.

Timberlake asked Sarah what kind of people Larry and Elisa were. "I mean," she said, "were they normal kind of people?"

"Yes and no," Sarah said. "I mean, Larry . . . [seemed] weird to [me] . . . Kind of, 'Oh, Blanche?' You know?"

"Who's Blanche?"

"Is that what he called her?" Links asked.

"They called each other 'Blanche,' " Sarah said.

The interview lasted for another forty minutes or so, with Sarah speculating that Larry had joined a cult, or was off on one of his infamous "runners." Timberlake and Links only nodded. It was clear that neither detective thought Larry had joined any cult, no matter where it was, or even that he was off on some sort of binge. It had simply been too long since anyone had seen him.

"Okay," Timberlake said, as the interview was nearing an end. "Do you think Elisa hurt Larry? That she killed him?"

"I don't think so," Sarah said. "You know, I hope she wouldn't do that."

Sarah gave the detectives some additional information

on what she knew of Elisa's background—that Haylei's father was supposed to be a Colombian, involved in growing coffee . . . that Haylei had been born in Florida . . . that Elisa's mother was somewhere in Florida . . . that Elisa and her mother didn't get along with each other . . . that she had several brothers and sisters, "including a brother named Loren . . ."

As the interview was concluding, Links said that until then, she had been very suspicious of Sarah.

"I have to tell you right up front," Links said, "that until I met you today I pretty much figured you were in on just about everything she's doing, because it's hard for me to believe that you can be this close to this woman and not know what she's into."

Sarah sighed. "I'm . . . starting to think I don't know her at all, either, you know . . . I mean, Greg told me that some detective told him that she has five aliases."

"We're not sure who she is yet," Timberlake said.

"I'm kind of believing your story," Links added, "because you look like you're really kind of surprised at what's going on."

The detectives advised Sarah to send certified letters to Elisa at the Woodbridge house and the leasing company, demanding that Elisa return the Jaguar. Sarah should also report any fraudulent credit card activity involving unauthorized use of her name. That way she could avoid any trouble later, they said.

"This gal is on the lam," Links told Sarah. "Okay? She's running. She's hiding. For whatever reason. Either something's happened to Larry . . . or Larry is on his own. I have a real hard time believing that Larry is gone on his own because he has cut off all ties with everyone since September tenth. Do you know that's the last time anyone has seen him, September tenth? That's a long time to be missing . . . Something's wrong."

Five days later, Links would find out just how wrong

things really were, when Larry finally resurfaced, in a vineyard almost eight miles due south of Whalen's ranch, down
a lonely road some twelve miles southeast of the Woodbridge house, now left silent and vacant after Elisa's own
mysterious disappearance the month before.

Scheffel

By the late afternoon of February 5, 2002, San Joaquin County Sheriff's Homicide Detective Deborah Scheffel decided to button things up for the day. The light was fading fast, and Scheffel didn't want to overlook anything in the gloom. The body would keep—it had been there for some time and wasn't going anywhere. Not now.

The call had come in around 4 in the afternoon. A dog belonging to several farm workers had "keyed in on" something in a low swale of the vineyard they were working in, according to the San Joaquin County Coroner's Office's later report. The three farm workers looked to see what their dog was so excited about, and discovered a human leg bone sticking out of the ground. All the flesh had been gnawed off by insects and small animals.

The farm workers returned to their houses, not far away, and called the vineyard's owner, who in turn called the sheriff's department. As it happened, it was Detective Scheffel's turn to be up on the homicide rotation, so she went out to the scene in the late afternoon.

Scheffel at first suspected that she knew whose body it might have been. She had just finished testifying in a rather complicated serial murder case involving two killers who sometimes acted together, sometimes separately. Police had been unable to locate all the victims of the disgusting pair, and Scheffel guessed this was probably another one of those lost victims. She hoped so, for the sake of the families whose loved ones had still not been accounted for.

But when she arrived at the scene in the vineyard off Frazier Road near Clements Road, northeast of Lodi, she realized that the victim had been far too recently buried to be one of the serial killers' victims. Those people had been missing for several years, and this body hadn't been in the ground for more than a few weeks.

In order not to lose any valuable information while recovering the body, Scheffel decided to wait for better light the following day.

By the next morning, Scheffel had rounded up several experts—a pathologist, Dr. Terri Haddix; a forensic anthropologist, Dr. Roger LaJeunesse; and a criminalist from the state department of justice—to remove the body from the ground. The work began when the forensic anthropologist strung up grid lines around the grave site, exactly as if he were excavating an ancient burial mound. As dirt was removed, first by shovels, then trowels and eventually a small butter knife, it was put into buckets. The buckets were taken to a screen mesh to be sifted for any potential trace evidence, such as hairs and fibers, or other small items that might otherwise be overlooked. A pair of rusty scissors with red handles was found near the grave, along with a beverage bottle produced in Mexico.

Within a short time, much of the body was uncovered, and Scheffel realized that the victim had been a man of middle age, rather large, and clad only in boxer shorts and part of a tee-shirt, which appeared to have been cut, possibly by the red-handled scissors. The man had a distinctive tattoo on his upper arm. What was strange was that the dead man seemed to be lying on his back, in a near-fetal position—that is, his knees were drawn up toward his chest, arms crossed, and his head was bent forward.

Scheffel began to consider the possible identity of the victim. One that popped into her mind almost immediately was the missing Sacramento lawyer, Larry McNabney, whose case was then receiving substantial publicity and air time in central California.

Dr. LaJeunesse, the forensic anthropologist, did the

majority of the excavation. He soon formed the opinion, based on the relative lack of decomposition, that the body had not been buried for very long. He asked if the detectives were looking for someone.

"And they said, 'We have an attorney that we are looking for, but he's been missing since September,'" LaJeunesse said later. "And I said, 'Well, from this grave, I don't think that would be the individual, because this body has not decomposed to that extent,' which I would have expected had that individual been buried in September."

Apart from the relatively intact condition of the body, LaJeunesse pointed to the yellowed grass that had been unearthed from the grave. The grass had probably grown in December, he said, and when the body was buried, the grass was buried with it.

At length, the exhumation was completed, and the body was taken to the San Joaquin County forensic pathology facility—the morgue—south of Stockton in French Camp, to await an autopsy by Dr. Haddix.

That began the next morning, February 7. Dr. Haddix was immediately struck by the absence of any obvious fatal injuries to the body—no gunshot wounds, no stabbing, no clear evidence of blunt trauma. Like LaJeunesse, Haddix was convinced that the remains had been buried relatively recently. In fact, some of the blood in the body was still in a liquid state. Probably the only overt sign of injury Haddix noticed was a surface hemorrhage in the muscles of the upper back area. But that was it—no broken bones, no internal injuries.

Meanwhile, Jose Ruiz, an evidence technician for the sheriff's department, took fingerprints of the corpse. Within a short time, Ruiz had matched the prints of the dead man to a set of fingerprints given to him by Scheffel.

The dead man was Larry.

But how could it be Larry? Larry McNabney was supposed to have disappeared in early September, and this body had only been buried for a little over a month. If the body was Larry—and the fingerprints proved that—where had he been all that time? And more to the point, how had he wound up in the vineyard, when he'd last been seen in southern California?

Haddix, LaJeunesse and Scheffel discussed the matter, trying out the possibilities. If Larry had died in early September, Haddix was convinced, there was no way that he had been in the vineyard grave since that time—the body was too well preserved.

Preserved—that started people thinking. Had the body been frozen? No, Haddix said—otherwise there would be evidence of tissue damage from the freezing process. Well, what about a refrigerator?

That would do the trick, Haddix said—assuming that one could find a refrigerator large enough to contain a six-foot, two-hundred-pound man. They recalled the way the body had come out of the ground, folded up—as if he had been compacted. It fit. So did the hemorrhage across the upper back, which might have come from the interior surface of a refrigerator as the body was crammed inside.

That raised another possibility: had Larry been *alive* when he was put into a refrigerator? The hemorrhage suggested that it was possible, since bleeding generally stops once the heart stops. That meant it was possible that Larry had actually suffocated to death. But if that had happened, Larry had been so near to dying, no other evidence of suffocation was apparent.

How would a previously healthy 53-year-old man get into a refrigerator to die? The obvious answer was, after some sort of poisoning that left him either dead or too weak to resist. Haddix took samples of organ tissues, the hair, blood, stomach contents, and portions of the brain, along with the shorts, tee-shirt, and mud that had adhered to the body, and sent them all out for testing. There was an explanation for what had happened to Larry McNabney, and Haddix was determined to find it.

The same day as the autopsy, Sarah was again being interviewed by the Sacramento Sheriff's Department. She called Lori Timberlake and told her that she'd just remembered something from the events of September 11. Timberlake invited her to come in and share it; she did not tell Sarah that Larry's body had been found. But by the time this interview took place, an investigator from the San Joaquin County Sheriff's Department, Robert Buchwalter, had arrived in Sacramento. Buchwalter had been to the vineyard and had observed the autopsy. Now he had some pointed questions for Sarah.

Timberlake introduced Buchwalter, and told Sarah that San Joaquin County was going to take over the investigation.

Before Sarah could say anything to this, Buchwalter asked her: "Do you know why?"

Sarah said she had no idea.

Timberlake told Sarah there were some "inconsistencies" from the previous interview that needed to be cleared up.

"Oh," Sarah said.

"Regarding . . . mainly regarding Larry's disappearance," Timberlake said.

"Uh-huh."

Buchwalter wanted to go back farther than that, however. He wanted Sarah to tell once more how she had come to work for the McNabneys. Sarah gave the basic background information all over again.

"Anything else?" Sarah asked. "I'm trying to think of what else you—" She acted as though she wanted to leave immediately.

"We're just getting started," Buchwalter told her, ominously. "We haven't even gotten to the good stuff yet."

Buchwalter made Sarah discuss her work for the law firm. Sarah said that while she was working part-time and going to school, she had a salary of $3,000 a month, along with the use of two cars, the BMW and the Saab. It was clear to Sarah that Buchwalter thought the terms of her employment were highly unusual for an inexperienced 21-year-old art student. Eventually they came to the mystery weekend in the City of Industry. Once again, Sarah said she'd driven back to Sacramento on September 9, and returned by air on September 10.

"And that was when Larry was like . . . I had told you about . . . first time I drove down, he was acting really strange, like from the first time I got there, acting kind of crazy, you know . . ."

"Okay," Buchwalter said, "you're describing strange . . . I don't know what strange is to you."

Sarah said that weekend was the first time that Elisa had told her about Larry's drug use.

"She said, 'Larry uses drugs,' and I'm like, 'Okay, well, what does he do?'" Sarah said. "And she was like, 'Well, he does cocaine . . . I mean, he does 'em when he has 'em, like sometimes he'll really do a lot of drugs . . .' She told me that, like up in Reno he won a big case, and he left for, I don't know, a couple of weeks. And with that money he went and bought like crank [methamphetamine] and stuff and did a whole bunch of drugs, like over a period of a month. And she didn't know where he was until she hired a private investigator to find him."

Buchwalter said he didn't understand where all the money was coming from if Larry was busy doing drugs day and night for weeks and months at a time.

Sarah said she was being paid out of different smaller settlements that kept coming in while Larry was missing. Buchwalter turned back to the events of Larry's disappearance.

"And she flew you back down on the tenth?" Buchwalter asked.

"Right. And she said that Larry was in and out. And I'm like, 'What do you mean he's in and out?' She was saying, 'Well, he's leaving and he's coming back.' I'm like, 'Well, what's the matter?' She was like, 'I don't know, Sarah, he's freaking out on me.'

"And I'm like, 'Okay, he's freaking out.' And she was like, 'You know, the drugs.'"

"Uh-huh," Buchwalter said.

"And so I didn't actually stay in the room that night," Sarah said. "I was like in the car pretty much all night long . . ."

"The car?"

"Her . . . her truck."

"*Her* truck?" Buchwalter asked. He knew that the truck had been registered in Larry's name as the owner.

"Uh-huh," Sarah agreed. "But she was like afraid for me to go in there [the hotel room]. You know what I mean?"

The next morning, Sarah continued, she asked Elisa where Larry was.

"She said, 'He's gone,' You know, this was early in the morning, and she said, 'He's gone.' I'm like, 'Okay, well, is he coming back?' And she said, 'I don't know if he's coming back.'"

She went to the horse show, Sarah said, and then Elisa came to her there.

"And she said, 'Larry's back in the room and he's acting crazy.' And I said, 'Well, what do you mean by acting crazy?' And she's like, 'He's all over the room and he's running around and making a mess of everything and kind of being crazy,' you know what I mean? And Morgan, I think, she had Morgan in the room and . . ."

"Morgan?" Buchwalter asked.

"Her dog. And he was saying how he was going to throw Morgan off the balcony, kept joking, 'I'm gonna throw Morgan off the balcony.' I mean, Larry's just— And I said, 'What's wrong with him?' And she said, 'Drugs, Sarah, drugs, drinking, all that crap, and it's just messing him up.' And so she said, 'We're gonna go check into a different hotel, because he's embarrassing me and all my friends are here and Morgan's barking all the time and we're gonna get kicked out of this hotel room 'cause it's a nice hotel.' And so . . .'"

Now Sarah made the second significant adjustment to her story from the earlier interviews. Where she had told Cranford on Janaury 15, and Timberlake on January 31, that she hadn't seen Larry at all after returning from Sacramento on the night of September 10, she was now about to admit that she had, too, seen him, and even talked with him.

"I guess he was in the room and was . . . She said he was falling all over the place, and so she said, 'I want to get him out of this hotel room, he's embarrassing me . . .' Larry always kind of embarrassed her by being drunk and stuff in public, she hated that, just hated that. So she said, 'I want to get him out of here,' and I'm like, 'I don't really want to help you if he's acting crazy.'

"And so she said, 'I'm going to go get a wheelchair and help him out, because he really can't walk.' And I said, 'Okay.'"

They went to a medical equipment rental place not far from the hotel, Sarah said, and rented a wheelchair.

"Well, she found the place," Sarah continued, "and she had my ID, and so they said, 'They need you to sign something,' so I went in and signed something and put the wheelchair in the back of the truck and we drove back to the hotel. And we went up to the room and I told her, 'I'm not going to go in there,' you know, 'if he's acting insane I'll get help for you,' in case he tries hurting her or something. And so she went in there and put him in the wheelchair and she pushed him out, and I helped her push him out to the truck, and as we were walking through the lobby he, like, started swinging his hands around and stuff like that. And I'm like, 'Oh my God, Elisa, he's insane!' She's like, 'Oh my God, just help me get him in the truck.' So I helped her get him into the truck. And in the truck he started like, you know, saying, 'I'm gonna kill you, Elisa, I'm gonna kill you,' acting, mumbling, 'cause he just reeked of alcohol.

"So I said, 'I'm not gonna be in the car with him. He's crazy.' And so she dropped me off at the corner in front of the horse show and I jumped out." Elisa drove off with Larry in the truck. Sarah said she believed that Elisa had checked Larry into a motel, and then came back to pick her up some minutes later.

"Let me ask you this," Timberlake said. "When you guys were bringing Larry out in the wheelchair, out of the lobby, you said he was flailing his arms around . . ."

"Yeah."

". . . and screaming and yelling?"

Sarah didn't say anything.

"Did he argue with you guys, to get him into the truck? Was he okay with getting into the truck with you guys?"

"Well, yeah. She's like, 'Larry we're gonna go to a different hotel, you're embarrassing, you're embarrassing.' "

Larry "jumped into the back seat," Sarah said.

Buchwalter asked how Elisa had gotten Larry into the wheelchair.

"I didn't go in there," Sarah said. "I didn't go in there."

It seemed that Sarah definitely didn't want to admit that she'd been in the hotel room. "I was standing outside the room," she added. "I wasn't going to go in there because I didn't know how cooperative he was going to be about that. I mean, I'm like, 'Okay, he's acting crazy but he's gonna get in a wheelchair?' So I waited outside. And then, you know, she pushed him out."

After Elisa dropped her off at the horse show and drove

off with Larry, Sarah said, she met an acquaintance at the horse show and talked with him for fifteen or twenty minutes before Elisa returned, this time without Larry.

"She says, 'I put Larry in bed.' And I'm like, 'Okay, is he doing better?' And she's like, 'Yeah, he's okay.' And so then we drove back up [to northern California]. And she's . . . we're talking about other stuff, because . . . it pissed her off to talk about Larry, the way he acted."

Sarah said that Elisa drove her all the way back to Sacramento, where they stopped at the office to pick up the Saab. Then Elisa drove back to Los Angeles, and Sarah drove the Saab to her apartment.

A day or so later, Sarah continued, she was driving the Saab back to the horse show when she wrecked it in the accident. Jason came to pick her up, and the day after that she flew back to Los Angeles, where Elisa and Greg picked her up at the airport.

"So I flew back down there," Sarah said, "and that was when Elisa and Greg were like, 'Larry's gone, Larry's gone.' And I'm like, 'What do you mean, Larry's gone?' And Elisa said, 'Oh my God, I'll have to tell you all about it. Larry, he took off.'"

Sarah now told how Elisa had sold the dually to the Van Vliets.

They had then driven back to Sacramento in the rental car, and Elisa began trying to operate the law office, Sarah said. When she asked if Elisa had heard anything from Larry, Elisa told her that he was probably with the cult or off on "a runner." Elisa told her, Sarah said, that she would get hang-up calls from the office that she guessed were from Larry. She told Sarah that she had been served with divorce papers.

By December, Sarah said, the money began running low at the law office. Elisa had given her a paycheck that bounced, and asked her to get a loan to pay for the new BMW.

"Where's Larry at this whole time?" Buchwalter asked.

"I don't know," Sarah said.

"You know, the hardest part I have with this, Sarah," Timberlake said, "is, there is so much going on in that office that probably wasn't on the up-and-up . . . You had to know. We've gotten information that not only Elisa, but you yourself were practicing signing Larry's name to things."

"Who said that?" Sarah demanded.

"Okay, you know what?" Buchwalter asked. "I think it's a real good time to let you know something. You realize that I do not work for Sacramento County. Okay? I work for San Joaquin County Sheriff's Department."

"Right," Sarah said.

"Larry's dead."

"Oh, my God."

"This isn't a joke anymore. All right? We've known since this whole thing started that you're very close to Elisa, okay? She's flying you all over the place. She's flying you back and forth from overseas. She sells the truck when you're in the middle of this. She's paying you three grand a month. You guys are renting cars you aren't even using, and shelling out all this money. Where's Elisa at?"

"I don't . . ."

"Don't even start. Okay? Let's get something understood. This is not a missing persons investigation any longer. This is a homicide."

"Oh my God."

"Okay? You're in this right up to your eyeballs. Understand that? It's not a game anymore. You're young and it sounds like you got drug [sic] into something and went along for the ride. You're living good. You're flying all over the place. You're running with a rich crowd. You're driving expensive cars. Elisa's dirty, okay? And you're in this up to your eyeballs. I do not believe that you have no idea where Elisa is at. Not as tight as the two of you were and all of a sudden, poof . . ."

Sarah said it was hard to remember things.

"Don't even go there," Buchwalter said. "You're not eighty years old with Alzheimer's. Your memory's not that bad. See, there's a problem here. When people tell lies, it's very difficult to remember what lies you told, and tell the same thing all over again."

There were inconsistencies between Sarah's first, second and now third statements, Buchwalter said.

"Sarah, think about what you're doing," he continued.

"I'm telling you I have not heard from her. I swear to God. I've not heard from her. You know how much I would like to get that car back and get that thing away because I can't pay . . . I mean I would love to find Elisa. I—"

"Get what car back?"

"The Jaguar."

"The Jaguar's the least of your problems," Buchwalter said. "Did you hear what I told you? I'm here because Laurence McNabney was found in a hole. He's dead. All right?"

Sarah insisted that she had no idea where Elisa was. Not even Greg knew where she was, Sarah said, and Greg was her best friend.

"Best friend? Come on, Sarah, let's be honest. It's time to be honest here."

"He was her horse trainer and it was kind of like a father–daughter thing," Sarah said.

"Sarah, Elisa's not the daughter type," Buchwalter said.

Over the weekend after her autopsy, Dr. Haddix began thinking of possible ways Larry might have died. The lack of any overt mechanism for death made a form of poisoning a strong possibility. Moreover, it would have to be a poison that wouldn't be readily apparent at the autopsy, which ruled out the garden-variety killers like strychnine, arsenic and cyanide, all of which would have left tell-tale evidence of their use. When Haddix heard that Larry and Elisa had been involved in the show horse game, and that Elisa had been overheard asking about acepromazine, she assembled a list of veterinary medications that potentially might cause a human being to die—including ketamine, or "Special K"—and forwarded it to the laboratory which had been hired to perform the tests on Larry's blood and tissue samples.

The autopsy took place on Thursday, February 7, just before Sarah was undergoing her third interview in Sacramento, as recounted above. By the first part of the following week Haddix had some information back from the Central Valley Toxicology laboratory: the tests for "Special K" and acepromazine were negative. But there *was* something unusual in the blood sample. "I was told that they believed they had identified xylazine," Haddix said later, "and they were quantifying the result."

Xylazine? What did this mean? Haddix researched the drug and found there was fairly little understanding of how it might affect a human being, as opposed to a 1,500-pound horse. Certainly, the stuff hadn't made it into the illicit drug culture—the number of xylazine poisoning cases reported in the literature could be counted on fingers.

As Haddix read more about xylazine, it was difficult not to be impressed, that is, if one were looking for a chemical that was almost certain to be fatal if left untreated. Widely available in horse circles under various trade names, its use had been almost exclusively restricted to horses and cows, or to catch wild animals with tranquilizer darts. There was virtually no information on the "recreational use" of xylazine—it was simply too deadly to have made it onto the street.

Haddix read that several people—all of them farmers or ranchers or horse people—had attempted to commit suicide with xylazine, and in at least one other case—in Florida, no less—it had been used in a particularly gruesome double murder. The stuff generally came in a liquid form and was most often injected in the animal intramuscularly. One cow that had been treated with a relatively small amount of xylazine was still unresponsive to pain stimuli nine hours after she was injected. The drug also came in a powder form, which meant it could be mixed with another liquid—like wine, or even soup.

A human being who received the drug would ordinarily notice its effects within minutes of ingestion. First would come disorientation, followed by difficulty breathing. Blood pressure would rise and the heartbeat would slow. Body temperature would decrease. If nothing was done to reverse the effects, the person would slip deeper and deeper into unconsciousness, almost as if he had entered into a hypnotic trance that became more and more debilitative. Yet at least at first the person would still have some control over his limbs—something like a person trying to move spasmodically underwater—and retain some limited power of speech, at least at first. But eventually a coma would set in, and then death from circulatory collapse and respiratory depression. At the same time, there was some evidence that the drug caused damage to the heart.

While there wasn't much in the literature to suggest what a person who had been given xylazine might be thinking, it seemed likely that it would feel much the same as a particularly intense, albeit slow-motion dream, that would eventually end as the victim felt like he was drowning.

But the kicker was—it took hours for the drug to kill, and only then when left untreated. If Larry had been given or taken xylazine—and that's what the lab seemed to be saying—his whereabouts in the hours before he died would be critical, at least from the perspective of criminal intent. Had Larry been taken to a hospital within even ten or twelve hours, his life could have been saved.

Which made Sarah's contradictory accounts of what had happened at the horse show potentially significant—almost as significant as the fact that the horse trainer, Greg Whalen, had a "vet kit" loaded with horse drugs, almost certainly including xylazine.

Even as Haddix was learning that the lab had found xylazine in Larry's autopsy samples—the exact amount was still being determined—the San Joaquin County detectives were visiting Greg Whalen's ranch. Whalen had been at a horse show in Los Angeles over the weekend when he first heard that Larry's body had been found. Mary had called him and asked if he knew whether Larry had had any tattoos, saying that the detectives were pretty sure it was Larry's body that had been found in the vineyard south of the ranch. Then, when Whalen returned to his ranch the next week, the detectives wanted to talk to him and to his workers. They wanted to know whether Elisa had given him anything, including, specifically, a refrigerator. Whalen wasn't happy to see the police, and was somewhat less than cooperative. He showed the cops Larry's golf clubs, and said that he intended to hold them for "Joey," Joe McNabney. The police took them, and also his vet bag. But Greg said nothing about the refrigerator that Elisa had given the workers in early January as she was moving from Woodbridge.

Whalen explained later that some of his workers were

"wet," as he put it, and he didn't want to get them into trouble with the immigration authorities. There was no sense in getting everybody into an uproar over Elisa, he thought, especially now that she was gone for good.

Later, however, Greg admitted that he'd been taken in by Elisa.

"She had a way about her," Greg said. "Mary and I both liked her up until we found out what she done. We had always thought she was nice and she was Larry's wife, and, you know, we didn't know what she had done to Larry . . . we were mad at her for the credit card thing, but we were done with her showing out of our barn . . . so, you know, we just let it go."

"So you just sent her on her way down the road to burn someone else, is that right?" Greg was asked.

"Well," said Greg, "that's the way they sent her to us."

"That's the way who sent her to you?"

"State of Florida," said Greg.

Over the next two weeks, Scheffel and Buchwalter, along with a wide assortment of other investigators, labored to assemble as many facts as possible about the elusive Elisa, the law firm of Larry McNabney and Associates, and the horse set. By now the rumors were running wild through the horse crowd, gaining english as they were spun. Soon the gossip was that Larry had been murdered by Elisa and that his body had been buried in Greg's breeding barn. Now, not only were Greg and Elisa supposed to have been having an affair, but she and Greg said to have done poor Larry in. Scores of people contacted the police to tell Greg and/or Elisa stories. One woman told about seeing Greg and Elisa kissing at the Lancaster show; others talked about Greg and Elisa's conflicts at the world show.

At the same time, efforts were made to get a handle on the law business—where had the money come from, and where had it gone? The investigators soon developed a portrait of an office that was being used as a cash cow by Elisa and Sarah.

The detectives also served a search warrant on the McNabney horse trailer, looking for some indication of who Elisa really was, and where she might have gone. Latent fingerprints were found all over the vehicle, and it was expected that some of the prints might be those of Elisa, in which case they could begin to figure out who she really was. That would be a long stride to figuring out where she might have gone.

On February 20, 2002, the toxicology lab came up with its initial assessment of the amount of xylazine that had been present in Larry's system: 8 milligrams per liter of blood, a substantial amount given that death had occurred in one woman at less than .3 milligrams; in other words, Larry had almost twenty-seven times what was known to be a lethal dose in another case. The big shocker, however, was the amount of xylazine found in Larry's liver—69.2 milligrams per kilogram. There were some reports of death by xylazine poisoning of only .26 milligrams per kilogram. That meant the portion in Larry's liver was at least 270 times greater than that of a man who had also died. This was certainly overkill. It seemed impossible that Larry could have ingested such a large amount of xylazine through any sort of self-infliction. He would have passed out long before. Significantly, Larry's blood alcohol content was less than .06, well under the legal limit, and even that a probable by-product of the body's decomposition. If Larry had indeed "reeked" of alcohol when Elisa and Sarah had wheeled him out of the hotel, a lot of time had passed before he died.

How much time? That would loom as a critical question as the next few weeks passed, and it would come to bear on one of the major mysteries of the McNabney murder: exactly when, and how, did Larry get such a huge dose of xylazine, and who gave it to him?

By the third week of February, Scheffel was ready to talk with Sarah. Some people in the department wanted her to do this sooner rather than later, but Scheffel wanted to establish the right sort of psychological conditions before attempting to get the real story from her. She began by interviewing Jason Cataldo's mother, asking her questions about Sarah and Jason, knowing that Jason's mother would tell Jason, and that Jason would tell Sarah. (Jason and Sarah had gotten back together after Elisa had fled.) When reporters came across Sarah's name in researching the McNabney saga and asked Scheffel about her, Scheffel downplayed Sarah's importance, calling her a bit player in the law office. She wanted to make Sarah worried without alarming her so much that she would get a lawyer. It was a fine line. She eventually went to Vacaville to talk to Mark Dutra—at that point Scheffel did not know about Mark's problem with the earlier embezzlement—and suggested to Mark, "You need to talk to your daughter."

Scheffel's idea was that Mark would tell Sarah what she'd said. If Sarah were truly innocent in Larry's death, she would then be likely to contact the sheriff's department voluntarily. If she were involved, she would probably hire an attorney. But Scheffel did not consider Sarah's disinclination to take any advice from her father. Whether this was a result of her residual contempt for him because of his earlier difficulty, only Sarah knows.

When three or four days passed without either event happening, Scheffel decided to initiate things. She called Jason's cell phone and left a message: Sarah could call the department and make arrangements to get her clothes from the McNabney trailer.

That did the trick. Within a few hours, Sarah called Scheffel and made arrangements to come in on Saturday to pick up the clothes.

On February 23, Sarah arrived at the San Joaquin County Sheriff's Department headquarters in French Camp, just south of Stockton. Scheffel invited her to sit down in an interview room rigged with a hidden video camera. Sarah brought Ralphie once again.

Scheffel's idea was to treat Sarah in a manner much different from the one Buchwalter had used two weeks before. Where Buchwalter was accusatory, disbelieving, Scheffel hoped to convince Sarah to cooperate. At that point, Scheffel wanted Elisa far more than she wanted Sarah. True, it seemed apparent that Sarah was deeply involved in the criminality at the law office—after all, she'd enjoyed the fruits of the frauds with the travel and the BMW and all the new clothes—but it wasn't clear that Sarah knew exactly what had happened to Larry. That she knew *something* was apparent, because her story kept changing. But maybe Sarah was lying only to protect herself from being arrested for the frauds, and nothing more. Scheffel hoped to induce Sarah to trust her. At least, Scheffel figured, even if Sarah didn't tell her what had actually happened, she'd be pinned down once again to a story that could later be taken apart and analyzed for its discrepancies. Eventually those discrepancies would have to be explained, and that was when, Scheffel was sure, Sarah would crack.

This would be a particularly long interview, although not nearly the longest, and run for almost five hours. Scheffel wanted to put Sarah at ease, to encourage her to tell everything she knew. If anyone ever caught up with Elisa, Sarah would almost certainly be the key witness in any case against her. But before she could be used as a witness, the authorities would have to know everything Sarah had done. Scheffel wanted to make this as painless as possible for Sarah.

"Getting a confession is always easier in a non-threatening environment," Scheffel said later. "You get more flies with honey." And even if Sarah didn't come clean, at least Scheffel would be able to lock her into whatever lies she might choose to tell.

Scheffel began by saying that the detectives really just wanted to get to know Sarah better. "Although," she added, "we know you pretty well . . . we've amassed files . . . we have probably thirty detectives working on the case, in conjunction with the FBI." Scheffel wanted to give Sarah the idea that any further lying would be fruitless, that the police effort so far had been so thorough that she would never be able to lie and get away with it.

To encourage Sarah to spill, Scheffel began by casting Elisa as the evil one, and suggesting that Sarah had been duped.

"The level of her deceit and taking advantage of people is widely based," Scheffel said. "It's not just you. You're in really good company. But unfortunately for you, Sarah, she is a very street-wise and worldly-wise older woman, who, in our opinion, has taken advantage of a twenty-one-year-old college girl . . . who just got dazzled by the glamor and the money and the [social] circles . . . you got sucked into something that's causing you to learn a life lesson the hard way . . . you may have signed on for the glamor and the red cars, and the fun, like any of us would at your age, but what you didn't sign on for, nobody will make me believe you signed on for, was murder."

Sarah didn't say anything, but shook her head no.

"You didn't have anything to gain by it, sweetie," Scheffel added.

Sarah started crying. "I trusted her, you know," Sarah said. "And I feel like, I feel stupid because I . . . Maybe there were things I should have said, hey . . . but I'm just a trusting person."

"Yeah," Scheffel said. "But I talked to your dad [Mark], and he's behind you, your mom's behind you, your brother's behind you, and we want to work with you. But here's the thing, Sarah, and this is going to be hard, and this is where you're going to have to be really mature and make some good, solid decisions here. You've made some mistakes, everybody makes mistakes, but there's a world of difference between a person who makes a mistake and admits it, and somebody who will hide behind a lie. And here's the dangerous thing about fibbing even a little bit in a homicide investigation . . ."

Scheffel explained that if Sarah lied on virtually any point, her value as a witness against Elisa would be severely damaged. Even one lie would make it possible for Elisa's lawyer to say that Sarah was the person who'd actually committed the murder, because once Sarah's credibility was shot, no one would believe her if she said she wasn't involved in Larry's murder. And in fact, Scheffel added, that's exactly what Elisa would do—point the finger at Sarah.

"That is something you absolutely do not want to happen," Scheffel said. "You do not want to be a defendant in a murder case, and that's what Elisa's plan is. She wants to put it on you." That was why Elisa had run off, leaving Sarah on the hook for the Jaguar.

Sarah said she understood. But to make the point even more clear, Scheffel told her that she and Elisa had been widely observed during the days at the City of Industry horse show and its aftermath.

"You're pretty and flamboyant," Scheffel said, "and so was Elisa, so people remembered the red truck and the two pretty ladies . . . they remember you guys. You're very pretty, so it's hard to forget you, even in a sea of faces." They'd taken photographs of both Sarah and Elisa to various locations in southern California, and people readily identified them, Scheffel said. Search warrants had been served on telephone records, she added, and on bank accounts and credit card companies. The police had so much information at that point that it would be futile to try to lie, Scheffel said.

"Am I really gonna get my clothes back today?" Sarah asked.

"Probably not," Scheffel admitted—the police had to analyze them to see if there was any trace evidence, such as human blood or tissue on them. What Sarah had to focus on now was telling the truth about everything that had happened, even if Sarah felt it might embarrass her. "All we want is the truth, regardless of what it is, okay?"

Sarah nodded her head yes.

Scheffel now took Sarah back to the beginning of the story, when she'd first responded to the McNabney firm's ad for office help. The detective did most of the talking, summarizing what she knew about Sarah's relationship with the McNabneys, as Sarah confirmed her descriptions.

"Okay," said Scheffel, "now we're going to start talking about things that are really hard to talk about, and again, don't back off—stick to the truth no matter how bad it makes you look or how bad it makes you feel . . . trust me, you signed on for some fun, and you got caught up and pulled into some kind of shady things, but nothing prepares me to believe that you signed on for murder, okay? And that's the end goal here, to separate yourself from someone who did. Don't—don't—go down with her for something you didn't bargain for, okay?"

"Okay," Sarah said.

Scheffel took up the issue of what had happened down at the City of Industry. As Scheffel zeroed in on the pertinent questions, Ralphie began to whine.

Sarah described the dinner at the Olive Garden restaurant, when Larry had gotten drunk and called her a bitch. Scheffel asked what Larry was like when he'd been drinking.

"He would talk about himself a lot," she said. "Especially when he was drunk, he would . . . cut in on a conversation, 'because I did, dah dah dah,' you know, talking about himself, and everyone's going, 'Jesus Christ, he's not talking about himself again?'"

Sarah described Larry calling Debbie Kail "a bitch," and said that Elisa was embarrassed and the Whalens offended. Then she'd driven back to Sacramento, and the following night Elisa had asked her to fly back. Sarah said she'd agreed to return because Elisa was both her friend and her boss, and she felt obligated to do what she asked.

Elisa met her outside the hotel, Sarah said, after she'd arrived from the airport in the taxi. "She's telling me how Larry's acting crazy," Sarah said. That was when they'd decided to spend the night in the dually, smoking pot.

Sometime in the early morning—"maybe once or twice," said Sarah—Elisa had gone back to the room to check on Larry. "I walked up with her," Sarah said. That was when she'd heard Larry yelling at Elisa, "I'll kill you, I'll kill you," Sarah said.

At this point Scheffel realized that Sarah was not going to tell the truth. Already she was backsliding from what she'd told Buchwalter two weeks earlier, when she'd said that Larry had said, "I'm gonna kill you, I'm gonna kill you" to Elisa when they'd gotten to the truck on September 11, not the night before as she was saying now. It was a small discrepancy, but one sufficient to tell Scheffel that Sarah was trying to make up a story.

Sarah went on to describe the events of the morning of September 11, when she, Elisa and Greg had come into the Whalen hotel room across the hall from Larry and Elisa's room. Scheffel wanted Sarah to explain what Elisa had meant when she told Debbie that Larry had run away to join a cult, when in fact they hadn't yet removed him from the hotel in the wheelchair. Elisa's statement to Debbie was evidence that Elisa had intended to murder Larry, or at least make him seem to disappear. At the very least, Sarah had to have known that Elisa was lying to Debbie when she said this.

Sarah tried to explain. What Elisa meant by telling this to Debbie was that at the time, Elisa had *thought* Larry had run away to the cult, but he'd actually come back a few minutes later, so he hadn't left after all. Of course, that meant Sarah had to explain how Larry had been ambulatory at 7 A.M. and so paralyzed, he needed a wheelchair two hours later, but Sarah didn't think of that. Neither, it appears, did Scheffel. But then, Scheffel already knew that Sarah intended to lie about what had happened, so her interest at this point was in getting Sarah pinned down to as many details as possible, even if they were lies.

Sarah told the wheelchair story next, saying Elisa had been too embarrassed to continue staying with Larry at the hotel.

"So," Scheffel said, "do you go anywhere else or buy anything else, while you're out and about?" She wanted to see if Sarah would tell her about buying the shovels. At that point, the detectives already had receipts showing that Elisa and Sarah had bought two round-pointed shovels at a nearby hardware store after they picked up the wheelchair.

Sarah said she had a vague recollection of going to a store, but couldn't remember what they'd done there.

Scheffel decided to try to buck Sarah up, to get her to face the reality that it wasn't going to be possible to lie her way out of the fix she was in.

"Because we're gonna end up facing all this in a courtroom in the months and years to come," Scheffel said, "and trust me . . . I mean, I wish I could just reach into your heart and give you the strength to stick to the truth. I'm an old woman with grown children [Scheffel was 48!], and I'm seeing you as a young woman on the verge of—being afraid and making a mistake, afraid to tell the truth. And if I can give you the courage to stick to the truth, no matter how bad it might make you appear to be, the truth is gonna stand you in a lot better stead than the lies. I just don't want you to make a mistake, Sarah."

"Okay," Sarah said. But she was still unable to remember what they'd bought at the store, so Scheffel asked her to describe what had happened when they got back to the hotel to pick up Larry with the wheelchair.

"Could you hear him talking back to her?" Scheffel asked. "And this is very important, Sarah."

"Yes I could," Sarah said. "He was saying, 'Okay, Blanchie, okay.' "

"Huh?"

" 'Okay.' And, 'Okay, Larry, I got you a wheelchair, so we can help you out to the car,' but he said something about getting more to drink. And I thought, 'Gosh, he's just drinking so much, I've never seen anyone drink that much, just keep drinking and drinking . . .' So she pushes him out to the car and I helped."

Scheffel asked Sarah what Larry had been wearing. Sarah said he'd had on a tee-shirt.

"And boxer shorts?"

"I don't think he had boxer shorts," Sarah said. She thought he'd been wearing jeans and tennis shoes.

Sarah described wheeling Larry out to the truck, with him waving his arms.

"I don't know what he's trying to do," Sarah said. "He's just, like, throwing his hands up like that and then, I was like, 'What's he doing?' and she's like, 'He's drunk, Sarah, he's just drunk.' And I'm like, 'Jesus Christ!' You know?"

After they'd put Larry in the back seat of the truck, Sarah told Scheffel, she was afraid to ride with him. Elisa told her that she'd drop her off at the horse show. They came to a stop light, Sarah said. "He started, I'm trying to remember what, exactly, what he was saying to her. He was— Larry didn't want me there, so he was saying something like, 'Get her out of here, get her out of here,' but he was, like, mumbling under his voice. I could smell alcohol."

"Uh-huh."

"And so, at the light, I jumped out of the truck."

As she had told Buchwalter and Timberlake two weeks earlier, Sarah now said that Elisa had driven off with Larry, and that was the last time she'd seen him.

This of course was the sticking point: Scheffel was convinced that this was Sarah's first big lie. There had to be some explanation for why Larry's body had wound up in a vineyard twelve miles from the Woodbridge house, and judging from all the parties' perambulations from September 11 to the following Sunday, September 16—the Whalens' undisputed, uninterrupted presence at the horse show for the whole week, the repossession of the BMW, Sarah's accident with the Saab, the sale of the dually to the Van Vliets, and the return to northern California in the rental car—there was only one period when Larry could have been moved, and that was the day of September 11. And since Sarah had already said that Elisa drove her back to Sacramento on that day, that meant that Larry had to have been with them, either dead or alive.

But Sarah stuck to her story, that the last she'd seen Larry, Elisa was taking him to a motel near the horse show, and then returning to pick her up some minutes later. They'd driven back to Sacramento and stopped at the law office so Elisa could pick up the title to the dually, she said. Then they'd driven back to Woodbridge, and that was when Sarah heard about Mark and Karen taking the BMW and the dog. She'd driven the dually to Vacaville, picked up Ralphie, and then driven back to Woodbridge. She'd spent the night at the Woodbridge house. In the morning, Elisa had driven the dually to the Whalen Ranch, where Sarah picked up the Saab to drive to the office in Sacramento, and Elisa had driven the dually back to Los Angeles to sell it to the Van Vliets.

After her accident in the Saab on Thursday, September 13, Sarah said, she'd returned to southern California by air the next day. The following Sunday, she'd gone with Elisa to sell the truck, and then they'd all returned to northern California, Sarah driving the rented green Mustang.

Scheffel asked Sarah what Elisa had been saying about Larry when she'd returned to the horse show on Thursday. "Greg's kind of saying, you know, 'God, what's up with Larry being gone?' " Sarah said. "And I'm like, I kind of look at Elisa, like, *What?* And she's like, 'Oh my God, Sarah, oh my God,' you know, and so we, I'm trying to remember now, we went back to, she was staying at a different hotel . . . and in the hotel is where, you know, I asked her . . . what was going on. And she said that Larry took off . . .'"

Elisa told her, Sarah said, that Larry had left " 'because he's a drunken fool, and drugs, Sarah,' and you know, she was so disgusted at that."

Scheffel asked Sarah why Larry would take off when he'd just been ranked number one in the nation in amateur halter horse showing. "I didn't know that," Sarah admitted.

As the fall unfolded, Sarah said, she never saw Larry again, although Elisa told her that she'd heard from him, and that she'd been served with divorce papers. Elisa told her that the divorce made her sad, "because I did everything for him."

Then, in early January, when she'd gone to the airport to fly to Scottsdale, she'd discovered that the ticket hadn't been paid for. After finding Elisa's telephone numbers disconnected, she'd called Mary Whalen and tracked down Greg.

"Eventually Greg got hold of me and said that Elisa is gone," Sarah said. "He's like, 'She left.' And I asked him, 'Why did she leave?' And he said, 'Well, she was on the cell phone and she had gotten some calls, and she looked really worried, and she left.' And so, I guess he went back to the hotel to see if she was there, and she wasn't, she was just gone.

Greg went to pay the hotel bill, and he was trying to say, 'I'm here to pay Elisa McNabney's or Elisa Jordan's hotel bill,' and they said, 'We don't have anyone staying here under that name.'"

That was when Greg discovered that Elisa had checked into and then out of the hotel under the name Elizabeth Barasch.

S cheffel asked Sarah what Elisa had done with the refrigerator that had been in the garage of the Woodbridge house. Sarah said she didn't know.

"I didn't . . . I didn't really go in the garage or anything," Sarah said.

Scheffel accepted this and moved on. She asked Sarah what she knew about the discovery of Larry's body. Sarah said she only knew what the police had told her. "They said he was found in a shallow grave," she said.

Scheffel said that Larry's body had been found in a grave less than fifteen minutes' drive from the Woodbridge house and the Whalen Ranch.

"Of all the places," Scheffel said. "I mean, the last place you saw him was where?"

"Down in L.A.," Sarah said, starting to cry.

"How do you think Laurence McNabney got into that shallow grave?" Scheffel asked, "so close to the house in Woodbridge and so far from the place you last saw him alive?"

"I have no idea," Sarah said.

"Okay," Scheffel said. "You are the last person to have seen him alive. Do you understand what I'm saying? Let me tell you this, and you're going to need to pay real close attention, okay? When we found him, he'd only been in the ground three to six weeks. Okay, now we found him on February the fifth, which means he was put there around the first of January. So the question is, where's Larry been, from the last time you saw him? No one else has seen him either. Has he been held captive somewhere, tied up and fed?"

"Did someone kidnap him?" Sarah asked.

"But he was found fifteen minutes from his house in Woodbridge," Scheffel reminded her. She added that only two sets of people knew how Larry had died—the killer or killers, and the police. But, said Scheffel, rumors were already rampant in the horse set that Larry had been killed with a horse tranquilizer. She told Sarah about the time that Elisa had asked Debbie Kail about "ace" two days before Larry disappeared.

"You're kidding," Sarah said.

"That brings me to how much loyalty you're feeling for Elisa McNabney," Scheffel told her. "Trust me, Sarah, we're going to catch her. She is not going to be able to escape us. What do you think she's going to tell us when we get her? Who do you think she's going to blame this on when we catch up with her? Do you think she's going to stand up and take responsibility for what she did, or do you think she's gonna try and put this off on someone else? And who do you think, of all the people around you, around her, is the person that she could set up to take the responsibility for what happened to Larry McNabney?"

"My name's on everything," Sarah said.

This opened up another lane for Scheffel. She asked if Sarah had ever signed Larry's name to anything—like checks.

Sarah admitted that she had. She'd done it because Elisa had told her to, and said it was all right. She said she and Haylei had practiced signing Larry's name, and then burned the practice sheet. She'd only signed Larry's name because she felt like she had to, Sarah said. It was the only way they could get paid. She'd also signed Larry's name to the back of a settlement check.

This was a little progress, and it left Scheffel thinking that maybe Sarah was getting ready to tell what had actually happened to Larry. She steered the conversation back to the discrepancy between Larry's disappearance and the fact that he'd only been buried three to six weeks. What would Sarah guess had happened?

"Don't they keep, like, cadavers in cold places?" Sarah asked.

"Refrigeration?" Scheffel suggested.

"Are you trying to say he was in a refrigerator someplace?"

"No, I'm asking," Scheffel said. "I'm asking you."

"I have no idea," Sarah said, "where he could have been, or under what circumstances."

Scheffel showed Sarah a photograph of the folded-up body.

"Oh my God," said Sarah. She looked away from the picture.

"That's how we found him. See how curled up he is, Sarah?"

Sarah burst into tears. "I can't see that, I'll be sick."

"Well, this is the reality of homicide, okay? And the last time you saw Laurence McNabney, he didn't look like this, did he?"

Sarah shook her head. "I have a really weak stomach," she said.

"This is the reality of what's happened," Scheffel said. "This is not a game. I don't know—has Elisa threatened you, that if you tell on her, she'll implicate you in some way? Does she have something on you?"

"No," Sarah said.

"Okay, the way to deal with a terrorist who's holding something over your head is to take that power away from them," Scheffel said. "To tell the truth, to stand with us against them."

"I can't look at that," Sarah said again, meaning the picture.

"Laurence McNabney, a viable, living human being with faults like all of us, did not deserve to end up where we found him, in the manner we found him. And I'm sorry to have to press you, Sarah, but I can't be sure that Elisa McNabney isn't holding something over your head, or threatening your family so that you will stay silent about anything that you know about her involvement in this. I can't read your mind."

"I swear, I don't know."

"I know what killed him, and I don't think you're the one who did it, but I do think there's a possibility that you know more than what you're saying. And that's because you're afraid to say. Has she got something on you? People who make threats like that, they're counting on you remaining silent."

All the evidence pointed toward her involvement in Larry's death, Scheffel told Sarah.

"Sarah, I don't think for a minute that you signed on for anything more than just a good time," Scheffel said. "There's a world of difference between being sucked in to making errors of judgment versus committing homicides. Even if you helped cover it up after the fact, that can be dealt with. But I can't help you fix what's wrong unless I know what happened, and there's only two people who know that, and that's you and Elisa. If all you did was get involved after the fact, that can be dealt with. I'm so afraid that you'll make the wrong choice, that you'll be too afraid to step forward and say what it is that you know, because you're afraid that if you'll implicate yourself you'll be in serious trouble. Because I have no doubt that's what Elisa told you."

"What else do you want me to say?"

"I want you to say the truth, whatever it is . . . but if you make me come after you, too, trust me, the evidence that we're compiling will implicate you right along with her, unless you set yourself apart and say, 'No, I signed on for a good time, I did not sign on for murder.' "

There was a bit more to the interview, and near the end, Scheffel was pretty sure she'd gotten Sarah right up to the edge of telling the truth. A little more time—perhaps another talk with Mark and Karen—and Sarah was likely to crack, Scheffel thought.

"Can you say to me categorically, 'There is no way that Laurence McNabney's body was in that truck on our trip to Sacramento to pick up the Saab and drop [me] off'? . . . Can you tell me that there is no way that Laurence McNabney's body was in that truck?"

"I mean . . . in the back of the truck, you're saying?"

"Can you tell me there is no way that Laurence McNabney's body was in that truck on the trip back to Sacramento?"

"No," Sarah said.

"Is it possible?"

"It could be."

And in fact, was there any way that Sarah could assure her that Larry's body hadn't been in the refrigerator in the garage in the Woodbridge house for three months before it was buried in the vineyard near Lodi?

"It could have," Sarah admitted.

At last, a ray of light, Scheffel thought. Now she just needed to give Sarah a chance to think things over, and she'd be ready to tell what really happened.

Scheffel told Sarah that she would be allowed to go home for the day. But, Scheffel added, she could be sure of one thing: that Elisa was going to blame her for everything. Sarah needed to figure out where she stood before that occurred.

"I'm going to give you my card," Scheffel said. "Every

day starts over, new and fresh. If you give this some thought, and what I've said makes any kind of sense to you at all, call me, and we'll sit down and get it on the record, and let it go from there. Otherwise, I'm going to continue to dig, and continue to interview, and continue to pull records in, and the chips are gonna fall where the chips are gonna fall."

Sarah and Ralphie left, both sniffling.

Scheffel's seed bore fruit the very next day. Jason Cataldo had been scheduled for an interview. When he arrived, Sarah was with him. She was crying.

"I have to tell you," she told Scheffel. "I have to tell you something."

Scheffel tried to calm her. "Jason's here, Ralphie's here, and we're gonna get through this," she soothed.

"I have to have this just be with law enforcement," Sarah said. "It can't get out to the media, otherwise my life could be in danger. Please, will you promise me that? I need to know that you promise."

Scheffel said she wouldn't say anything to the media. Whatever Sarah had to tell her, Scheffel said, they'd do their best to protect her.

With Sarah sobbing and Ralphie yipping and whining, the story began to come out.

Elisa had told her never to tell anyone about the wheel-chair, Sarah said. "I asked her why . . . and she said, 'Don't ask me why, just don't ask me,' and then I can't understand what's going on . . . but you know, 'If it's going to help Larry, that's fine.' And so she was gonna drop me off at the horse show and . . . then she said, 'No, stay in the car, we're going to Sacramento,' and I asked her . . . 'Well, isn't Larry going to the hotel?' And she said, 'No.' "

"Scoot closer to her," Scheffel told Jason. Sarah was now sobbing almost uncontrollably. Scheffel thought Jason could comfort her.

"I said, 'What's going on?' " Sarah continued, when she

recovered her breath. "And I just . . . at this point I was starting to get scared because Larry was acting so weird."

"He was still alive at that point?"

"Yes. And so she said, 'Just drive,' and so I was driving and I was so scared I could barely drive and she said . . . 'You need to forget that Larry was in this car,' and I said, 'What are you talking about, what's going on?' And I started crying, and I was going, 'God!' and she said, 'It's in your best interest to forget that he was in this car,' and I said . . . 'I don't understand, I just don't understand what's going on,' and she said, 'It doesn't involve you, you don't need to worry about it.'

"I was so scared . . . scared, because I was wondering, What is she doing? . . . Why is she doing [this]?, and so we went to the office and we pulled over a bunch of times and stopped because I . . . I couldn't drive, I couldn't even concentrate, I had to stop and have a cigarette break, and get fresh air all the time, so it took us a while to get home. And so we got to the office and, you know, I got out and she went in there and, you know, and got all that stuff, that's all true."

"And where's Larry?"

"And Larry is still in the back of the truck."

"And is he still alive at this point?"

"Yeah." Ralphie started screeching. "He was, like, nodding on and off and sitting up, and, you know, he was just kind of talking back with Elisa, but he was kind of mumbling.

"We went back to her house in Woodbridge, and I got a message on my phone from my parents about them taking my car and all that, so I called Jason, and she [Elisa] said, 'Stay in the car,' and so she and Larry went into the house."

"How did she get Larry into the house?"

"She walked him in. She walked him in and I stayed in the car and she came and she said, 'You are to forget Larry was ever here,' and I said, 'What's going on?' And I said, 'Please, Elisa, please, Elisa, what's going on?' And she said, 'It's in your and the people you love's best interest that you forget about this.' And she had the most horrible look in her eye and I was scared. Because I was thinking, 'I wonder if she's going to hurt me.' "

Sarah had made the call to Mark and Karen about the car and the dog. "And Elisa came down and she ends up listening to every word I said. And then before I drove away I said, 'Elisa, what's going on? Do I need to go to the police?' She said, 'That's the last place you will ever go. Otherwise there will be problems for you and the people you love,' and I was just so scared . . . "

Well, with this, Sarah had gotten halfway across the bridge—she'd finally admitted that Larry had come with them in the dually back to northern California; and she'd implied that Elisa had bad intentions, and indeed, had threatened her. But that didn't address the remaining question of what had actually happened to Larry—how he'd come to have a massive amount of xylazine in his system, and how he'd been refrigerated for three months, or how he'd wound up in the vineyard. And, beneath all the tears and gasps and sobs and yipping Maltese terrier, there was something so melodramatic about Sarah's story that one could almost imagine the sinister Elisa in a black hat with a whip and a mustache, tying poor Sarah to the railroad tracks.

Apparently Sarah heard something false, too, because she soon rushed up reinforcements.

"I was like really scared [Ralphie was really setting off a racket now], like, if she knows I'm going to the police, something could happen to me."

"Nothing's going to happen to you," Scheffel said, appropriately but inaccurately.

" 'Cause she knows people," Sarah went on. "She's told me before that she knows people, like when she grew up in Florida that she's dated, you know, Mafia-type people . . . that her brother was a big cocaine dealer [untrue], and all that type of stuff, so I didn't ever doubt that she would know somebody."

"Okay," Scheffel said.

"And when I came back that night, I said, 'Where's Larry?' and she said, 'Don't worry about it,' and so she'd already made up a bed for me downstairs on a couch and I slept there and didn't ever hear anything and I woke up the next morning and I said, 'Where's— What's going on? and she said, 'Just forget about it, don't ever ask me.' And she had this look in her eye that I can't describe."

Now Elisa was giving Sarah the evil eye. Next would come the Black Spot.

"Yeah," Scheffel said.

"I was so scared," Sarah continued. "I was so scared now, I'm so scared to tell you because I don't know if it's going to get out, because I don't want them to hear that I'm telling you this."

Now Elisa had become "them."

This interview would continue on for almost three hours, but the salient facts were now out on the table. In this latest version, Sarah had last seen Larry walking into the house with Elisa. "He seemed happy to be home," Sarah said. She'd driven to Vacaville, picked up Ralphie, and then returned to Woodbridge and seen Elisa.

"And where did she— Did you see where she went?" Scheffel asked.

"No, I just held Ralph and I went right to sleep, I was so scared."

"Was she in bedclothes, nightclothes, or was she dressed in street clothes? Or do you remember?"

"I don't remember," Sarah said.

"Okay, how was she acting? What was she saying when you got there?"

"Nothing really."

"Anything about Larry?"

"No. I said, 'Where's Larry?' She just looks at me . . . and said, 'Don't worry about it, just don't worry about it.' I was thinking, Oh my God, oh my God . . ."

"Okay," Scheffel said.

"And I wish I knew more, but I don't."

"Okay."

"And I woke up the next morning. There was nothing. And I was afraid to say anything to her. I didn't hear anything."

"You don't hear him, he's not calling her 'Blanche,' or he's not down in the kitchen fixing breakfast or getting anything to drink, or anything?"

"Huh-uh."

"Do you go upstairs at all? Is that where their room is?"

"Yeah, it was upstairs."

"But you don't know?"

"I—I didn't go up there."

"Once you saw her take him into the house?"

"I never saw him again."

After Jason, Sarah and Ralphie left, Scheffel began to consider the probability of what Sarah had said. It rang true to an extent—at least the movements did, although not the threats. Those, Scheffel was sure, Sarah had made up to explain why she hadn't come forward sooner. If Elisa was so scary, why had Sarah enjoyed spending all the money in October, November and December? Why had they taken trips to all the horse shows together? Why, indeed, had Sarah been so distraught to learn that Elisa had abandoned her at the airport?

So Sarah was lying, still lying, this time about the threats from Elisa. But why? When you stripped the story back to its relevant facts, the net effect was . . . nothing. There was nothing in Sarah's story that implicated anyone. No one had done anything illegal. Larry, albeit wobbly, "seemed happy to be home." Apart from making faces at Sarah and issuing dire-sounding edicts, Elisa hadn't done anything either. Why then was Sarah so shook up? The tears, the sobbing, the angst were real—even Ralphie knew that. So what was Sarah still hiding?

It could only be what had actually happened to Larry, and how he'd wound up, first in the refrigerator in the garage, and later in the vineyard. Had Sarah helped bury him? Somehow, Scheffel didn't think so. Sarah's shock at seeing the disinterred Larry was real. The refrigerator, though—that was probably another story.

Where *was* the refrigerator? The evidence seemed to be that Elisa had moved all of the appliances out of the Woodbridge house in early January. Who had helped her? Whalen's workers. The chances were, despite Greg's denials, that was where the refrigerator was, or at least had been.

On the following Monday, Scheffel and her colleagues drafted a search warrant for Whalen's ranch. On the following Thursday, the last day of February 2002, a team of police swarmed over the ranch in search of the fateful icebox.

Whalen was unhappy once more as the cops poured through the gates of his ranch. "The raid," as he later called it, was disrupting his business. Even worse, it was adding fuel to the rumors that he and Elisa had conspired to kill Larry. Already Whalen had had his lawyer send letters to four horse show people, telling them to stop spreading rumors about Greg and Elisa and Larry or face the prospect of being sued. Now here came the cops, about twenty of them, accompanied by dogs, and armed with their warrant. As the searchers prowled through the house and out among the barns, Detective Javier Ramos asked Whalen to come down to the sheriff's department in French Camp, some forty minutes away, to answer questions.

"You are not under arrest," Ramos said, when they were seated in the interview room with the hidden camera. "You are here freely and voluntarily."

"Oh, really?" Whalen said, sarcastically. "I'm here 'voluntarily'?" He shook his head. "You told me to come here, that's why I'm here."

Ramos told Whalen they needed to have some things cleared up. First of all, Ramos said, he needed to know: had Whalen ever obtained a refrigerator from Elisa's Woodbridge house?

Whalen said he hadn't.

Well, Ramos asked, had he ever been to Elisa's house, helping her move stuff?

Whalen denied that he had.

Ramos said that there had been witnesses who saw Greg at the house.

"I don't care how many people saw me there, I was not

there except the one time when they moved in," Whalen insisted.

Ramos told him he needed to tell them the truth, that it was a murder investigation. Ramos said they had information that Greg had indeed accepted a refrigerator from Elisa.

"I'm tired of you guys harassing me," Whalen said. "Show me—show me the witness who says I was at that Woodbridge house helping load up a refrigerator. Show him to me." A thought appeared to strike him. "Was it Sarah?" he asked.

Ramos sidestepped the question.

"I need you to tell me the truth," Ramos said. "Did you have any kind of affair with Elisa McNabney?"

Greg glowered at Ramos. "I never had sex with that woman," he said, perhaps unconsciously echoing a more infamous phrase. "If you guys keep accusing me of things, I'm going to get a lawyer and it will stop," he said.

Meanwhile, back at the ranch—really—the searchers had readily located a white refrigerator in the bunkhouse used by the workers. Mary Whalen said that maybe Elisa *had* given the workers that refrigerator.

Criminalists Jenny Thomas and Bill Hudlow examined the appliance.

"We found some red-brown stains in the refrigerator in the bottom of the door and the bottom of the refrigerator that tested positive, [on a] preliminary test for blood, and we found some hairs and some fibers," Thomas said later. They noticed that the inside of the refrigerator appeared to have some "sticky substance, like tape adhesive," on the inside. There were some cracks in the bottom of the refrigerator that made Thomas think that a great weight at one time had been stored inside it. Thomas and Hudlow talked it over: was the refrigerator large enough to hold a six-foot-tall, two-hundred-pound man? They decided that with determined stuffing, it was.

Other searchers in the house located and opened a safe. There they found a significant amount of cash. Later, when he was asked to explain why he had this money, Greg said that the horse business was often a cash business. One never knew when money might be needed to close a deal, he said.

The blood and hair samples were packed off to the state's DNA laboratory for further testing.

The next day, Scheffel tried to get the San Joaquin County District Attorney's Office to ask for a warrant for Elisa McNabney's arrest for the crime of murder in the first degree. That office declined to approve one. She didn't have enough for probable cause, Scheffel was told. That didn't deter Scheffel. She took her proposed affidavit directly to Judge Bernard J. Garber of the Superior Court. Garber, a former prosecutor, looked over Scheffel's affidavit and approved it. The official hunt for Elisa McNabney, or whatever her name was, was on. What no one then knew was that Elisa was on her last journey—on her way home.

Shane

As they drove out of Scottsdale in the new red Jaguar convertible on the night of January 10, 2002, Haylei pressed her mother to tell her why they were leaving in such a hurry—why, in fact, the police wanted to talk to her.

Elisa told Haylei that she was wanted for kidnaping—when they'd left Florida in 1993, she'd taken Haylei out of the state in violation of a child custody order. That was also why they had to change their names, Elisa added. From then on, she told Haylei, she would be . . . Shane Ivaroni. Who did Haylei want to be?

"Penelope," Haylei said.

All right, Elisa said—from then on they would be the Ivaronis, mother and daughter, Shane and Penelope.

On through the night they drove. Elisa had very little in the way of liquid assets. She did have a check for a small amount of money that had come from the Lodi furniture dealer from the sale of the living room furniture, and according to Haylei's version of the events, recounted later, about $300 in cash given to her by Greg, who had supposedly advised her to "Git to gittin'." Other than that, Elisa was close to being tapped out. Not even the fabulous red Jaguar could be converted to cash, since it was leased in the name of Sarah Dutra.

Elisa and Haylei discussed where to go next. According to Haylei, they decided to go to Charleston, South Carolina. But first they had some places to stop.

By the middle of the same night, Elisa and Haylei were in New Mexico. Elisa looked in the rearview mirror and saw red lights.

"And I pull over," Elisa said later, "stopped for speeding, and I just figure, it's pretty much over now . . . I don't even have a driver's license."

But Elisa turned on her charm, and the trooper let them go with a warning.

By the next day they were in Denver, where Elisa tried to cash the check that the furniture store had given her. They went to another horse show, where Elisa met a friend, and told her she needed to do something to make some money. She did a little work at the show, earning a small amount of cash, and then she and Haylei headed farther east, still in the Jag.

"We went to Kentucky," Elisa said later, after the police finally caught up with her. "Kentucky had good [horse] tracks and I knew I could work there." Then, after a week or so in Kentucky, they drove on to Nashville. There Elisa pawned Larry's ring, a gold horseshoe studded with diamonds. Elisa again turned on the charm, and the pawn shop owner was excited by her. "If she had asked me to go home with her," he told police later, "I would have, there and then, even though I'm a married man."

Elisa couldn't find a job in Nashville, so she and Haylie drove on to Mobile, Alabama, and then Biloxi, Mississippi. By Biloxi they were tapped out again, and Elisa couldn't find any work. They went to a homeless shelter in a church—probably the only time in history two homeless women had driven up to a homeless shelter in a nearly new red Jaguar convertible.

By late January, Elisa had been to the welfare department for help, and had cadged some used clothes to help her interview for a job; she'd had to use the last of her cash to buy new shoes for the interview.

"I was driving down the highway," she said, "and this guy's Jaguar comes by. And he says, 'Nice car,' and I said, 'Nice car, too.' And he smiled. And I smiled. And he takes me across the street to a casino, and he made like three thousand five hundred, so he gives me four hundred. Then later, he takes me to another table and makes fifteen hundred and gives me a couple of hundred. And it was good."

The man who had picked her up owned a furniture store in the Florida panhandle town of Fort Walton Beach. He asked Elisa if she'd go with him to a golf tournament the following day, and Elisa said yes.

One thing led to another, and soon the man invited Elisa and Haylei to live in a condominium he owned in Destin, Florida, just across the opening of Choctawhatchee Bay from Fort Walton Beach. Elisa and Haylei decided to accept the man's offer. This was as good a place as any to rest until they piled up some more money for the trip to Charleston.

By early February, Elisa had found a job in Destin at a nice restaurant, Destin Chops, a place frequented by lawyers and stockbrokers. On February 8, even as Scheffel and her colleagues at the San Joaquin County Sheriff's Department were beginning to try to figure out what had happened to Larry, Elisa had taken a part-time job in a law firm located on the main highway just east of Destin. Haylei developed a close friendship with a boy in Fort Walton Beach. Things were finally looking up for Shane and Penelope Ivaroni. But then, just as safety finally seemed to beckon, the old Laren came back.

As the authorities pieced the story together later, after living with Haylei for about a month and a half in the rich man's condo, Elisa had some sort of dispute with the furniture store owner. One thing led to another, and he soon discovered that Elisa had taken out credit cards in his name: authorized user, one Shane Ivaroni. When the man also discovered that "Shane" had run up a large bill on the bogus cards, he demanded that she and her daughter get all their stuff out of the condominium at once. Elisa made some complaints about the man, too.

Not content with evicting mother and daughter, the

furniture store owner called the law firm where Elisa had
been working. He told people there that "Shane" was a
crook, that she had stolen from him, and they'd better watch
their own petty cash. Someone at the law firm confronted
Elisa with the accusations; as she had done in Reno, Elisa
heatedly denied them, then took off in the Jaguar. But someone had written down the Jaguar's license plate number, and
soon was on the telephone to the Okaloosa County Sheriff's
Department. On Friday, March 15, the Okaloosa department
checked the national crime information computer and discovered that the Jaguar was registered to Sarah Dutra, a
known associate of the wanted fugitive Elisa McNabney.
The Okaloosa authorities told their San Joaquin counter-
parts that they were closing in on their murder suspect.

Elisa was much too street-wise to think that the police
wouldn't now be looking for her everywhere—especially in
the hot red Jaguar. That night, she located a man she had
met in the restaurant, the owner of a dry cleaning establishment in Fort Walton Beach. Using her charm once more,
Elisa managed to get the man to invite her home with him.
That night as he slept, she removed $600 from his wallet,
some of his credit cards, and the keys to his Dodge Dakota
truck. Then she picked up Haylei and ran for the Georgia
state line.

The first the dry cleaner knew about having been taken to the cleaners by Elisa was the following morning, when he discovered that his truck was missing. In its place he found the red Jaguar. Not knowing what else to do, he drove it to work, where it was soon spotted by a roving police patrol. It was a car that was very difficult to conceal, and the dry cleaner wasn't even trying.

By the time the police put the red car under covert surveillance, Elisa and Haylei were halfway across Georgia.

Haylei, it appears, was perturbed by the abrupt departure. As they made their way east on U.S. 84, through Valdosta and Waycross, she peppered her mother with questions. Why were they running again? What had gone wrong *this* time? Elisa tried to make some excuse, but Haylei wasn't buying any of it. Every time she made any friends—every time she got a boyfriend she liked—something happened, and they were off on the road again. It wasn't fair—she was 17 and had a right to a life, didn't Elisa understand that?

All the way through Georgia, the discussion continued, growing alternately heated and teary. By that night they had reached Charleston, where they found a place to spend the night.

The more Haylei talked and cried, the more Elisa could see her points. She'd made plenty of mistakes in her life, Elisa knew; but was it fair that Haylei had to pay a price for them, too? Wouldn't it be better for Haylei to have her own life? She was almost an adult. Elisa—Laren—had tried her best, doing whatever she'd had to do to take care of her

daughter, and now there wasn't much she *could* do, anymore.

Except, Laren thought, tell her the truth—about running
away from Florida when Haylei was just a little girl, about
marrying Larry, about the trust accounts, about killing Larry,
the refrigerator, the burying—all of it. By morning Laren had
told Haylei everything, or at least most of it. And then she
had come to a decision—she would take Haylei back to
Florida, back to Destin and Fort Walton Beach, and let her
go. It was time for Haylei to live her own life, time for Haylei
to be grown up, just as it had been for Laren at the same age
so many years before.

Back they drove in the stolen truck across Georgia,
pulling into Destin in the evening. Laren called a taxi for
Haylei. The cab came and took her away, back to her friends
at Fort Walton Beach. Laren sat on the front seat of the truck
and wrote an 8-page letter to her daughter for her coming
of age:

> *Dear Haylei—*
> *I am so sorry for dragging you through the life I took*
> *you through. You have always loved me no matter*
> *what and that means everything to me. Since telling*
> *you the real truth about everything last night, I hope*
> *you can make your life good. Don't steal and don't*
> *lie. I did both for as long as I can remember and look*
> *what I did to myself . . .*

Laren told her daughter that leaving her was the hardest
thing she had ever done—that she wasn't leaving because
she didn't want to be with Haylei, but so "you can have your
life." She didn't know what came after death, Laren said,
but if Haylei lived honorably, she wouldn't have to "face
any more of the craziness you've lived with in your life."

Laren gave Haylei some practical advice, too—what to
do about school, what to do about men. Marry someone for

love, she said—not because she thought she had to do it. When Haylei needed help, she should never be afraid to ask for it. But as for Laren, she couldn't go on.

> *I wish I were strong enough to face all this, I just don't feel I deserve to live anymore. If I am out of your life, you have a better chance of making it . . .*
> *You can open your heart now and not be afraid you will have to run. The running is over.*

Laren recalled that Haylei had asked her to promise her that she would call if she felt suicidal. Now, said Laren, she wanted to explain why she intended to kill herself—"I am too weak," Laren said, "to face myself in the mirror everyday and hate myself for what I have done to you and others around me." Haylei should always tell the truth, no matter what, Laren said. That way she could never go wrong.

> *By ending my life, I am washing you clean . . . I will always be in your heart!*
>
> > Love,
> > Mom

When she was done, Laren took the rest of her pot and crossed the highway, heading for the beach, not far from the condominium where she and Haylei had lived before their eviction by the rich man.

Her plan was simple: she would walk into the ocean and start swimming, swim until she was exhausted. By that time she would be too far from shore to make it back. By then, she would be too tired to want to live anymore. Laren began walking toward the sea.

Haylei arrived in the taxi at the house of her friends in Fort Walton Beach. The police had the place under surveillance, and when she arrived and paid off the cab, they intercepted her. Everyone went into the house, where Haylei's friends were also calling the police. Everyone was worried for Haylei's safety. Haylei told the police that she was worried that her mom was going to do herself harm.

Where was she when you left her? Haylei was asked, and Haylei told them that her mother was sitting in the truck at the Winn-Dixie store, just across the highway from the condominium.

Within a few minutes, police units were rushing to the area. The truck was soon sighted, and uniformed officers spread out across the beach, looking for the woman who had been the object of a coast-to-coast search. At just before 10:15 P.M. on March 18, Laren was arrested by Okaloosa County sheriff's deputies as she smoked the last of her marijuana on the beach. If there was one thing that Laren had learned about life, it was that you'd better use it all up, because you can't take it with you.

The interview of Laren Renee Sims Jordan Redelsperger McNabney, also known as Elisa McNabney, began at 11:15 P.M., Florida time, in a room wired for video at the Okaloosa County Sheriff's Department in Shalimar, just up the road from Fort Walton Beach. Back in California, it was three hours earlier, and Scheffel couldn't get into the office for nearly an hour. FBI Agent Victoria Harker and Sergeant Don Amunds of the Okaloosa County Sheriff's Department asked the California authorities if they wanted them to ask the prisoner some questions.

Cognizant of the need to get a statement, if the woman they knew as Elisa was willing to talk, the California people said sure, go ahead. Because neither Harker nor Amunds knew much about the McNabneys' history, they were in no position to confront their prisoner over any lies she might tell. Laren's objective at this point seemed to be to induce the two investigators to feel sorry for her, and to that end she soon began to paint a very unflattering portrait of Larry, which was, inevitably, not the truth.

Because circumstances made this the only recorded statement Elisa would ever make about the events surrounding Larry's death, it calls for careful parsing as to its potential accuracy. It's often when the asserted facts are reassembled in their proper order that lies become most apparent. Harker and Amunds didn't have the background necessary to do this, at least that night in the Okaloosa County sheriff's station. But their purpose wasn't to evaluate Laren's story, it was to get it.

In her appearance and demeanor, Laren seemed a sympathetic figure. She had lost a considerable amount of weight since the prior summer. In fact, with the wind-tousling of her hair from the beach, she looked positively wraith-like.

The FBI's Harker asked most of the questions. After establishing her identity as Elisa McNabney, wanted on the fugitive warrant, Elisa admitted that her true name was Laren Renee Sims Jordan, and that she had grown up in Brooksville, Florida.

"I've been running for nine years," she sighed.

When she'd seen the police on the beach, Laren said, she'd known it was all over. "I knew something needed to happen, either I needed to put a bullet in my head or I needed to deal with it . . . and did I kill my husband? Yes, I killed my husband."

Harker asked Laren when she'd married Larry. "I married him February sixth, 1995, in Reno, Nevada," Laren said, getting the month as well as the year wrong. She said she'd known Larry a year before marrying him.

"I told him I had left Florida, and I had credit card fraud and all that, checks, and dealing with stolen property and blah blah blah . . . and he later [unintelligible] and we stayed married. He had an alcohol and drug problem and when things were good, he used to go on runners, like when you disappear for four or five or six days at a time."

Laren said Larry had begun to hit her "on July second, 1995," and threatened that if she left him, "they" would take custody of Haylei away from her.

By the summer of 2001, Laren said, Larry's drug problem had gotten out of control. "Everything," she said, "coke, meth, smoked heroin . . . 'Special K'. . . ."

To get Larry something to do other than drugs, Laren said, she'd decided to get him a horse. While Larry enjoyed showing the horse, it hadn't dented his appetite for drugs, she said. Then Larry took $10,000 from the client trust account, she said. Over the next year, she went on, Larry continued to raid the trust account; the implication was that he was using the money to buy drugs.

In June of 2000, Laren said, she'd hired "this secretary named Sarah Dutra . . . Is she in custody in California?"

"I don't know yet," said Harker.

"Do you know where she is?"

"She's not in custody," Amunds said. "We know where she's at, but she's not physically in custody."

"Sarah and I are good friends," Laren said. She continued with her story, describing Larry's DUI and subsequent depression. Laren said Larry had tried to shoot her with a gun during March of 2001, but shot a hole in the floor of the Elk Grove house instead. Laren said she'd told Larry he had to go to rehab, and he'd agreed to go for thirty days. But six days into the rehab, they'd begun group therapy, Laren said, and Larry had called her to come and pick him up. He said group therapy was too freaky for him, she said. She'd driven down to the rehab place near Los Angeles and Larry had told her to drive around the back. He went over the wall and jumped into the back of the car, telling her to "Go! Go! Go!" just like a prison escape movie, Laren indicated.

Things just got worse during the summer of 2001, Laren said, with Larry pulling a knife on her in a restaurant in front of Greg Whalen (this seems to be something Laren made up, as she did in telling the Florida investigators that Larry was a "convicted domestic batterer," which was also untrue).

"So we go to L.A. to a horse show," Laren continued, "and we're at the hotel and we're there for like eleven days. He started drinking at ten in the morning and he started showing at nine, and so at ten . . . my dog, I really love my dog . . . he took my dog and hung him out the balcony on the ninth floor and he goes like, 'I'm gonna kill him,' because we were [arguing] . . . he brings the dog in and beats the crap out of me . . . and Sarah was coming that day and she said, 'Come on, come on' [inaudible].

"Sarah said that?"

Whatever Laren had told them that Sarah had said was too mumbled to be picked up on the tape, but it appears from the context that this was where Laren first claimed that killing Larry was Sarah's idea.

"So, Sarah's idea or your idea?" Harker asked.

"Initially [inaudible] talked about it. It was probably both of us, you know, for some reason. My daughter told me that Sarah told her—'cause I told my daughter the truth last night about everything—and she told me that Sarah told her that they should have him killed, because he was so horrible. And I thought, 'Why is she telling my daughter that?' I love Sarah, so I know I couldn't betray Sarah, or anything like that."

"But both of you started talking, you gotta get rid of him?"

"What are we going to do with him? . . . We couldn't send him back to rehab, he's gonna bust out . . . We gotta get the business straightened out, we have so much stuff we have to do, and I was dealing with a jeopardized past anyway and I didn't want to [attract attention]."

She and Sarah first began discussing getting rid of Larry on Friday or Saturday while they were at the horse show at the City of Industry, Laren said. Larry was "out there," meaning spaced on drugs. "He was taking drugs from my horse trainer," Laren said.

"What do you mean?"

"He was taking horse drugs from the horse trainer."

"What kind of horse drugs?"

"Taking them out . . . the 'Special K' is a tranquilizer . . . he was taking them out of the trainer's box, you know, so we knew he was doing that, so . . ."

So she and Sarah decided the best way to get rid of Larry was to give him an overdose of the horse tranquilizer he was already taking.

There are a couple of problems with this story of Laren's, at least as she had told it thus far. First, of course, was the fact that Whalen never had any ketamine, as he later swore, and as his vet did also. Second, Whalen kept the horse drugs in his vet kit, which was inside the locked trailer. Laren knew the combination to the trailer lock, but Larry did not, according to Debbie Kail (although Whalen said Larry did know the combination). So if Larry was taking "Special K," he was probably not getting it from Greg Whalen's vet kit.

But it nevertheless seems likely that Laren *believed* that Larry was getting "Special K" from the vet kit. "I looked it up," she told Harker and Amunds. "I wanted to know, is he going into stroke or something? It can paralyze you . . . because his face kept drooping, over the last month and a half, and I kept thinking, what is going on with him, did he have a stroke, or what?"

This was reminiscent of Sarah's description of Larry at the Olive Garden dinner—"water on the brain," the vacuous, drooping-mouth stare Larry had displayed.

"Did he tell you he was taking it, or you saw him taking it?"

"I saw him."

Putting this together, it seems likely that Larry had been taking the drug volitionally, that is, to get high, for some time. When Laren noticed this, Larry had told her he was taking "Special K." When she asked him where he'd been getting it, he had told her he'd been getting it from the vet kit, even if that wasn't actually so. Then, when Laren sought to give Larry an overdose, she'd gone into the vet kit herself, not knowing the difference between ketamine, acepromazine, and xylazine, and had pulled out the bottle of xylazine marked as "TranquiVed," a sedative. To Laren, "Special K" was a generic term for *all* horse tranquilizers. That was why, months after Larry was dead, Laren continued to believe that she'd given him an overdose of "Special K." She didn't know the difference between xylazine and a xylophone.

• • •

"So here we are in L.A.," Harker said, "in the hotel, he's pretty much passed out . . . What did you do to him? Was he awake?"

"Half awake," Laren said.

"You and Sarah were . . . Where are you in the hotel room?"

"We're still in the other bed."

"He's in one bed, you two are in the other bed, talking about what to do with him? What did you guys decide to do with him?"

"Well, we said that nobody would miss him, because everybody hated him and we said . . . if we kill him, nobody's gonna miss him . . ."

"Were you going to do it like that day or were you going to do it some other time in the future? When were you guys planning on doing it?"

"Right then."

But Laren was, for some reason, confusing two different nights. It was on Saturday night, September 8–9, that Sarah had stayed in their room. On September 10–11, two nights later, Laren and Elisa had spent most of the night in the truck, not in "the other bed" in the hotel room. This was a significant elision. It appears that Laren was attempting to take two different series of events and make them appear to have happened all on the same night. In short, it appears that Larry was drugged not once, but three different times, as we shall see: Saturday night, early Tuesday morning, and the fatal, final time on Tuesday night or early Wednesday morning.

Laren resumed her story. On the night Sarah had flown down from Sacramento, Laren said, they had sat in the truck, trying to decide what to do with Larry, who was asleep in the room on the ninth floor of the hotel. They considered holding a pillow over his face to suffocate him, but ruled that out because he was too strong. They went up to look at Larry. He was asleep.

"Sarah's standing over by the door and I'm, like, leaning over to see if his eyes were open or closed," Laren said. "He jumped out of bed, I mean, *jumped* out of bed. Sarah's, like, screaming and runs out of the room. I get out of the room, and that's when we said, 'Screw it,' and so we went down to the trainer's truck and . . ."

Harker asked if Laren and Sarah had made any verbal agreement to poison Larry.

"Well, no," Laren said. "We were just so scared . . . Like, we can't deal with him anymore, you know, we have to do this . . . It's the only way out. We went down to my trainer's truck and I got the medicine bag out and I got the tranquilizer out of it and I got a syringe. I went back over to my truck and I said, 'I don't know how we're gonna do it to him.' Sarah said, 'Put it in the Visine bottle,' so I squirted Visine out of the Visine bottle and I stuck the syringe in there . . . Oh God, it seemed like a good idea at the time, but, oh my God, it's so horrible . . ."

"Sarah put it in a Visine bottle?"

"She emptied the Visine bottle and we put the syringe . . ." Laren indicated that they'd filled the plastic bottle with tranquilizer with the syringe. Then they'd put the bottle of tranquilizer back in the vet kit and returned to the ninth floor of the hotel.

They went into the room, Laren continued, and "Sarah went to the closet and stood in the closet, and I was waiting to see if he was awake or not. And then I told her he was asleep, so she came out, and then, she watched him on one side and I watched him on the other. He was sleeping on his back. Then I put, like, three drops in his mouth and then I got all freaked out, so Sarah put some in there. And then we got scared and put [inaudible] . . . we got scared and then we went to sleep and at six in the morning he was just mumbling, you know . . . and then he got up and showed his horse and he wouldn't talk to Sarah . . . so he told my trainer he was really unhappy and he was going to go back up to Washington . . ."

It's difficult to square this explanation with the known facts, however. For one thing, Larry didn't show his horse the following day, which under this explanation of the events would have been September 11, using Sarah's flight down on the night of September 10 as the reference point cited by Laren. By the morning of that day, the 11, he was being wheeled out of the hotel in the wheelchair, and was on his way to the Woodbridge house in the back of the dually. Harker and Amunds had no way of knowing this, however, so they couldn't ask questions to clarify what Laren meant. Further, after showing the horse on Sunday, Larry had said nothing to Whalen about going back to the cult, but instead had talked about showing the horse in the East.

Based on the known facts, it's possible that Laren may have been indicating that she and Sarah put drops of "Special K" into Larry's mouth on *Saturday* night, when they planned to "make sure Larry has enough to drink so we can go out and party." This would have been the first instance of doping. The following day, Larry did show Justa Lotta Page—the day that Debbie Kail noticed that Larry wasn't his usual self, and the day of the night that Larry was so drunk at the Olive Garden restaurant that he fell down on the way back to his truck.

Certainly, if they had given Larry xylazine before the last showing of Justa Lotta Page, on Sunday, September 9, that meant that Larry had been under the influence of the xylazine for three full days, almost four, before dying. That seems impossible.

Given that everyone else who had ever taken xylazine was nearly comatose within a matter of hours—and the tests showed Larry had a huge amount in his system—either Larry hadn't been given xylazine on Saturday night, but some other drug, possibly "ace." The only alternative is that Larry had set a new world record for ambulatory survival on xylazine, which was almost always fatal within hours if left untreated. It's also worth remembering that on the Monday following Larry's last showing, Elisa had been overheard asking Debbie Kail if acepromazine would kill a person. That seems to suggest that Larry had been doped with "ace" the preceding Saturday night, and by Monday, Elisa was wondering why the Rasputin-like Larry hadn't dropped dead yet.

That therefore suggests very strongly that in southern California there were *two* different doping attempts, one on Saturday night, with "ace," and the second on early Tuesday morning, after Sarah had returned from Sacramento. By doping Larry twice, the evidence of intent to commit murder was effectively doubled, which may have been one reason why Laren cobbled the two dopings into a single incident.

She continued:

"Then, that day he showed his horse, and I remember going back to the hotel. He told me that he was going to leave, and I said, 'Okay, if you're sure,' you know, blah blah blah. So then we go back to the hotel thinking that he's gone, but he's not gone, and we went in there and he was doing his own drugs and he said, 'I'm dying, dying, dying,' and says, 'Here's how to do it, I'm dying,' and he was, like, trying to reach him and whatever . . . and that night, that was the night of the terrorist attack."

This really confused matters. If Laren was telling the truth, she and Sarah had first given Larry horse tranquilizer the night before he showed the horse, Saturday; he'd then shown the horse on Sunday; and on Sunday afternoon or evening had begun doing his "own drugs," and "trying to reach him," whatever that meant, as if Larry were trying to call someone. But that was *two* nights before the terrorist attack, not the night of, and also the night that Sarah was driving back to Sacramento. And Laren would say a few minutes later that Larry had wanted to kill himself, and that she'd helped him by telling him to take the rest of the "Special K," that "here's how to do it," and given him the Visine bottle, which he'd then chugged—all of which she said had taken place at the Woodbridge house after they'd returned on the night of September 11—"the night of the terrorist attack."

It therefore seems as though Laren for some reason had smashed together events from four days: the eighth, the ninth, the tenth, and the eleventh. Sarah, of course, hadn't been present on the night of the ninth or the morning or afternoon of the tenth, because she had gone back to Sacramento. If Laren was combining the events of Saturday night with those of early Tuesday morning—the Saturday drugging by the non-fatal acepromazine and the second drugging on early Tuesday morning—that might be evidence that while Sarah was present for the first, non-fatal drugging (so they could go out and party), she was nowhere around for the second drugging, that she was, as she insisted, never in the hotel room that night, while Laren was inside allegedly being kicked and threatened by Larry.

That in turn would account for Sarah's steadfast denial, to the bitter end, that she had anything to do with fatally poisoning Larry, and that her only crime was helping her friend to cover it up, once he was dead. And even Elisa admitted that Sarah wasn't anywhere near Larry on the night of September 11, when, in the bedroom of the Woodbridge house, he had allegedly told her he wanted to kill himself. That was evidence that, if the final, fatal xylazine poisoning had actually taken place that night, Sarah had nothing to do with it.

But in turn it raises the question: Why would Elisa want to implicate Sarah in the murder at all?—unless, as she said, it was Sarah's idea to begin with.

As the night wore on, Laren continued with her version of the events down at the horse show at the City of Industry.

"That night [Monday] he goes to sleep, the next morning [Tuesday] he's, like, lying there, and I thought he was dead. So I wake Sarah up and I say, 'I think he's dead,' and she pushes him and says, 'No, he's not dead.' " This was reminiscent of Sarah's story—that Larry was pushing *her*, calling her "Blanche." Only in this version, it's Sarah pushing Larry, to see if he's dead.

And again there is the problem: Laren wakes up Sarah, who is sleeping in the hotel room, when by all accounts, they'd actually spent most of Monday night and early Tuesday morning in the truck. The inconsistency in the story is another indication that Laren, for some reason, has combined the events of two different nights into a single story.

Laren continued. She said she'd gone downstairs with Morgan the dog, where she encountered Whalen on the grass strip in front of the hotel. When she returned to the hotel, she'd heard about the terror attack. Larry was still alive at that point, Laren said.

"Larry was stumbling around and so he wanted to go home," Laren said. "So I said, 'I'll take you home, we'll take you home right now,' and we couldn't get him up, so we went down the street and rented a wheelchair, and I got him dressed, put him in the wheelchair and we rolled him out to our truck and put him in that."

"Now, is he dead or alive?"

"He's alive."

Laren said she and Sarah switched off in driving the truck back to northern California, arriving "thirteen hours" later. Of course, if Larry had been given xylazine in the early hours of that same morning, he should have been dead by nightfall, according to all the studies of the deadly tranquilizer. But he wasn't.

"He was in the back seat, and we ended up going by way of San Bernardino, and you could go up to Yosemite on the back road. We went back, we thought he was going to die in the car. We didn't know what to do, so we just wanted to get him home, we were freaking out at that point. So we got home to my house, which is in Lodi. We get Larry in the house, get him upstairs . . ."

"Was he walking or were you guys carrying him?"

"He's half-walking and I told him I was going to call poison control because I thought he was O.D.ing, and he was like, 'I'm not fucking O.D.ing.'" Again, the fact that both Elisa and Sarah agree that Larry walked into the house appears to show that whatever tranquilizer he'd been given early that morning, it couldn't have been xylazine.

"Okay, what's this? He says, 'I want to die.' What's that all about?"

"He always says that."

"Okay . . . and you say, 'If you want to die, all you have to do is take this Visine'?"

"Yeah," said Laren. "'If you want to die so bad, Larry, go take it.'"

"Okay, and did you tell him what was in the Visine bottle?"

"No."

And this is a point where it might be worthwhile to freeze the action for some speculation. If the first two dopings were non-fatal—as the evidence suggests they were, and if the second one did not involve xylazine, as the evidence suggests it did not—what was going on with the Visine bottle? It seems possible that after the second doping proved non-fatal, that someone replaced the Visine bottle's non-fatal contents with the more powerful xylazine between the early Tuesday morning doping and the final, fatal doping late Tuesday night.

Laren's description of the events once they were home moved on:

She said Larry had taken the Visine bottle from her and squeezed the remainder of its contents into his mouth. She said she'd told him she would take him to the hospital, but Larry refused to go.

"Then he laid down on the foot of the bed and I got a blanket for him and a pillow and I covered him up and I went downstairs." She'd gone to sleep on the couch, Laren said.

"I guess I fell asleep. I heard the front door and I thought, 'Oh my God,' and I run to the front door, I look out, he's walking down the street, and I said, 'What are you doing? Where are you going?' And he's like, 'I'm gonna die, I'm gonna die,' and I'm like, 'Come back into the house,' and I know my mind wasn't working properly or I'd never done that to him in the first place, but I keep thinking I'm gonna take care of him."

"So he's out the front door and walking out and he's barefoot?"

"Oh no, he's down the street. In his boxers, in our six-hundred-thousand-dollar-home neighborhood, and so I say, 'Let's go in, let's just go back in the house.'"

Larry came back inside. Laren said he'd soiled himself. He saw Sarah, Laren said, and lunged at her, saying he was going to kill her. "I'm like, 'Come on back upstairs.' He doesn't want to sleep on the bed, he wants to sleep on the floor." Then Larry got up and went back downstairs and started touching Sarah, Laren said. "She says, 'Tell him not to do that.'"

"I thought you guys wanted to kill him?" Harker said. "I don't know, I get confused here."

Indeed, now it sounded like Laren was saying that Larry actually committed suicide.

"We don't want to kill him, we just want to be away," said Laren. "We don't want to kill him, just wanted him to stop being so mean and so horrible. So I went back up there [to the bedroom] and his pants were gone . . . then when six o'clock rolls over, the sun starts coming out and Sarah sleeps late, and so I immediately go up there and he's dead. And I run back downstairs and I said, 'He's dead,' and she went up there and she says, 'He's dead.'"

"Okay," said Harker, "and this is like forty-eight hours after he's taken the 'Visine'?"

"Oh yeah," said Laren. "Oh yeah."

But it seems more likely that Laren had conjoined three

separate drugging events, the Saturday drugging, the early
Tuesday morning drugging, and the drugging at the Woodbridge house, and had then tried to implicate Sarah in the first
and second, non-fatal incidents, in order not to go down
alone. But then, Elisa had said it was Sarah's idea to begin
with.

Harker and Amunds tried to unscramble all this confusion of dates and movements, but didn't make much headway. Laren didn't seem to know herself. They moved on to the morning of September 12.

"Six A.M.," said Harker, "he's dead. Okay. So what do you do with him at that point?"

"We say, 'What are we going to do with him?' and I say, 'I don't know.' And she says, 'Well, take the sheet that he's lying on,' and we wrapped it around him. And we took duct tape and wrapped it around him, and he was, like, in a crouch position . . . in my garage we had this one refrigerator." She and Sarah dragged the body down to the refrigerator in the garage, took out the shelves, and stuffed Larry's body, still wrapped in the sheet and duct tape, inside. Then they closed the door.

Laren said she then drove back to Los Angeles. Sarah was supposed to return to the horse show the next day.

"I called her," Laren said, "and said, 'Can you go by the house?' And she told me [later] that she went by the house and that the refrigerator had come open, so she had to [put] him back in there, and [close it] with duct tape all the way around."

"Because it was a tight fit?"

"Yeah. And so she was driving down, she got into a car accident . . . the next day she flew down to L.A. and then we just told everyone that he went back to the cult." They sold the truck, Laren said.

"Were you gonna bury him in the back yard, or—?"

"No . . . we talked about burying him in the back yard,

we talked about burying him over at the trainer's, we talked about taking him to the desert and burying him. We didn't know what to do, and then time starts going by, a month, a couple of months, and then, this girl we hired, it's my understanding, called the police and said she thought that Larry was abusing me, because she knows that . . ."

This was a reference to Ginger Miller, and how Laren would know about Ginger's November 30 tip to the Sacramento Sheriff's Department that Larry was missing is curious. It's possible that Larry's lawyer Georgeann McKee may have told Laren about Ginger when she first called in December to tell Laren to have Larry call the police. But for Laren to explain why Ginger would have called meant going into why Ginger was mad, which would have opened all the fraud problems, undercutting Laren's attempt to establish the battered-spouse defense that she'd already clearly embarked upon. It was better to tell Harker and Amunds that Ginger had "known" that Larry was abusing Laren (even though Ginger had never met him) and let it go at that.

Harker and Amunds nevertheless zeroed in on the operation of the law office, and soon Laren admitted that money was moved out of the client trust account into the general account, and then out the door to pay for things. She indicated that Larry was in on this. Harker asked how much money had been moved around this way, and Laren said it was about half a million dollars over the previous two years. Laren said probably $350,000 had been replaced in the client trust account over the two-year period, leaving it about $150,000 short. That was the same amount that had been ripped off from the Carters, of course.

By December, Laren continued, when the Sacramento Sheriff's Department started asking about Larry, she and Sarah had realized they needed to do something about the body in the refrigerator. The day after Georgeann McKee called and told Laren that the police thought Larry was dead—that was December 12—she and Sarah decided to take the body to Las Vegas and leave it there.

"The next day we were supposed to be going to Las Vegas, so we put him in the trunk of the car."

"Which car was that?"

"The Jaguar."

Harker and Amunds wanted to know how they'd managed to get the body into the trunk.

"We took a trailer tire," Laren said. "A tire for the horse trailer. We played the tire down in front of the refrigerator, opened the refrigerator door, slid him out, put him on the trailer tire . . . back up the Jag . . . and pushed him off the tire into the trunk. And he was shaped like this, you know [folded from the refrigerator], and we closed the trunk and went off to Las Vegas."

When they got to Las Vegas, Laren said, they drove into the parking structure of the Bellagio hotel.

"We pulled up to the parking garage and there was a security guard there, and they said, 'Can you pop the trunk?' Sarah was driving, and I said, 'What did she say?' 'Pop the trunk.' [Sarah pushed the button to open the trunk.] Well I jumped out of the car at this point . . . and I said, 'We're looking for the Mirage,' and I just pushed the trunk closed."

"What was Sarah thinking?"

"She was just freaked out, she didn't know, we were, like, living for every day after that happened."

Laren said her plan was to bury Larry somewhere near Las Vegas. She said they had a shovel with them in the Jag.

The first night in Las Vegas, Sarah stayed in the hotel with Ralphie and Morgan, while Laren went out looking for a suitable spot to bury Larry. She couldn't find anyplace, so she went out again the following night.

"I thought, *Okay, I can do this*, and I started digging," Laren said, but she couldn't do it. "So I went back to the hotel and I told her, 'I can't do it,' and the whole time he's still in the trunk and the valets are parking us, and it's not good . . ."

Laren said the ground was too hard.

"So we came home that night, Sunday, and Sarah says, 'You have to bury him today.'" Haylei wasn't around, Laren said. "So I told her [Sarah], 'I will take care of him' . . . so I got up at four in the morning, and it was raining and . . . I dug a hole."

"How big of a hole did you dig?"

"Not big enough, obviously."

She'd dug the hole in the rain and mud, but quit before long, Laren said. Laren indicated that Sarah was with her.

"Sarah said, 'Make sure you take all his clothes off and then take off all the clothes that you're wearing and get rid of them,'" Laren said.

"Why did she say that?"

"For DNA and so on."

"Did she say DNA?"

"Yeah, because she didn't want her hair on him and she has a lot of hair."

"So you took all his clothes off?"

"Well, I couldn't because of the sheets and the duct tape . . . I couldn't."

Laren mumbled something inaudible. It appears that she indicated that Sarah cut off the sheet and the duct tape with the red scissors that had been found at the scene.

She'd pried the body out of the trunk with two pieces of plastic, then down onto a blanket, Laren said. "I rolled him onto the blanket and I dragged the blanket down to the hole . . . I had to pull and push and turn and pull the blanket the whole way down there and it was deep in mud the whole time."

"So you're getting stuck as you're going?"

"Yeah, we . . . and then, Sarah said, 'Pull.' So I cut the stuff off him and then I rolled him into the hole, but not [deep enough]." There was no light to see by, she said.

"I just couldn't chance it. I couldn't see anything, and so there was a lot of water and then we covered him up the best I could and I took, like, this grass . . . and I couldn't find the scissors."

Laren said they looked for the scissors for about an hour, fruitlessly.

After disposing of Larry's body in the vineyard, Laren drove all over the area, even going far east of Sacramento, dumping clothes and shoes in Dumpsters to get rid of the evidence.

She got back to the Woodbridge house about 8 in the morning, Laren said. She and Sarah cleaned the Jaguar bumper to bumper. Then they started on the refrigerator.

The next day, Laren continued, Sarah told her they hadn't buried Larry deep enough. That afternoon they drove back to the scene in one of the BMWs. They saw a number of cars in the vicinity. Laren was sure the police had found the body. "So I just, like, lose it, and we go back to the house and I say, 'I think it's time . . .'"

Laren meant that it was time to get out of town.

For the next two weeks, as she tried to organize her departure from the Woodbridge house, Laren said, she kept thinking that at any moment someone was going to find the body. She began driving by the vineyard every day, looking for some sign that someone had found Larry. Her relationship with Sarah began to deteriorate, she said. Both of them were nervous and afraid, especially since the police were now actively looking for Larry.

By early January, Laren continued, they'd cleaned out the house, and had driven to Scottsdale for the horse show. Sarah was supposed to call her from Sacramento, Laren said, but when she didn't call, Laren began to wonder whether the police had started talking to her. On the night of January 10, she was in the hotel with Greg in Scottsdale.

"And then my trainer receives this phone call, and I see him walk over around the bar, and I'm like, 'Something's going on' . . . he said that the sheriff's department had come to the ranch and asked him, asked his wife, where he was . . . that they understood I had given him some golf clubs . . . and [Mary Whalen] was asking where the golf clubs were."

Laren said Greg told her not to worry about it, that it was

some sort of mistake. He told her to go take a shower, and then they would get together for dinner.

"So then, we go have dinner . . . Greg tells [his clients] that they [the sheriff's department] are harassing me for investigation in the disappearance of Larry. Greg says we [Laren and Haylei] need to go home and deal with this. And I said, 'Okay, we'll go home.' "

Greg gave her $300, Laren said, to go with $200 she already had. Then they got in the Jag and took off, down the road that led home, to Florida.

It was nearing 2 in the morning, Florida time. Laren seemed done. She gave a few more details: on the day of the long truck ride back to northern California, they had stopped in Yosemite, she said. Larry had tried to attack Sarah, she said. "He hated her, he just hated her." Sarah had a shovel. She stopped the car and began digging a hole to bury Larry, Laren said, but he was still alive. She told Sarah that they couldn't bury Larry alive. Sarah had agreed, Elisa said. But that day, she added, "Sarah was in control . . . I was too freaked out."

Then, the next day when Larry really was dead, Laren said, they knew they couldn't call anyone, not even poison control, because there would be too many questions. The chances were good that someone would figure out who she really was. And besides, making Larry disappear for a while would give them a chance to get the law business straightened out.

So they'd decided to put Larry in the refrigerator until they could figure out what to do, and the weeks had turned into months, and the money stopped coming in, and then people started looking for Larry, and then the only thing to do was get lost. They had come to Destin, had been found, and now it was time to face everything that had happened.

"I'm totally prepared to . . . I know I'm gonna spend the rest of my life in prison or to the electric chair or whatever it is you do with people . . . I mean, I know that, I know I killed him and I know I'm guilty, and I'm prepared to deal with the repercussions of it," Laren said.

At about 2:20 in the morning, Harker wrote out a statement for Elisa to read:

> *I, Laren Jordan, provide the following statement because it is true. I was not forced to make this statement, nor have I been threatened or promised anything.*
>
> *I, Laren Jordan, along with Sarah Dutra, planned to overdose Larry McNabney with a horse tranquilizer in a hotel in Los Angeles, California. After giving him horse tranquilizer, he was still alive. Dutra and I didn't want to leave him in the hotel for the housekeepers to find. We, Dutra and I, began driving Larry McNabney home. We stopped in Yosemite and Dutra began digging a hole with a shovel we had bought. I told Dutra he was alive and we could not do this. We drove home together.*
>
> *After we arrived at home, Larry McNabney went to sleep on the floor upstairs. Part of his face had been frozen the prior month, his face was drooping and one of his hands was cramped. During the evening before he fell asleep I told him I was going to call poison control. He told me not to call. I realize I could have called 911. I could have called poison control. The next morning Larry McNabney was dead.*
>
> *Dutra and I wrapped him in a sheet and duct tape and placed him in the refrigerator in the garage for three months. I then took Larry McNabney's body, cut off his clothes and buried him in a shallow grave in a vineyard. I then threw his clothes, my clothes and plastic wrappers in approximately ten different Dumpsters.*
>
> *I understand Dutra and I killed Larry McNabney by giving him the horse tranquilizer, knowing he*

mixed this with other drugs and alcohol, and not get-
ting him the help he medically needed.

   Dutra and I together discussed how to discard the
body. I alone buried McNabney's body.

Laren Jordan
March 19, 2002

Laren read the statement over and signed it. The time
was just past 2:30 in the morning on March 19, and even as
she was signing, Detective Deborah Scheffel was on her
way to Sarah Dutra's apartment in Sacramento.

Scheffel and four other detectives pulled into the parking lot of Sarah's apartment building just after midnight. By that point, Laren—Elisa, as far as Scheffel was concerned—had given her confession to Harker and Amunds in Florida, and in fact had signed the statement written for her by Harker. Scheffel, however, did not know the details of what Elisa had said, only that she had been taken into custody and was talking.

Scheffel was accompanied by Detective Lori Darneal, her sergeant, Joe Herrera, and two other deputies, Larry Gardiman and John Williams. All were in plain clothes and armed. Scheffel wanted to get Sarah's permission to search the apartment. They also hoped to interview Sarah once more.

Leaving the three men down in the parking lot, Scheffel and Darneal went to the upstairs apartment and knocked on the door. Jason Cataldo answered. Sarah was in another room working on a school project. Jason invited them in. Scheffel told Sarah that Elisa had been arrested, and that there was no longer any reason for her to fear.

Scheffel thought Sarah seemed glad to hear that. She asked if Sarah objected to a search of the apartment—for anything that Elisa might have given her, she said—and Sarah said she didn't. The other three deputies were summoned. Sarah signed a permission-to-search form. She was calm and cooperative.

After they'd looked around, Scheffel told Sarah that she needed to ask her some more questions. She said that now that Elisa had been arrested, she would be making statements to the police, and that if there was anything Sarah hadn't told her before, now was the time to unload it.

"I knew I needed to talk to Sarah before she had an opportunity to hear about Elisa's statements on the news or in a newspaper, so that anything she would tell us wouldn't be tainted by what had been released to the media," Scheffel said later.

Scheffel now invited Sarah to come with her and Darneal down to the car in the parking lot. Sarah agreed, but pointed out she was only wearing her slippers. Scheffel said that wasn't a problem, that they'd bring her back when they were done. Sarah left the apartment and went down to the parking lot. She got in the car, Scheffel started it up, and then drove it out of the lot, on the way back to French Camp, forty-five minutes away.

Later this maneuver by Scheffel would excite the opprobrium of Sarah's lawyer, Kevin Clymo. Clymo contended that the minute Scheffel had removed Sarah from her apartment she had effectively placed her under arrest, and was therefore obligated to give her the standard Miranda warning—the right to remain silent, the right to consult with an attorney. But prosecutors said that wasn't so, that Sarah was not under arrest at any time—at least, not until much later the next morning. Scheffel wasn't overly concerned with the nuances of custody interrogations. All she knew was that this was a big case, that Elisa was talking and probably trying to shift the blame onto Sarah, and that she wanted a videotaped interview of Sarah responding to the things that Elisa would probably be saying. It was the only way Sarah could hope to avoid being charged as an accomplice if not the actual perpetrator, Scheffel thought. She thought that Sarah would finally be eager to tell her side of the story.

This final interview began at just before 2 in the morning. Elisa's interview in Florida had been over for over two hours. Scheffel began by warning Sarah that she had to tell the truth, for sure, this time, because Elisa and Haylei were both talking.

"Is she, like, incriminating me?" Sarah asked.

Scheffel sidestepped the question, saying she hadn't yet talked to the detectives who were talking to Elisa. She said the best thing Sarah could do for herself at that point was tell the truth.

"What do you mean, the best?" Sarah asked. "I don't understand."

Scheffel said the evidence—that is, the level of xylazine in Larry's body—indicated that he couldn't have been alive when they had driven back to northern California from the Los Angeles area.

"Yes he was, yes he was. I swear Larry was alive, I swear to you, Larry was alive."

"And why were you crying and upset all the way back from Los Angeles?"

"Because she was telling me I'm to forget about this and I was trying to ask her what was going on, why is he acting so strange? . . . the two of them were just kind of talking and it felt weird, I was scared. I was scared and when she said, 'It's none of your concern,' that scared me, because honestly, Larry was alive, he was sleeping most of the time, and then awake some of the time, I swear to you."

Scheffel now fired one of her bullets.

"Do you remember," she asked, "was there a big rodeo going on?"

"Yes, in Las Vegas."

"Okay, tell me about that Las Vegas rodeo. When was it?"

"Oh my gosh," Sarah said.

Scheffel asked some more questions about the trip to Las Vegas in December, but it was plain that Sarah wasn't going to volunteer any information about Larry's body having been in the trunk at the time. After establishing that they'd driven the Jaguar to Las Vegas, Scheffel decided to go at it head on:

"Okay. Does that car have a trunk?"

"Oh yeah."

"And what was in the trunk?"

"You know, I never opened the trunk, I don't think we ever used it, we just kept the stuff in the car."

So—either Elisa was lying about Sarah helping her put Larry's body in the trunk, or Sarah was lying.

Scheffel moved on to Sarah's trip back to the horse show in the Saab, before she'd wrecked it. Sarah said she'd stopped by the Woodbridge house on the way, because Elisa had asked her to make sure everything was locked up, and to pick up some marijuana that was at the house.

Well, that checked—Elisa had said Sarah returned to the Woodbridge house. But then Elisa said Sarah told her she'd had to wedge Larry's body back into the refrigerator because it had come open, and had to seal it tight with duct tape.

"Is there any reason why your fingerprints would be on duct tape?" This was a shot in the dark—they had no prints on duct tape, but Sarah couldn't be sure of that.

Sarah said she wanted to think about it.

"Okay," Scheffel said, and she left the room to get an update from Florida.

When she came back, Scheffel tore into Sarah for lying. "Don't sit here and lie to me anymore, okay? It's too painful to be around."

"Could I go to jail?" Sarah whispered.

"Yes you could," Scheffel told her.

"I wanted to come to the police." Sarah said she was still afraid of Elisa, even if she'd been arrested.

"Then stand up and tell us . . . you need to explain some of these things. Are you a cold-blooded killer?"

"God, no. I can't go to jail, not for something when I was scared for my life."

"That's a possibility," Scheffel said. "We're talking about a man's life."

"I don't know," Sarah said, "maybe I need to talk to a lawyer."

Which is exactly what Sarah should have done at that point—although Scheffel almost certainly would have placed her under arrest to prevent her from leaving. Not that she could leave anyway, since she had no transportation back to Sacramento. But if Sarah had invoked her right to a lawyer, Scheffel would have had to stop questioning her. Scheffel decided to play it casual.

"Okay," she said, acting as if it were a matter of indifference to her.

One could see the wheels turning in Sarah's mind: if she insisted on a lawyer, there was a good chance she'd be arrested. On the other hand, maybe she could explain things in a way that Scheffel would accept, and they'd let her go. Sarah decided to roll the dice.

"I want to tell the truth," she said.

"Then do it, Sarah," Scheffel said. Now Scheffel decided to tidy up the record. She asked Sarah if she'd been threatened in any way, or had any promises made to her, and Sarah said no.

"You're here of your own free will, Sarah," the detective said.

Well, that was something of an overstatement under the circumstances. Sarah hadn't had any choice when Scheffel started the car and drove off to San Joaquin County. Where was Sarah going to go at 2:40 in the morning—in her slippers yet?

Sarah played for time to think. She asked for a cigarette, but Scheffel kept the pressure on.

Sarah began to cry.

"I never wanted anything to happen to Larry," she said. "God, please don't think I could do that to someone."

Scheffel eased up a bit and told her that she didn't believe Sarah was the guilty person, that it was Elisa's doing.

"I mean," Sarah said, "if I tell you what I've done, I could be put under arrest and everything?"

"You could be—I don't know what you're going to tell me."

"But if my life was put in danger . . . ?"

It all depended on Sarah's motives for doing whatever she had done, Scheffel told her.

"But you can obviously see that there is no motive, I have no motive," Sarah said.

Scheffel said she could see that Sarah was in turmoil.

"Elisa's an evil woman," Sarah said.

"Well, here's your chance to set the record straight," Scheffel said.

"After this cigarette, I'll tell you everything," Sarah said.

Not yet, the detective said. She suggested that Sarah give a quick summary first.

"Okay," Sarah said. "She took Larry inside that night."

"In Woodbridge." Sarah nodded.

"And he was alive."

"Okay."

"He was alive."

"All right."

"And I went to my parents' house, and that's when she was telling me, 'You're to forget that he was here.' God, the next morning she told me to come upstairs."

Sarah started crying.

"And I said, 'Why?' And she said, 'Come here,' and Larry was laying there in the ground [sic], and I go, 'What's the matter?' and she said, 'He's dead,' and I said, 'Oh my God, we better call the police.'

"She said, 'You go to the police and I'm going to kill you, you're gonna end up just like him.' I said, 'Oh my God, I've never seen a dead person. I can't handle that kind of stuff, my stomach . . .'"

Sarah started gagging. "It scared the shit out of me," she said when she came up for air.

"And how is she acting, Sarah?"

"Very calm."

"Is she crying and upset?"

"She said, 'Larry's dead.' And I was like, 'Oh my God, how did he die?' And she'd, like, she didn't say anything. Oh my God, I can still see him. He was, like, on his side, he was lying on his side . . ."

Sarah started crying again.

"Do you remember what he was wearing?"

"No . . . I remember he was wearing shorts. Like boxer-type shorts. Can I get that cigarette now?"

"Sarah, that's the hardest part," Scheffel said.

But it wasn't.

Still, Scheffel felt they were making progress. The last time she'd talked to Sarah, on February 24, Sarah had insisted that the last time she'd seen Larry, he was alive, going into the Woodbridge house with Elisa. Now that she had finally admitted that she'd seen him in the morning when he was dead, it would be much easier to get to the refrigerator, then to the vineyard.

Sarah still wanted her cigarette, but Scheffel kept pressing her. Scheffel knew that she had to keep going, and Sarah's by-now ravening desire for a cigarette was a weapon she could use to her advantage.

But first Scheffel gave a backhanded delivery of the Miranda warning, saying she didn't know what else Sarah was going to say, but she *did* have a right to speak to a lawyer "if you're a suspect in a case."

This probably had the effect of mostly reminding Sarah that she was a suspect, not that she had a right to a lawyer.

"Just get it over with, Sarah," Scheffel told her. "Spit it out and get it over with and put it behind you."

"Okay. Okay. Okay." Sarah was calming down. "Okay, so she put him in a sheet, oh my God . . . I've never seen anything like this, okay? And she said, 'Grab the sheet and then we carry him down the stairs,' and I'm like, 'What are you

doing? We have to call the police.' She said, 'We are not calling the police, if you call the police, you're gonna be so sorry
you ever did.' I said, 'What are you doing? What are you
gonna do?' And she said, 'I'm going to put him in the refrigerator downstairs.'"

Now there were two versions of the same events. When
Elisa had told her story, it was Sarah who had taken the lead
on deciding what to do about Larry. But in Sarah's version,
the idea woman was Elisa.

Sarah said she felt paralyzed. She said she didn't want to
help Elisa move Larry's body, but that Elisa insisted.

"She's like, 'If you don't help me . . .' She had a horrible
look in her eye and so I . . . I didn't understand how she could
do that to him. I don't understand how anybody could kill
anybody, that's sick."

They managed to get Larry's body downstairs to the
garage, Sarah continued, and up to the refrigerator. The refrigerator was normally used by Larry to store his Chardonnay wine.

"Now she says, 'Take all his stuff out, take all the things
out,' so I help her take them out . . . I'm like, 'Please, why
don't you call the police?' And she's like, 'No, I will not call
the police,' and I thought, 'You are crazy, you are crazy. You
are not going to get away with this,' and she's like, 'Yes I am.'
I'm like, 'What if I go tell the police?' [and she says] 'You
won't, because you have your life in front of you, and you
want to keep it that way.' My God!"

"And now that all the stuff is out of the refrigerator, now
what do you guys do?"

"She, like, sets him in there."

"In the sheet?"

"Yeah."

Scheffel was now relentless, prodding Sarah to tell exactly how Larry had been put into the refrigerator, in what
position, how he was wrapped—all the details that Sarah
said made her sick to talk about. Scheffel insisted that Sarah

explain just what she did when she'd helped to wrap Larry's body up before putting it in the refrigerator.

"God, I don't want to end up like him," Sarah said. "I thought, God, she was sick and that she would do something . . ."

"Tell me what happens next."

"So then she was holding [his] clothes and she was saying, 'Grab that tape and wrap it around him.' I did it, I just wrapped it around it."

"Wrapped the duct tape around the refrigerator?" Scheffel misunderstood—Sarah wasn't talking about the refrigerator, she was talking about Larry's body.

"Yeah," Sarah said, "she put some stuff first on the side like this and then she was like, 'Oh, that's not going to hold,' so then she grabbed that and wrapped it around—"

Sarah now had a burst of hysterics and began panting things out in fragments, sounding a bit like Dutch Schultz, or at least a Beat poet. "Police, and I told her to, and I told her so and I said, 'Elisa, I can't handle this,' it was going to Oklahoma, I said, all the money. It's eating me up inside, if you go to the police they will put you in jail forever . . ."

"Do you need a break?" Scheffel asked.

"Yes," Sarah said.

Just after 3 in the morning, Scheffel formally advised Sarah of her Miranda rights, which in Scheffel's system of thinking meant that Sarah was now on notice that she was a murder suspect. Interestingly, the transcript of the interview does not show that Sarah ever acknowledged those rights, or formally waived them. Instead, after reading them, it appears that Scheffel began asking more questions.

This time, Scheffel wanted to take the story from the top—from when Sarah had first arrived at the City of Industry in the BMW.

The story came out once more, this time in more detail. Sarah recalled going back to the hotel room three times with Elisa on the night she flew back to the horse show, rather than the one time she had said before. When they had removed Larry in the wheelchair on the morning of September 11, he was docile, almost friendly, greeting her with a "Hi, Sarah." Sarah had helped put him in the truck, and a few minutes later Elisa had told her to keep driving, straight on back to northern California. On the way, Elisa had told her to forget about seeing Larry in the truck that day.

By now Scheffel had heard the Yosemite story—that Elisa had said that they'd stopped in Yosemite, and that Sarah had started digging a grave for Larry, but that Larry wasn't dead yet. She wanted Sarah to tell her side of this story, but without telling her what Elisa had said.

Sarah said nothing had happened in the mountains.

"Okay, she doesn't suggest that maybe you guys leave Larry up there in the mountains?"

"No."

Scheffel gave up and moved on to the return to Woodbridge. Sarah said Elisa wanted to sell the truck . . .

"When does she start talking about selling the truck?"

"She was talking about that before, when I was in L.A.,
that people were looking at his truck," Sarah said. This was
confirmation that Elisa's plan to sell the truck had begun
even before Larry was dead.

Over the next hour, Sarah went back over the events of
the fateful weekend, but little new was added. They took another break about 4 A.M., and Scheffel got another update
from Florida, where it was then 7 A.M. After the break,
Scheffel bore in on Sarah once more.

"I know some things you're still holding out on, because
the evidence tells me that," Scheffel said.

"Like—like what?"

They started all over again with the body, this time with
Scheffel prodding Sarah to provide more details, urging her
to drop her fear reaction and tell what she saw. Sarah added
little that she hadn't already said.

They went on to the horse show, and Elisa giving
away Larry's boots and golf clubs. "I just remember her
saying, 'Larry doesn't want these boots anymore,' and her
saying, 'Larry ran away.' "

"And how does that make you feel, Sarah?"

"I just remember looking at her, thinking, God, you are
so sick, how can you stand there with such a normal look on
your face? Because I was freaking out, I mean, I could
barely handle myself."

Scheffel asked about Larry's jewelry—his Rolex watch,
and his horseshoe diamond ring. Sarah said she remembered Elisa removing them while they were driving back
in the dually. Scheffel turned to the subject of the shovels.
Sarah said she couldn't remember anything about shovels.

The talk turned to the world show in Oklahoma City.
Sarah remembered Elisa giving jewelry to various people,
and going to parties. Sarah said she thought Elisa was sticking

close to her to prevent her from spilling the beans about Larry. On the way to the show, while they were driving in the Jag, Sarah said, she brought up Larry to Elisa.

"I told her, I said, 'Elisa, I can't take it anymore. It scares me every night, like all the time.' She said, 'You are to forget about that, everything is fine.'" Elisa told her again she would only ruin her life if she went to the police.

Scheffel asked Sarah if she could remember what had happened in December. This was another attempt to get at the Las Vegas burial try, and eventually the vineyard. But Sarah said that as far as she knew, Larry had stayed in the refrigerator. She had no knowledge of how he'd wound up in the vineyard. After Oklahoma City, Sarah said, she'd told Elisa, "I'm done." She wanted nothing more to do with Larry's body. "I didn't want to think about it anymore."

"You just assumed she'd deal with it, huh? Sarah, did she ever ask you to help bury Larry McNabney?"

"No!"

"Not in the desert? Not in Yosemite?"

"No!"

"And not out there in [the vineyard]?"

"No, no, no!"

"Absolutely not?"

"Absolutely not."

She had never looked inside the trunk of the Jaguar when they were in Las Vegas, Sarah insisted.

It was nearing dawn, but Scheffel kept on pushing. She veered into the law firm finances.

"Did you ever wonder what was happening to the money in the firm after Larry died? I mean, she bought you a Beamer."

"I never really watched the dollar amounts coming in and the dollar amounts going out," Sarah said.

They got ready for another break. Scheffel said that she thought Sarah was still holding out.

"I know that Elisa asked you to help her get rid of the body, and I need to hear it from you," Scheffel said. "I can't tell that story for you. You have to do it for yourself. There is no such thing as ninety-eight percent truthful, you are either one hundred percent truthful or you are not truthful. Just say it and get it over with."

Sarah started to protest that she had told the truth, but Scheffel cut her off.

"Don't even go there, not after all you've been through. Don't stop now, don't make a poor choice. You've shown a lot of guts in coming up on what you did."

"Yeah, I'm probably going to go to jail for the rest of my life."

"Why, Sarah?"

"Because. I mean, I should have gone to the police, but I was too scared to."

"That doesn't make sense."

Another barrier fell down, and Sarah decided to tell about the trip to Las Vegas.

Scheffel rewarded her with another cigarette break. It was just after 6 A.M.

"That morning," Sarah said, "she was getting everything ready, you know, packing up for Vegas, and she said, 'Sarah, come out here and help me load up the car,' and there was a black tarp on the ground . . ."

Scheffel sighed.

". . . and it was him," Sarah finished.

Sarah had another fit.

"She said, 'I need your help.' I said, 'I'm not helping you, I'm not doing that.' It's like she put me right into it. Like, I walked out there, and he's laying on the ground."

"Oh my God," said Scheffel, sounding like Sarah.

"I just wanted to die. I just wanted to go, 'I can't handle any more, I can't handle seeing it,' and I said, 'What are you . . . ?' I say, 'I'm not helping you . . . do that.' I say,

'I helped you put him in the refrigerator and that was way too much.' Then she said, 'I'm not asking you to do that, just help me lift him into the trunk,' and so I did and, God, I didn't want to go to Vegas. She said, "You're going to Vegas . . .'"

"Oh my God," Scheffel said. It *was* catching.

That was the last time she saw Larry, Sarah said, when she got her composure back. She'd thought she was going to die in Las Vegas herself. "I was wondering if she was going to bury me, too."

When they got back from Las Vegas, Sarah said, she'd told Elisa she would get no more help from her.

There was one more area Scheffel wanted to cover: somewhere along the road the detectives had heard that Sarah and Elisa had talked with one another about overdosing Larry with horse tranquilizer—before it had actually happened. This was really the money question. If Sarah admitted that they'd talked about it beforehand, there was evidence of premeditation. Scheffel believed that such a conversation had taken place before the horse show. If she could get Sarah to confirm it, she would have a clear first-degree murder case—at least against Elisa, if not Sarah herself.

Scheffel tried all manner of approaches, but Sarah wouldn't bite. Finally Scheffel suggested that if Sarah and Elisa had had such a conversation, Elisa might have secretly taped it. It might have been Elisa's way of getting some blackmail on Sarah—a way to hold her in place when the going got rough, Scheffel suggested.

Bit by bit, Sarah acknowledged that there might have been such a conversation, but never seriously. There had possibly been loose talk about poisoning Larry, after his DUI, Sarah admitted. But Scheffel said the talk was more specific than that. Eventually Sarah realized that Scheffel was talking about horse tranquilizers.

"Sarah," Scheffel said, "what's 'Special K'?"

"'Special K' is, it's a drug that a lot of kids use these

days. I don't know what the main drug is, but I had a friend who was really big into it, and Elisa had asked me one time about 'Special K' . . . It's a horse tranquilizer."

"Really?"

Scheffel made Sarah swear that if there was ever any evidence offered that she'd had a conversation with Elisa about deliberately overdosing Larry on horse tranquilizer, it would have been merely idle talk, and one that she could not remember. Sarah said it was true—she might have had such a conversation, but if she did, it wasn't serious, and anyway, she couldn't remember it.

Scheffel now made preparations to return Sarah to her apartment. In Scheffel's mind, Sarah had emerged as her key witness against Elisa. Now was the time, Scheffel thought, to ease off of Sarah and welcome her into the fold.

"Okay," Scheffel said, "let's take you in and get you fingerprinted . . . and we'll get you home, 'cause I know it's been a long night."

And at that point, Scheffel really did intend to take Sarah home.

After the fingerprinting, Scheffel took Sarah to a small room with a pile of stuffed animals. This was where the police conducted their child molestation interviews. At that point, Scheffel had the schizophrenic notion that Sarah was both a child and a suspect in a cold-blooded murder, and likely a star witness to boot.

"It was just chairs and a table and the waiting area upstairs, the place where we have our children wait," Scheffel said. "It's more comfortable. I got her a blanket so that she could lay down if she wanted to. And she did in fact lay down in this pile of stuffed animals and covered up with the blanket that I had given her." Scheffel turned off the lights so Sarah could take a nap. Sarah was worried about the college paper she had to finish. Scheffel told her they would write a note to the instructor, giving her an excuse. Scheffel said she did have some concern about Sarah trying to flee, especially since it appeared that Sarah had broken the law, at the very least being an accessory after the fact, in helping to hide Larry's body. Sarah assured her that she would not try to flee—she had no money, anyway, she said. Scheffel told her that she didn't think Sarah would try to run away either, and because she wasn't a danger to the community, Scheffel would be taking her home.

Scheffel called the Florida authorities for another update, and was sent a fax containing Elisa's statement, the one that had been written by Harker. Then she went to talk to San Joaquin County Sheriff Baxter Dunn, briefing him on where they were. Dunn had called a press conference for that morning. He wanted Scheffel to appear with him. At the press conference, Dunn announced that Elisa had been arrested, and that she had implicated Sarah as an accomplice. He read the confession that Elisa had signed.

Scheffel was asked about Sarah.

"She got caught up in the glitz of a high-end horse world," Scheffel said. "The McNabneys took her to and from horse shows and she got a taste of a richer life. She saw a lot of glitz and made a lot of poor choices."

Scheffel was asked about the money that had supposedly been looted from the law firm—did Sarah have any of it? No, Scheffel said.

After the press conference, Dunn and Scheffel conferred again. "I told him that I had more work to do on this case," Scheffel said later. "That I didn't—I still felt that Sarah wasn't being completely truthful with us about what had happened, but that I needed more time to either corroborate or disprove the things that she had given us during this latest interview. He expressed to me that he felt that I had more than enough to arrest her and that it was his order that I place her under arrest. I told him I had already given her my word that she was to go home, and that I was going to be taking her home. And he overrode that and said, 'Place her under arrest.'"

Scheffel returned to the stuffed animal room and woke Sarah up. She took her out of that room and to another interview room. Now Scheffel produced the confession and confronted Sarah with it—particularly the assertion that Sarah had helped plan the poisoning, and that she had started to dig a grave for Larry while they were in Yosemite. At that point, Scheffel again read Sarah her rights, and told her she was no longer free to leave. She did not say what she might be charged with. Sarah seemed to think that she could still talk her way out of this, however.

Eventually, Scheffel's sergeant, Joe Herrera, came in and took up the questioning, which ran past the noon hour. Sarah admitted that Elisa had told her to bury Larry at Yosemite, but that she hadn't been able to do it. She also said that Elisa had told her that she'd given Larry a horse tranquilizer for the first time while they were sitting in the dually on Monday night, around midnight. Sarah said she didn't believe it at first—she wasn't sure if Elisa meant that she was doping him to keep him sedated or if she really meant to kill him.

Like a closer in a car dealership, Herrera stepped up the pressure on Sarah. He said they had enough evidence already to make the charge that Elisa and Sarah together had killed Larry.

"The only thing that's missing," he said, "is whether or not you were manipulated . . . Did you kill Larry McNabney?"

"No."

"Are you a murderer in the first degree?"

"No."

"Then don't be one," Herrera said. "Don't be one. Because when we walk out that door today, and you walk out there in handcuffs, that's what's going to happen, unless you use this last opportunity to tell me, or anyone else you want, the truth of what happened. We know that you knew that she was poisoning him, but did *you* do it? Did *you* poison him?"

"No."

This was really and truly her last chance, Herrera told Sarah.

"When is the first time you knew she gave him some drugs?"

"When I came to the hotel that night," Sarah said.

"Was it your idea?"

"No."

"How did she administer it to him?"

"She told me she put it in his mouth."

"How?"

"I don't know."

"Okay, did you see her do it?"

"No."

Where had Elisa told her this?

"It was after we were in the truck, and I was asking her what's going on, and she said, 'I can't handle him anymore,' and I [asked] her, 'What are you doing?' and she said, 'I'm giving him poison,' and I thought, Oh my God . . .'"

"And here you are," Herrera said.

"God," Sarah said, "she's talked about it before, but now she was *doing* it. And I thought, 'Why me? Why is she pulling me into this?'"

Sarah said she went up to the hotel room with Elisa, and watched as she bent over his sleeping form. Sarah said she was thinking the whole thing was unreal, like it was some sort of dream. But the dream just kept getting stranger the following morning, with the wheelchair, and in the background the news reports streaming in about the terrorist attacks at the Trade Center and Pentagon.

As they drove north, Sarah said, Larry came partially awake.

"Do you think he knew he was being poisoned?"

"Yes he did," Sarah said, rushing her words together. He said, 'Blanchie, what's going on? Blanchie, why are you doing this to me?'"

"Did he blame you?"

"No, he didn't say anything to me, he didn't say one word. He just said, 'You're not going to get away with this, Blanche.'"

When Larry said he was thirsty, Elisa would pass him her water bottle, which he drank from, Sarah said.

"What did you think about the water? What did you really think about the water?"

"I think that's what she poisoned him with, was the water bottle," Sarah said, "giving him water."

"Why did you think that?"

"Because she told me she was poisoning him, and she had her water bottle and she said, 'Okay, here,' and she gave it to him."

So now here was a fourth possible doping—on the trip

north in the dually, when Larry drank from Elisa's water bottle.

Sarah described driving the rest of the way back to Woodbridge, then going to pick up Ralphie in Vacaville.

"I wanted to stop at the police," she said.

"Why didn't you?" Herrera asked.

"Because," she said, now crying again, "I could just hear her voice saying, 'You do not want to go there. It's in your best interest not to.' I could only think, I started to think, God, if I go to the police, it could go on the news, and if it goes on the news, what if something happens to [my family]?"

"It was a tough decision," Herrera said.

But when the interview was over, the San Joaquin Sheriff's Department had also made a tough decision. They asked the district attorney's office to charge Sarah with first-degree murder.

Nearly three thousand miles away, Laren was infuriated by Baxter Dunn's press conference, which had gone out over the national airwaves. Already, people were starting to call her a "Black Widow," she complained to Amunds, who went to see her after Sarah was arrested. It wasn't like that at all, Laren said—she'd had to kill Larry before Larry killed her. And she was perturbed for a second reason.

"She told me it was her idea that she could sell her story to the movies," Amunds said later. "She said it was the only way she could take care of her children, but now that sheriff [Baxter Dunn] had ruined her chances by giving it all away for free."

That afternoon, Amunds recalled, two San Joaquin County detectives arrived in Destin. Amunds said he thought he had good rapport with Laren, and offered to introduce the detectives to her. They eagerly agreed. But when Laren was brought out from the holding cell to talk to the two California investigators—after they'd read her rights to her—Laren told them to perform an anatomically impossible act. She wouldn't say anything further until she talked to her attorney—Tom Hogan of Brooksville, as it turned out.

Amunds later thought the whole situation could have been avoided and Laren persuaded to talk with the San Joaquin County detectives if Dunn hadn't given his press conference. He thought the rush for publicity back in California had in effect prevented anyone from challenging Laren's initial version of the events, and thereby had left it as Laren's word against Sarah's. Had Laren been questioned by someone who

knew more of the facts, Laren's assertions about Sarah might
have been significantly undercut.

But now Laren was lawyered up.

Within a week or so, Laren was transferred back to
Brooksville, where she had to face the old probation violations that had caused her to flee so many years before.
There, in the Hernando County Jail, Laren finally had a reunion with her family: her mother Jackie, her father Jesse,
and her siblings and nieces and nephews. Her mother and father were overjoyed to see her after so many years, as they
were Haylei. For nearly a decade, both Laren and Haylei had
been among the missing, but now they were found.

In the meantime, Laren met with Tom Hogan, the Sims
family lawyer who had represented her so many years before,
and who Laren had called before she married Larry. Laren
described her marriage to Larry, indicating that Larry had
used her past against her to keep her from leaving him, and
saying that Larry routinely beat her. Hogan began to believe
that Larèn had a defense in the murder case. He told reporters
in Florida that Larry had been an abusive husband, and that
Laren had feared for her life. When the probation violations
were dropped in order to speed Laren's extradition back to
California, Hogan indicated that Laren would fight being sent
back.

On March 29, 2002, Laren wrote a letter to Hogan. It
was in an eight-by-eleven envelope, and had two 34-cent
stamps on it.

Laren began the letter by telling Hogan about several
people in Reno and California who might substantiate her
claims that Larry had abused her, and that he was a severe
drug abuser and alcoholic. But then she went on.

"Tom, I think we both know that it doesn't matter what
kind of man Larry was, we murdered him. Of course, I should
spend the rest of my life in prison. Sarah should too. I wish I
could change what happened, but I can't."

Laren told Hogan how she'd had a crush on him years before, even before he had represented her on the old stolen property charges. Then she asked Hogan to watch over Haylei, even become her guardian if need be.

"I only want Haylei protected," Laren wrote. "Will you try to make her understand that I cannot put her through having a mother in prison for life, or worse, a mother on death row? It would be so unfair to her to have to carry that burden."

Then Laren turned to practical matters: the jail, she said, wasn't doing what it was supposed to—it wasn't keeping her under close observation. Laren said that she and Larry had handled several tort cases involving deaths in prison in Nevada, and that the cap on governmental liability was $50,000. "I don't believe CCA would be included in the 'governmental clause,'" Laren wrote—meaning that if she died in the Florida jail, the private corrections company, Corrections Corporation of America, might be sued for more than $50,000.

"I'm not strong enough to face all of this," she continued. "I have tried to dig deep into myself and it isn't working. There is nothing left."

She didn't want to be a burden to her mother and father anymore, Laren said.

"My dad will understand. I am a coward, but he will realize it is the best thing I can do for him and my mom . . . I never fit the mold, Tom. The fact that they even acknowledge me is amazing. I am not good, like they are. I don't have that in me. I don't know why and I don't know if I ever did. I just know that I have always been a disappointment to them."

Now Laren gave Hogan more specific information about the jail. She was supposed to be observed every fifteen minutes, and that wasn't happening. The jail had a log book in which they were supposed to document their observations. They were supposed to provide her with access to a telephone and to a shower, but they weren't, she continued—she hadn't been allowed to take a shower for three days. All that should help Hogan file a lawsuit against the jail, she said.

She closed by thanking Hogan for everything he had done for her over the years.

"P.S.," she wrote. "Please tell my parents I love them."

Late that night, Laren tore strips from a bedsheet, braided them together, threaded the makeshift rope through an air vent in the ceiling, and hung herself. It appears that she went undiscovered for a substantial amount of time. Rushed to Brooksville Regional Hospital, she died the next day.

The Truth

On January 6, 2003, trial began in the matter of *People of the State of California* vs. *Sarah Dutra*, in which the state alleged that Sarah Dutra had committed first-degree murder in the death of Larry McNabney. The charge carried two special circumstances: that the crime had been committed for money, and that it involved the use of poison. Additionally, Sarah was also charged with being an accessory after the fact of the murder, in that she had helped Laren Renee Sims Jordan Redelsperger McNabney conceal evidence of the crime.

Laren's suicide had a paradoxical effect on the trial. In one way it hurt Sarah, because until Laren killed herself, there had been the chance that prosecutors would negotiate some sort of deal for Sarah's testimony against the woman she had known as "Elisa." But when Laren died, that left only Sarah to face the bar of justice.

Yet in another way, the suicide helped Sarah. The only evidence against her of intent to commit murder came from Laren's lips alone, and once she was dead, the statements that Laren had made that night while being interviewed by Harker and Amunds were inadmissible as evidence.

The key witness against Sarah was Sarah herself—the hours and hours of interviews that she had given to detectives like Scheffel were used against her with devastating effect. And although Sarah had steadfastly maintained that she'd had no idea that the woman she knew as Elisa had given Larry a fatal dose of horse tranquilizer, it was impossible to believe her when she said that she hadn't known for sure that Larry was dying. There had just been too many lies before that.

In the end, the jury agreed with Kevin Clymo, Sarah's defense lawyer, that there was no reliable evidence that Sarah had intended to murder anyone. But the jury was troubled by Sarah's indifference to Larry's plight. All the way north in the dually, there had been ample opportunity for Sarah to alert someone that Larry was dying. There was yet another opportunity that same night, when she drove the dually to Vacaville to pick up Ralphie—why hadn't Sarah told her mother and father what Elisa was up to, or at least what was happening with Larry? Sarah's assertion that she hadn't known that Larry was dying until he was dead didn't hold any water—especially in light of all the lies Sarah had told the police before her arrest.

As for the accessory after the fact charge—there was no doubt about that. Not after Sarah, on tape, admitted having helped put Larry's body into the refrigerator on the morning of September 12.

Sarah's jury deliberated for three days. According to accounts of some, the panel, six men and six women, divided bitterly over Sarah's guilt. The men, perhaps swayed by Sarah's youth and beauty, thought she had been brutally used by Elisa, that she was innocent of any crime other than helping Elisa cover things up. The women on the jury were far harder on her—they thought she was guilty of first-degree murder.

When it became clear that first-degree murder would not prevail, the jury began considering second-degree murder— where the intent is to murder, but there is no premeditation. That possible verdict, too, resulted in a deadlock, although eleven jurors supported it against a lone hold-out.

In the end, the jury decided, based on one of the judge's instructions, that Sarah was guilty of voluntary manslaughter— that while she had knowledge that doing nothing would cost

Larry his life, she still did not act. As for the accessory after the fact charge, that was easy: guilty.

A month later, San Joaquin County Superior Court Judge Bernard J. Garber sentenced Sarah to the maximum penalty allowed under the law: 11 years in state prison. Garber said the defining moment of the entire case came when Sarah admitted that she'd helped put Larry's body into the refrigerator. That, Garber said, illustrated the callousness with which Sarah had acted toward a man who had never done her any harm.

So now we are at the end of this story of the Blanches— Larry and Elisa and Sarah—and if there's a moral to the tale, it is this: no one really knows another person. We only think we do.

Larry thought he knew Elisa—even though that wasn't really her name. Elisa thought she knew Larry—but Larry had deeply hidden flaws that made him something less than the "wonderful, charismatic person" she thought he was when she'd met him. And Sarah never really knew either Larry *or* Elisa. She never knew the Larry who had been the consummate lawyer, or even the champion horseman; all she knew of Larry was Elisa's caricature, the drunken, apparently loaded sap that Elisa had portrayed him as, and all she knew of Elisa was what she yearned to believe Elisa was.

And who was Elisa, to Sarah? She was the sophisticated woman who knew how to use men; she was the woman who took her shopping for pricey items, who introduced her to rich horse owners, who confidently shuffled large sums of money by check and by wire, the woman who had taken a young, naive girl under her wing to show her how the world really worked. Sarah never saw the aberrational thinking, the inability to plan ahead that marked the course of her mentor's hidden life—at least, not until it was too late.

If there is a key to understanding this complicated triad, it lies in the question that Sarah had told Herrera she'd asked herself that fateful night in the dually: "And I thought, 'Why me? Why is she pulling me into this?' "

Why, indeed? Why, after having sent her away the previous evening, did Elisa suddenly need Sarah to come rushing back? Not because it was part of any plan—if there had been a plan, Sarah never would have left to begin with. The most obvious explanation is that Elisa wanted to tell Sarah what she had done—that she had, as they had talked about idly over the previous summer, actually, really and truly, had in fact given Larry an overdose; that she was killing him. Elisa wanted Sarah's approbation for her action.

And in this, Elisa did not really know Sarah: while they had giggled together like schoolgirls the whole summer, busily separating Larry from his money, and had spoken casually of giving him an overdose, Elisa had come to see Sarah as a younger, sharper, more ruthless version of herself— someone utterly capable of taking such a step and pulling it off. If there had been no Sarah, Elisa never would have had the courage to do such a thing. In short, Elisa projected her own idealized image of herself onto Sarah—what she wished she was—while Sarah projected her own giggly, impish self-image onto Elisa, at least when it came to the subject of murder. When Elisa mentioned to Sarah that she wished she was rid of Larry, and the idea of overdosing him first came up, Elisa thought Sarah was serious; Sarah thought Elisa was simply sounding off. She never dreamed that such a thing might ever happen.

Then the event actually came to pass: Elisa gave Larry the overdose. When she called Sarah to rush back to southern California, it was to tell her: *I did it, what we talked about.* And this disclosure was less for the purpose of enlisting Sarah's assistance as it was for moral support, for someone to tell her she had done the right thing.

There Sarah sat, that night in the dually, realizing for the first time that there was something mentally wrong with the woman she had admired; *Oh my God, she actually did it.* Realizing, too, that she was involved with Elisa up to her own neck in fraud and forgery, and even the seemingly vacuous discussion of murder, to Sarah, it was as if it were a *TV* crime show, but to others, it was utterly damning. In Sarah's mind, there was no other choice at that point but to go forward with Elisa, because Elisa was incapable of bringing the thing off by herself without Sarah's support, and if Elisa were caught, Sarah was certain to go down with her. There they sat, trying to figure out what to do.

If the facts unearthed by the investigators demonstrate anything, they demonstrate that the entire fatal episode was unplanned—that in fact, it occurred on the spur of the moment. But that was Laren/Elisa's way from beginning to end. Only rarely in her life did Laren ever engage in anything like long-term planning. Instead, all of her life, decisions were made up as the need came along, by the seat of her pants; it was Laren's curse that most of these decisions were short-sighted, intended to solve an immediate problem, but inherently self-destructive—whether shoplifting a hair-coloring kit, writing a bad check, or killing her husband, everything was done to meet an immediate crisis, and badly. And the crisis in this case: the fact that the money had run out, that Larry was certain to find out, that the Whalens wanted their money. The solution: sell the truck, sell the horse, and make Larry disappear.

Had the killing of Larry McNabney been the result of a plan, hatched secretly by Elisa and Sarah in the months prior to his death, the horse show at the City of Industry had to be one of the worst places to put such a plan into effect. If there had really been a long-term plan, how much better it would have been to poison him at home, then make him disappear, into a previously prepared grave, for example. In any event, there were literally hundreds of witnesses around to Larry's disappearance—not the sort of thing one wants when planning a murder. Consider, too, that neither Elisa nor Sarah had made any concerted effort to consider what to do with Larry's body until the moment they realized he was dead—and even then, they picked . . . a spare refrigerator? It was as if they were so surprised at the result of their actions that they couldn't think of anything else to do—so they decided to put Larry away as if he were a plate of unwanted leftovers, another one of Laren's short-term, disastrous solutions to an immediate problem.

In the end, one can only feel sadness for all three of the Blanches—Larry, whose life had begun with such promise, but ended in such misery; Laren, so bright, so beautiful, so personable, so tortured by something she herself never understood; and Sarah, so young, so talented, so unformed. Two lives wasted, a third blighted. For all his brilliance, Larry never fully realized that life wasn't a race, it was a journey— that it didn't matter much how fast one got there, but what one did along the way. Or Laren: "I am not good . . . I don't have that in me. I don't know why and I don't know if I ever did," she'd told Hogan. Even after all that she had done, even in death, there was something about Laren that made one want to love her. And Sarah: who grew up too fast, much too fast, so that one could only feel the most painful sorrow for the choices that she had made, and wish for something different.

Acknowledgments

This book could not have been written without the generous assistance of a great many people in several states, who freely gave much of their valuable time in assisting the author with interviews and obtaining vital documents, including thousands of pages of police and court records in several communities in three different states. For their irreplaceable help, the author wishes to thank—

In San Joaquin County, California: Detective Deborah Scheffel of the San Joaquin County Sheriff's Department, who gave an enormous amount of her time to explain what happened; San Joaquin County Sheriff's Detective Lori Darneal, who tracked the money; Dr. Terri Haddix, pathologist, for her assistance with the properties of xylazine; the Honorable Bernard J. Garber of the Superior Court, who granted the author's motion to unseal vital records; Gail Miller, clerk of Department 23 of that court, who cheerfully assisted in keeping track of the proceedings; and Tami Brown, certified court reporter, who provided valuable transcripts of the preliminary hearing and the trial of Sarah Dutra.

In Sacramento County, California: Kevin and Kirsten Clymo, who defended Sarah Dutra, and who explained what was otherwise inexplicable; Georgeann McKee, who provided a crucial interview; and Cristin Becker Olson, for the same.

In Reno, Nevada: Nancy Eklof, who provided recollections of Larry and Elisa McNabney in their heyday; Myra Nelson; attorneys Tom Mitchell, Ron Bath, Fred Atcheson, Fred Pinkerton, Patrick Flanagan and Pete Durney, who recalled Larry McNabney as the fine lawyer he was; Donna Becker, for her recollections of her marriage to Larry; Mark Combs; and the staffs of Washoe County District Court and the Washoe County Public Library.

In Las Vegas, Nevada: Mike Henderson, former reporter for the *Reno Gazette-Journal* newspaper; and Nancy Goodrich of Goodrich Investigations.

In Seattle, Washington: Jeffrey Moore, for his recollection of the events leading up to the marriage of Larry and Elisa.

In Okaloosa County, Florida: Sergeant Don Amunds of the Okaloosa County Sheriff's Department, for his recollection of the events surrounding the arrest of "Elisa"; and sheriff's department spokesman Rick Hord, for the same.

In Hernando County, Florida: attorney Tom Hogan; Hernando High School counselor Bob McClelland; and the staff of Hernando County Circuit Court, who helped assemble long-archived records of Laren Sims' past.

To all who helped shed light on the tragic events recounted in this book, again my thanks.

Carlton Smith
South Pasadena, California
July 2004